PENGUIN BOOKS

FROM THE FAIR

Sholom Aleichem was born Sholom Rabinowitz in the Ukraine in 1859. His first writing was in Russian and Hebrew, but between 1883 and his death he published more than forty volumes of novels, stories, plays, and literary memoirs in Yiddish. Best known for his wonderful tales of Tevye the Dairyman, which became the basis of *Fiddler on the Roof*, he was often referred to as the "Jewish Mark Twain." (On one occasion when the two men met, Twain returned the compliment by calling himself the "American Sholom Aleichem.") Sholom Aleichem's work has been translated into virtually every language and has established him as a cultural hero and a master storyteller. He died in New York City in 1916.

Curt Leviant is a prizewinning novelist, author of *The Yemenite Girl* and *Passion in the Desert*. His short stories and novellas have been published in many magazines and have been included in *Best American Short Stories*, *Prize Stories*, and other anthologies. He has won the Wallant Prize, an O. Henry Award, and is a Fellow in Literature of the National Endowment for the Arts. A frequent lecturer on Yiddish and Hebrew literature, he has previously translated three other Sholom Aleichem collections.

Sholom Aleichem and his father,
Nochem Rabinowitz,
in 1885

From the Fair

THE AUTOBIOGRAPHY OF
SHOLOM ALEICHEM

TRANSLATED, EDITED AND WITH
AN INTRODUCTION BY
CURT LEVIANT

PENGUIN BOOKS

PENGUIN BOOKS
Viking Penguin Inc., 40 West 23rd Street,
New York, New York 10010, U.S.A.
Penguin Books Ltd, Harmondsworth,
Middlesex, England
Penguin Books Australia Ltd, Ringwood,
Victoria, Australia
Penguin Books Canada Limited, 2801 John Street,
Markham, Ontario, Canada L3R 1B4
Penguin Books (N.Z.) Ltd, 182–190 Wairau Road,
Auckland 10, New Zealand

First published in the United States of America by
Viking Penguin Inc. 1985
Originally published in Yiddish
under the title *Funem Yarid*.
Published in Penguin Books 1986

This work was supported by a grant from
the National Endowment for the Arts.

LIBRARY OF CONGRESS CATALOGING IN PUBLICATION DATA
Sholom Aleichem, 1859–1916.
From the fair.
Translation of: Funem yarid.
1. Sholom Aleichem, 1859–1916, in fiction, drama,
poetry, etc.   I. Leviant, Curt.   II. Title.
[PJ5129.R2F83   1986]   839'.098309   [B]   85-26006
ISBN 0 14 00.8838 X

Printed in the United States of America by
R. R. Donnelley & Sons Company, Harrisonburg, Virginia
Set in Goudy Old Style

For
Erika
and
Dalya, Dvora and Shulamit
and
for my aunt
Julia Glinert

C.L.

ACKNOWLEDGMENTS

I wish to thank the late poet, folklorist and Yiddish language expert, Professor Wolf Younin, whom I consulted for rare and unfamiliar vocabulary in the text. I also want to record my gratitude to my late uncle, Monia (Eiser Mordechai) Dusawicki, for his kind assistance.

Finally, my appreciation is extended to our dear family friend Dr. Leon Merkin, שיבדל לחיים ארוכים, physician and author, for his counsel regarding words of Slavic origin.

CONTENTS

INTRODUCTION

This final work by Sholom Aleichem (1859–1916), the famed Yiddish humorist and one of the central figures in modern Yiddish literature, is by no means a traditional "Life." It reads like a novel, but is in fact a memoir. It avoids superfluous detail, and contains, as Sholom Aleichem remarked in a letter to a friend, "no eating, drinking, sleeping, jumping around." *From the Fair* takes us from Sholom Aleichem's childhood to his first love and his early attempts at writing fiction and drama. It gives us an incomparable picture of a lost world, and paints in storylike episodes a delightful, occasionally self-critical portrait of the hero, his family and friends. Here in one volume is the essence of Sholom Aleichem's narrative genius.

Sholom Aleichem (he was born Sholom Rabinowitz, and later adopted the popular Hebrew/Yiddish greeting meaning "How do you do," or, literally, "Peace be unto you" as his pen name) wanted his autobiography to be his best work and, in fact, considered it his crowning achievement. One might wonder how the man who gave us the immortal Tevye the Dairyman, the luftmentch Menachem Mendl, the lovable orphan Mottel the Cantor's Son, how the artificer of Kasrilevke and dozens of its townspeople could hope to surpass these magnificent creations. Nevertheless, Sholom Aleichem was confident about his memoirs. In his dedication of the work to his children, Sholom Aleichem called his autobiography "my book of books, the Song of Songs of my soul."

In telling us the story of his life, Sholom Aleichem purposely departs from the traditional first-person narrative, informing the reader that he will be writing an "autobiographical novel" and "memoirs in the form of a novel." He chose this format not to remember more readily events that never happened, or to embellish those that did, but because he felt the less pretentious third-person stance would enable him to gain perspective without compromising truth. This approach was not new for Sholom Aleichem. As early as 1908, when a Russian newspaper in Kiev asked him to write an autobiographical sketch in honor of his twenty-fifth literary anniversary, he wrote the article in the third person.

Sholom Aleichem may also have felt more comfortable with the fictional mode. Since the memoir, like his stories and novels, was published in serialized form, reader suspense and interest had to be maintained from week to week, from installment to installment. This is why, just as in fiction, the end of a chapter in *From the Fair* will arouse the reader's curiosity—often in the form of a newly introduced character or incident—about the next segment. Sholom Aleichem here adapts the up-and-down, success-failure themes of his fiction to the memoir. And with this work, he bridges the gap between fiction and nonfiction—in effect, creating a new genre in Yiddish literature: the novelized autobiography.

A fine synergy exists between Sholom Aleichem's autobiography and his fiction, not only because so many familiar characters and incidents appear in *From the Fair* in their earliest guises, but because the mode of storytelling and characterization, the narrative voice and linguistic playfulness, and even the gloom and darker side of the author can be found here. And his autobiography also reveals the origins of some motifs that recur in Sholom Aleichem's fiction: young love and heartbreak, obsession with a lost treasure and the grand prize in the lottery, problems with high school and the draft board, and love of music and musicians. The treasure leitmotif may be the most insistent theme in the work. Young Sholom often daydreams that he finds the treasure buried in his hometown and then is able to free his father of near-poverty and make his hard life easier.

From the Fair is not, however, merely a sourcebook for Sholom Aleichem's imaginative creations. The author also shows us his corner of Jewish life in the Russia of the 1860s and 1870s. As a child Sholom Aleichem went to a traditional cheder, where he first learned Hebrew reading, writing and prayers, and then Talmud and other advanced texts. Private tutors taught him Hebrew grammar and language (subjects that were not stressed in the cheder), and Russian and Hebrew calligraphy. The boy's impeccable, even artistic handwriting—of which his father was particularly proud—is mentioned several times, and the author always recalls his penmanship instructors with love and gratitude. After cheder Sholom Aleichem attended the Russian district school, but admitted he didn't learn much there.

The literature of the Haskala, the Jewish Enlightenment movement, was the main source of his education.

During the latter part of the nineteenth century, there was a lively cultural struggle between Hebrew, the language of the Haskala, and Yiddish, the folk language of Eastern European Jews. Hebrew is the ancient classical language of the Bible, of prayers, and of almost the entire body of Jewish literature throughout the ages. A member of the Semitic family of languages, it is also the language of modern Israel. Yiddish, which stems from Middle High German, was created by Jews who lived in Germany, and dates back to about the year 1000. Both Hebrew and Yiddish use Hebrew characters and are read from right to left; both are essentially Jewish languages, representing the spirit and values of the Jewish people. But there the similarity ends. Although fifteen to eighteen percent of the Yiddish language is made up of Hebrew words, a Yiddish speaker does not necessarily know Hebrew (though many do), and a Hebrew speaker can be absolutely ignorant of Yiddish (many are).

Proponents of the nineteenth-century Haskala denigrated Yiddish, which was their own mother tongue. Yiddish, they felt, was the language of women and of the uneducated masses. It was suitable only for daily conversation and cheap, throwaway fiction—not for serious literature. "A man was ashamed to be seen holding a Yiddish book lest people consider him a boor," writes Sholom Aleichem in *From the Fair*. Hebrew, however, was at once the ancient and future tongue of the Jews, and through it would come intellectual and, eventually, political emancipation. But however noble its intentions, the Haskala closed its eyes to practical considerations: most Eastern European Jews did not understand Hebrew. They could *read* Hebrew in the form of prayers, and were perhaps acquainted with Biblical Hebrew, but for them modern Hebrew literature was written in what amounted to a foreign language.

One of the leaders of the Haskala was Mendele Mocher Seforim (1836–1917), a founding father of both modern Yiddish and modern Hebrew literature. Idolizing Mendele and firmly believing in the Haskala, young Sholom Aleichem shunned Yiddish and began to write in Hebrew and Russian. Soon, however, both Mendele and Sholom Aleichem realized that a movement that was meant to revolutionize Jewish education could not use a language understood only by the intellectual elite. Reluctantly, they turned back to Yiddish, and made it a respectable tool for enlightenment.

In 1883, when Sholom Aleichem was in his early twenties, he began to write in Yiddish—"for the fun of it," as he said. Even though he considered that year as the inception of his literary career, he had begun to write for Hebrew and Russian-Jewish periodicals while still in his teens. He poked fun at the rejections ("the editors, thank God, had plenty of stuff to heat their stove"), but he also received letters of encouragement from Hebrew editors who published his works. Nevertheless, these pieces from his short-lived Hebrew period made no lasting mark on Hebrew literature. They are forgotten today, overshadowed by his prodigious output in Yiddish, and used only as a correlative to his Yiddish fiction.

That critical esteem was late in coming, at least from the English-speaking world, may be seen by the approach taken by the *Jewish Encyclopedia* (1904). This classic reference lists Sholom Aleichem in a brief, two-paragraph citation as a journalist and novelist, focuses on his Hebrew short stories, and observes that his work ranks "with the highest of their kind in neo-Hebrew literature." The second paragraph discusses Sholom Aleichem's Russian fictions of Jewish life, and only then mentions that he "is chiefly known by his contribution to Judeo-German literature." Note: Judeo-German, not Yiddish. The word "Yiddish," so indelibly fused with Sholom Aleichem, does not once appear in the encyclopedia's citation.

With Yiddish came success. Editors constantly besieged Sholom Aleichem for more material. He noted that he devoted so much time to writing that "I no longer belonged to members of my household but more to our literature, and to that larger family known as the reading public."

It was that "family," along with fellow writers, who pressed Sholom Aleichem to write his autobiography. Undertaken toward the end of his short life, it is the only autobiography in Yiddish literature that can stand beside the author's imaginative prose as a classical representation of his style and literary mastery. Sholom Aleichem planned to write not only his life story but also a cultural and spiritual history of the preceding fifty years. Indeed, the work explores a period of modern Jewish life that, owing to the exigencies of time and terror—German Nazism and Soviet totalitarianism—has been excised forever. Still, Sholom Aleichem's purpose and direction can be seen even in the three extant volumes. As clearly as in the photographs of Roman Vishniac, but as if viewing them through a wider lens, we see Jewish villagers, townsmen and farmers, children and teachers, paupers and intellectuals in all their pursuits. A human comedy as diverse as the characters in Sholom Aleichem's stories appear in *From the Fair*.

The idea for a book of memoirs had been in Sholom Aleichem's mind for years. In a letter to the Yiddish writer Mordecai Spector in 1895, Sholom Aleichem informs his friend and mentor of his plan for an autobiography. He does not intend to describe the mundane and insignificant aspects of his life, but would rather focus on the "rich episodes . . . that will not only interest me but the next person too." And when he began serious work on the memoirs in 1915, Sholom Aleichem adhered meticulously to his earlier principle.

However, he began his autobiography in 1908, in Nervi, on the Italian Riviera, where he sought respite from his tuberculosis. While celebrating the twenty-fifth anniversary of his literary debut he suffered a severe, almost fatal episode in his illness. Having just "had the privilege of meeting . . . the Angel of Death face to face," he felt it was time to start writing. But after completing only a few chapters of the memoirs, he set the work aside.

Five years later, when Sholom Aleichem was in Switzerland, a wealthy oil merchant promised to underwrite the cost of publishing the memoirs, and he wrote several more chapters. The third and final stage of his autobiographical work commenced in New York in 1915, a year before his death. He was hired by the Yiddish daily *Der Tog*—which, with great fanfare, ran ads announcing that it was the only Yiddish paper in the world that could claim Sholom Aleichem as a regular contributor—and his life story appeared in the newspaper in weekly installments (a method still used by the Yiddish press today).

The sunny atmosphere and good humor of the autobiography are remarkable because the Yiddish master, accustomed to the clean air and warm sun of Switzerland and Italy, the esteem of readers and friends, and a comfortable lifestyle, enjoyed none of these while writing in cold New York. The man who was a living legend, a culture hero among Jews, could not even afford to go to Arizona for the winter. Ill, forlorn and in poor financial circumstances, he was nevertheless able to look back in time, to his memories of Eastern Europe, and re-create his youth at the bitterest period of his life.

Sholom Aleichem died a year later, on May 13, 1916, and 150,000 people attended his funeral. Too late did the public adulation he had known in the old country manifest itself in America.

This edition marks the first time that the complete manuscript of Sholom Aleichem's autobiography has appeared in English. It is a translation of the final draft of the three-volume work entitled *Funem Yarid* (*From the Fair*), which appears in Sholom Aleichem's twenty-eight-volume *Collected Works*—the same version he had been serializing in *Der Tog* from mid-June 1915 until his death. An earlier English translation of part of *Funem Yarid*, published thirty years ago, was not based upon the definitive Yiddish edition of Sholom Aleichem's memoirs and, moreover, deletes lines, phrases and occasionally complete paragraphs. More important, that edition contained only the first two of the three volumes. With this new translation, the final volume of Sholom Aleichem's autobiography has been rediscovered for the English-reading public.

Sholom Aleichem's autobiography, which should have run to ten volumes and carried the author though his fiftieth year, was unfinished. But the telling of his life story may have been Sholom Aleichem's final consolation: the two concluding chapters were written during the last days before his death. Sholom Aleichem's "book of books and Song of Songs" is a touching and honest work, in which young Sholom's faults and quirks, talents and sensitivity mingle and fill his story with the good humor, satire and occasional sad reality that are so much a part of Sholom Aleichem's fictional world.

CURT LEVIANT

For My Children—A Gift

My dear, beloved children,

To you I dedicate my work of works, my book of books,
the Song of Songs of my soul. I know that my book, like
any man's work, is not free of defects—but who knows
better than you what it cost me? I've given it the best of
what I have, *my heart*. Read it from time to time. Perhaps
you or your children will learn something from it—how
to love our people and appreciate their spiritual treasures
that lie scattered in all the dark corners of the vast Dias-
pora in this large world. This would be the best recom-
pense for my thirty-plus years of faithful labors in our
Yiddish language and literature.

Your father, the author,
Sholom Aleichem

New York, February 1916

BOOK ONE

1. From the Fair

*A Kind of Introduction—Why the Author Chose to Write His
Autobiography—Sholom Aleichem the Writer Tells the Story of Sholom
Aleichem the Man*

Everyone wants to compare a man's life to something. For
example, a carpenter once said, "Man is like a carpenter. A
carpenter lives and lives until he dies—and so does man."
A shoemaker once opined that a man's life is like a pair of boots.
Once the soles wear away—you can kiss them goodbye. And it's
quite natural for a coachman to compare man's life to—forgive the
comparison—a horse.

So don't be surprised if a man like me, who has gone through the
ups and downs of half a century and is about to write his autobiography, compares his past to a fair.

But that's not quite the whole truth. "From the fair" implies a
return trip, or the results of a great fair. A man heading for a fair is
full of hope. He has no idea what bargains he will find and what he
will accomplish. He flies toward the fair swift as an arrow, at full
speed. Don't bother him, he has no time. But on the way back he
knows what deals he has made and what he has accomplished. He's
no longer in a hurry. He's got plenty of time. No need to rush. He
can assess the results of his venture. He can tell everyone about the
trip at his leisure—whom he has met and what he has seen and
heard at the fair.

My good friends have often asked why I don't tell the world the
story of my life. It's high time, they say, and it might even be
interesting too. So I listened and tried to begin a number of times.
But each time I soon set the pen aside. Once, however, when I
wasn't quite fifty, I had the privilege of meeting his majesty, the
Angel of Death, face to face. No joke, I almost packed and moved

to the place where there's no mail and from where you can't even send regards. So I said to myself:

"Now's the time. Seize the opportunity and write. For who knows what the morrow may bring? When you die, others who think they know you, will concoct things about you. What good will that do you? Better pick up a pen and write it yourself, for you know yourself best. Tell who you are and write your autobiography."

"Write your autobiography"—the real story, not an invented tale—is easier said than done. It means taking stock of your entire life for your readers and confessing to the whole world. Furthermore, writing one's memoirs is almost like writing a will. That's number one. Second, it's rather hard for a memoirist to withstand the temptation to publicly make himself a saint and show everyone he's a fine fellow who deserves a medal. That's why I chose a special form of autobiography: memoirs in the form of a novel. I'll talk about myself in the third person. I, Sholom Aleichem the writer, will tell the true story of Sholom Aleichem the man, informally and without adornments and embellishments, as if an absolute stranger were talking, yet one who accompanied him everywhere, even to the seven divisions of hell. I'll present this autobiography in separate incidents or episodes. And may He who gives man strength to remember one's entire life grant that I omit nothing and no one during my fifty years at the great fair.

2. The Town

The Little Town of Voronko—A Sort of Kasrilevke—A Legend from Mazepa's Time—An Old Church, an Old Cemetery, Two Fairs

Sholom, the hero of this autobiographical novel, grew up in Kasrilevke, which has achieved a degree of renown. In case you want to know, Kasrilevke is in Little Russia, in the province of Poltava, near the historic old town of Pereyaslav. Actually, it's not called Kasrilevke but Voronko. Write it down!

Like all biographers, I really should cite the name of the city and the date and place of our hero's birth. But frankly this doesn't interest me. Little Kasrilevke, or Voronko, interests me more, for no other village in the world impressed itself on Sholom's memory as the blessed Kasrilevke-Voronko. No other village in the world had as much charm. It was an unforgettable place, one he will remember forever and ever.

Which large city—Odessa, Paris, London or even New York— can boast of such a large market with so many Jewish shops, stands and stalls with mountainsful of fresh aromatic apples and pears, cantaloupes and watermelons? Goats and pigs (constantly shooed away by the market women) loved to nuzzle these fruits, and the schoolboys too liked all these goodies but couldn't get near them.

Which town has such an old, tumbledown bes medresh with a carved wooden holy ark graced with two lions who would have looked like birds if not for their long tongues and the ram's horns in their mouths? Old Jews say that our ancestors once locked themselves in this venerable bes medresh in fear of Mazepa, may his memory be blotted out. They stayed there three days and three nights, wearing tallis and tefillin and reciting psalms. Only this saved them from death. These same old Jews assert that the old rabbi had said the bes medresh would never catch fire—and that's why flames have never touched the building, no matter how many conflagrations roared around it.

Which city has a bathhouse that tilts downhill, right at the edge of the river, and a well whose waters never run dry? And don't forget the river itself! Where in the world can you find a river in which generations of Talmud Torah lads and gentile youths have bathed and frolicked, have learned to swim, catch fish and play pranks? Old Jews have plenty of stories to tell about this old bathhouse, which miraculously is still standing. Once, a gentile was found there hanging on a rope. He had become drunk and committed suicide, and the Jews were falsely accused of murder. This caused the town a pack of troubles. The authorities wanted to beat the most prominent Jews in town; perhaps they *were* beaten. But I don't want to delve into this too deeply because I hate sad stories, even if they are ancient tales.

Which town has a big hill near the bes medresh so high its peak almost touches the clouds, and behind which, as everyone knows, a treasure is buried from Chmielnicki's times? Old Jews say that the townsfolk tried several times to find the treasure, but they always had to stop work, for while digging they found bones—human limbs and heads in shrouds. Evidently Jews, perhaps even martyrs. Who knows?

Which place has such fine townsmen, small merchants and shopkeepers who draw their livelihoods solely from the gentiles and from
one another? Still, they all live well. Everyone has his own house,
family, and a seat in the bes medresh at the eastern wall or in the
first row. But it makes no difference anyway. If he isn't rich or from
a fine family, then he has a prominent or wealthy relative he constantly talks about and tells tall tales that make your head spin.

Is there another town that has such a large, old, imposing cemetery? Most of the graves are so overgrown with grass that no one
knows if people are actually buried at the site. Much can be told
about this cemetery. They aren't merry tales either. In fact, only
awful incidents that happened in ancient times, of course. But let's
not discuss this at night.

Voronko is small but beautiful and full of charm. With strong legs,
you can traverse the entire village in half an hour. It has no railroad,
no sea, no tumult—it hosts only two fairs a year, founded by Jews
for the purpose of stimulating business and making a living. Although
it's a small village, the many fine stories and legends about it could
fill a book. I know you prefer stories and legends above anything
else. However, we can't go into them. We must adhere strictly to
the biographical format. First, as is customary, we must introduce
you to our hero's parents. So be glad I'm starting with Sholom's
parents and not like other biographers with his grandparents and
great-grandparents.

3. Sholom's Parents

*A Voronko Rich Man with Many Businesses—A Gang of Youths—
Frume the Maid Lords Over Them—Our Hero Is a Mimic, a Prankster*

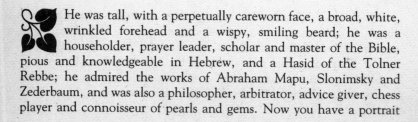 He was tall, with a perpetually careworn face, a broad, white,
wrinkled forehead and a wispy, smiling beard; he was a
householder, prayer leader, scholar and master of the Bible,
pious and knowledgeable in Hebrew, and a Hasid of the Tolner
Rebbe; he admired the works of Abraham Mapu, Slonimsky and
Zederbaum, and was also a philosopher, arbitrator, advice giver, chess
player and connoisseur of pearls and gems. Now you have a portrait

of our hero's father, Reb Nochem Vevik's,* regarded as the richest man in town.

The worth of such a Voronko grandee would be hard to estimate, but he had a pack of businesses. He leased land, supplied a sugar plant with beets, ran the local post office, dealt in grain, loaded cargo on Dnieper River steamers, felled timber in forests, and fattened oxen on malt grain. But he drew his sustenance from the dry goods store, which was a dry goods store in name only. He also sold haberdashery, groceries, hardware, hay, oats and homemade remedies for the peasant men and women. Actually, Father had nothing to do with the dry goods store. That Mama ran singlehandedly. She was a wonderful woman, active and extremely strict with her children. And there were plenty of them. More than a dozen. Of all sizes and colors. Children with black, blond and yellow hair. Usually, no great fuss was made over the children. No one was that anxious for them. And if God forbid they hadn't been born, it wouldn't have been such a great tragedy either. But since they were already here—why then, live and be well! They don't bother anyone, do they? Whoever survived measles and chicken pox and other childhood maladies grew up to become a Hebrew school lad. First he studied with Leib the primer teacher and then with Reb Zorechl the Talmud teacher. The one who didn't survive the thousand-eyed Fiend who lies in wait for infants returned whence he came. The mirrors were covered and the parents sat shiva, removed their shoes, and wept bitterly. They cried so long until they stopped. They recited the verse "God has given, God has taken!" Then they dried their eyes, rose from the ground and forgot their sorrow. Otherwise, with the tumult of more than a dozen children, one a bearded young man out on his own and another a child at the breast, it would have been impossible to go on.

Mama was very deft at raising such a gang and putting up with everyone's illnesses. Normally, a child would get as many slaps, smacks and blows as he could absorb. But if, God forbid, someone got sick, Mama wouldn't leave the child's bedside. "Woe is me!" she'd cry. But once the kid convalesced and was on his feet—"Back to school with you, you scamp."

In fact, the children studied in cheder from the age of four almost up to the time they were married.

*The possessive *Nochem Vevik's* is the equivalent of *Nochem son of Vevik*. [C.L.]

The greatest rascal in the family was the middle boy, Sholom, or Sholom Nochem Vevik's, the hero of this autobiography. Nevertheless, Sholom was not a bad boy. He was a better student than most of the others but also got more blows, cuffs, punches and smacks. No doubt he deserved them.

"Just mark my word, nothing good will come of him," Frume the Maid said of Sholom. "He's growing up to be a nobody, a nothing, the devil knows what! He's going to be an outcast, a drunkard, a glutton, an apostate, a scoundrel, a knave, the worst you can imagine!"

Pockmarked and blind in one eye, Frume was a very stingy and devoted servant. As a mark of her loyalty, integrity and extreme devotion, she hit the children, doled out food sparingly, and tried to make them decent, pious and honest, acceptable to people and to God. And because Mama was such a wonderful helpmate and was always in the store, Frume the Maid ran the household with an iron hand and raised the children like a mother. She woke them, bathed them, washed their hair, taught them their morning prayers, slapped them, gave them breakfast, brought them to and from school, beat them, gave them supper, said the nighttime Shema with them, whacked them again and bedded all of them down (including herself—don't think it a shame!) in one bed, the children next to each other while she slept across the foot of the bed.

With Frume around, the children were in miserable bondage. But the day she got married was a great holiday for them. Long live Ideleh the Ganev, who had a wild shock of hair greased down with goose fat and a flat nose with fused nostrils which he could never properly blow even if he had eighteen heads! Long live Ideleh (crazy chap!) for marrying blind Frume. And, mind you, he didn't marry her just like that. He married for love! He was head over heels in love with her. He wasn't marrying her because she was pockmarked and had only one eye but because she was connected to Reb Nochem Vevik's. Such a match was no feather on a scale! Chaya Esther herself (that is, Mama) hosted the wedding; she was the one in charge. She baked honey cake, brought in klezmer from Berezan, danced and enjoyed herself till dawn, and became hoarse in the bargain.

My, how the gang laughed and danced that night! They were celebrating not so much because a horse thief took a blind maid in marriage but because they were getting rid of Frume forever and ever. And they also laughed at the way the rascal (Sholom) mimicked the groom whistling through his nose and the way the bride looked at the groom with one eye, licking her chops like a cat who had swiped some sour cream.

At mimicking, imitating and making faces our Sholom was a veritable devil. One glance was all he needed to spot a flaw or a ridiculous trait. He puffed out his cheeks and found something to mimic. And the children burst out laughing. Whereupon Sholom's parents informed the cheder teacher, "The rascal imitates everyone like a monkey." The teacher, then, tried to break him of this habit. But to no avail. Some sort of demon had gotten into the child, for like an imp he imitated everyone, even the teacher taking snuff and his petite mincing gait; he mimicked how the rebbitsin pouted and blushed and twitched one eye as she asked the teacher for money for the Sabbath, which she mispronounced "Shabbath." Then the blows rained down, slaps were dispensed and whippings meted out. Whipping isn't the name for it! No end of them!

4. Shmulik the Orphan

Stories, Fantasies and Dreams—Kabbala and Magic

There are faces that God created to enchant you at first glance. Adore me, the face proclaims, and you adore it without knowing why. Shmulik the Orphan had that kind of adorable face. He had neither father nor mother, and was raised in the rabbi's house.

Sholom became attached to Shmulik the moment they met. They shared breakfasts and lunches and became bosom friends—literally one body and one soul. Why? Because of Shmulik's stories.

No one had more stories to tell than Shmulik. But stories are not everything. The narration itself is important. One has to know how to tell a story. And in this Shmulik had no equal.

How did this extraordinary youngster with the red cheeks and dreamy eyes know so many stories? Such rich, beautiful ones with so many extraordinary images? Had he heard someone telling these tales? Or were these absolute fantasies drawn straight from his imagination? To this very day I do not know. But one thing I do know: the stories poured out of him as if from an everlasting spring. Smooth as oil, the stories flowed from him, drawn out like threads of silk.

His voice and diction were as sweet as sugar. And his cheeks were red, his eyes dreamy and moist, as if covered with a slight film.

The two friends met on Friday afternoon, Sabbath after lunch or on a holiday evening at Voronko's highest hill, whose peak almost touched the clouds. The two lads would lie face down on the grass or on their backs looking up at the sky, and Shmulik would begin to tell one story after another.

He would tell a story about a prince and princess or a rabbi and a rebbitsin, a tale about a duke and his dog or a princess in a crystal palace. A story about twelve robbers in a forest or a ship that sailed on a frozen sea. He told stories about the pope who debated with the greatest rabbis and one about a chandelier from Prague. He told about beasts, imps, spirits, bands of demons, wizards, elves, were-wolves, vipers, half humans and half beasts. Each story had its own special flavor and unique charm.

Sholom listened with open mouth and never took his eyes off that extraordinary boy with the red cheeks and moist, dreamy eyes.

"How do you know all that, Shmulik?"

"That's nothing, dummy. For instance, I know how to draw wine from the wall and oil from the ceiling."

"How do you draw wine from the wall and oil from the ceiling?"

"That's a cinch too, dummy. I even know how to turn sand into gold and make diamonds and gems from shards."

"How do you do that?"

"How? By means of Kabbala. The rabbi is a Kabbalist. Who doesn't know that? He never sleeps, you know."

"Then what does he do?"

"At night, when everyone's asleep, he's up studying Kabbala."

"And you see what he does?"

"How can I see, silly, if I'm sleeping?"

"Then how do you know he studies Kabbala?"

"Who doesn't know that? Even a kindergartener knows that. Ask anyone. What the rabbi knows, silly, no one knows. If he wants to, the twelve wells of quicksilver open for him and the thirteen gardens of pure saffron—and gold and silver, diamonds and gems, are all around you like sand, so much that you don't even want any."

"Then why are you always hungry? And why doesn't the rabbi ever have enough for the Sabbath?"

"Because he doesn't want to. He wants to suffer in this world and repent. He's a penitent. He could be as rich as Korah if he wanted to. He could put a thousand Rothschilds in his pocket. Because he knows how to get rich. Everything has been revealed to him. He even knows where the town treasure is buried."

"Well, where is it?"

"Smarty! How should I know? If I knew where the treasure is hidden I'd have told you long ago. I'd have come to you in the middle of the night and woken you up: 'Come, Sholom, let's get the treasure. We'll scoop up gold by the handful and stuff our pockets!' "

As soon as Shmulik began talking about the treasure, his dreamy eyes lit up, his red cheeks flushed, and he became so excited and wrought up that Sholom too became agitated and stirred up. Shmulik spoke and his friend Sholom stared openmouthed at him and greedily swallowed every word.

5. Treasures

What's a Treasure?—A Legend from Chmielnicki's Time—Magic Stones

That there was a treasure in our village was an indisputable fact. Where did it come from? Chmielnicki. He buried it ages ago. For thousands of years people saved their treasures, and then along came Chmielnicki, who seized and hid them.

"Who was Chmielnicki?" Sholom asked Shmulik.

"You don't know Chmielnicki, you dummy? Chmielnicki, that evil man, that Haman, stole millions of rubles' worth of gold from the old nobles and from rich Jews, and had it all brought here to us in Voronko. And one night, by the light of the moon, he buried the treasure at the foot of the hill, near the bes medresh, deep deep in the ground. Now it's overgrown with grass and a spell is cast on it so no one can find it."

"And is it lost forever and ever?"

"Who told you it's lost forever and ever? If so, why did God create Kabbala? The masters of the Kabbala, dummy, know how to undo a spell."

"How?"

"They know. They have a charm and a verse from the Psalms which has to be chanted forty times forty times."

"Which verse?"

"Oh, dummy, if I only knew that verse! But even if I did know it—it wouldn't be so simple. First you have to fast forty days and recite forty psalms each day. And on the forty-first day at sunset you have to slip away without being seen. And you have to do it cleverly, for if someone sees you, you have to start your forty-day fast all over again. And only then, if you're lucky and don't bump into anyone, you go off on a dark moonless night to the foot of the hill, at the other side of the bes medresh. You stand there on one leg for forty minutes, counting forty times forty, and if you don't make a mistake in the counting, the treasure will reveal itself to you."

Shmulik somberly explained the secret of the treasure to his friend Sholom. His soft voice gradually grew softer; he spoke as if reading from a book, without even stopping for a second:

"And the treasure will be revealed to you by means of a little fire, a tiny flame. When the flame appears, approach it at once. Don't be afraid of getting burned. It's only a light—it's not hot at all. All you have to do is bend down and scoop up handfuls"—Shmulik shows with both hands how he scoops—"of gold and silver, diamonds and gems, and stones called Kadkod and Yoshfe."

"What's the difference between them?"

"Oh, you dummy, there's a world of difference between them. Kadkod is a stone that lights your way in darkness like a candle, and Yoshfe can turn black to white, red to yellow, green to blue. It can change wet to dry, hungry to full, the old to young, the dead to life . . . All you have to do is rub it on the right lapel of your jacket and say: 'I wish I had a magnificent breakfast!' Then a silver tray appears with two roasted pigeons and fresh pletzls made of the best flour. Or you can say: 'I wish I had an excellent supper!' Then a golden tray appears with all kinds of dishes fit for a king: roasted tongues and stuffed necks whose delicious aroma seeps into every limb. Fresh challa rolls materialize before your eyes and flasks of choicest wines, and nuts and carob and sweets without end—so much, you don't even want any!"

Shmulik turned away to spit. Judging by his friend's dry lips and dreamy-eyed, pale face, Sholom realized that Shmulik wouldn't refuse a piece of roasted tongue, a stuffed neck, or even a piece of challa. Sholom promised himself that tomorrow, God willing, he would bring him some nuts, a couple of pieces of carob and a candy which he'd pilfer from his mother's shop. Meanwhile, he asked Shmulik to tell him more and more. Shmulik didn't have to be asked twice. He wiped his lips and told Sholom more and more:

"And once you've had your fill of all these delicious foods and have drunk the choicest wines, you take the stone and rub it and say: 'I wish I had a soft bed.' And a bed of ivory appears. It's gold-plated, covered with a butter-soft featherbed, little pillows made of silk, and a satin-covered quilt. You stretch out and fall asleep. You dream of angels and cherubs and seraphs. You see the celestial Garden of Eden and the earthly Garden of Eden. Or you can rub the stone and you're lifted up, up to the clouds, above the clouds, and you fly up on high like an eagle, soaring into space."

It's hard to say if this poor orphan and his fantastic tales appeared later in the writings of his friend Sholom, when Sholom Nochem Vevik's became Sholom Aleichem. But one thing is certain: Shmulik enriched Sholom's imagination and deepened his perception. Shmulik's dreams about treasures, magic stones and other good things are still ensconced in Sholom's heart—perhaps in another form or guise, but he bears them within him to this very day.

6. The Rabbi in Paradise

The Friendship of David and Jonathan—The Leviathan and the Wild Ox—The Appearance of the Righteous in the Other World

Shmulik the Orphan's beautiful stories completely enchanted his young friend and prompted him to dream about princes and princesses who woke him, tugged him by the sleeve, and said: "Get up, Sholom. Get dressed and come with us."

Sholom also spent many of his waking hours with princes and princesses—in a crystal palace or on the frozen sea; on an island where savages reigned, or in the earthly Paradise with its twelve wells of quicksilver and thirteen saffron gardens, where gold and silver were scattered everywhere like dust; or lifted into the air above the clouds with the power of the stone Yoshfe. It came to the point where Sholom could name all these places and see them wherever he went.

A pile of planks sufficed to spark his fantasy. He fancied it was an island and he was its prince; the geese and ducks who strutted about in the yard were wild cannibals; he was their king, who could drive them wherever he wished and do what he liked with them, for they were his subjects. If he found a piece of glass his fantasy transformed it into a precious magic stone, a kind of Kadkod. A plain pebble picked up from the ground might very well be the real Yoshfe. Who knows? When no one was looking, he diligently rubbed it on his right lapel and, like Shmulik, said: "I wish I had . . ."

Shmulik's stories about treasures made the deepest impression on Sholom. He was absolutely confident that if he didn't discover a treasure today, he'd find one tomorrow. Naturally, he would give all the gold to his parents. Father would no longer have to worry and be so involved in his businesses. Mama would no longer have to freeze all day at the shop. With the power of Yoshfe he would build them a crystal palace surrounded by a saffron garden, in the midst of which would be a quicksilver well. A guard dog would watch the entrance; vipers, elves and wildcats would scramble up the trees. And he, the prince in all his glory, would dispense largesse to the paupers of Voronko with an open hand—he'd give gifts big and small, according to each person's due.

The two close friends never dreamed they would have to part permanently. First of all, why should friends separate? And, besides, they both swore to God while holding their ritual fringes that one would not travel anywhere without the other. No matter what happened to them or where fate would take them, they would always be one soul. Their love was the kind that bound David to Jonathan. Would you then expect the rabbi—who was indeed an old man, I'm afraid, perhaps even seventy—to suddenly lie down and die without warning and the orphan Shmulik to leave with the rabbi's widow for some godforsaken village, far off in the Kherson province, and to vanish as if there'd never been a Shmulik in the world?

Of course all this didn't happen that fast. A rabbi doesn't just lie down and die so quickly. The rabbi, who had always been in frail health, sickly from his self-imposed fasts and from just plain not eating, took to bed in his old age, lay there paralyzed for over a year, neither eating nor drinking, only studying and praying, struggling with the Angel of Death. Shmulik swore to Sholom by all that was holy that every evening, between the Afternoon and Evening Service, the Fiend himself flew in through a crack in the window, stood at the head of the rabbi's bed and waited for him to stop praying so he could nab him. But the rabbi outsmarted him. He didn't stop for a moment; he either studied Torah or recited prayers.

"How does he look?"

"Who?"

"The Fiend."

"How should I know?"

"You just said he came, so you probably saw him."

"Dummy! If you see the Fiend you're finished. So how could I have seen him?"

"Then how do you know he comes?"

"Really now! What then should he do? Wait for an invitation?"

When the rabbi died the two friends had a holiday. Only a rabbi in a small village could have such a beautiful funeral. Shops were closed, schoolchildren were dismissed, and everyone in town accompanied him to his resting place.

On the way back, the two beloved friends, David and Jonathan, were the very last mourners. They walked slowly, hand in hand, so that they could talk to their hearts' content. And there was plenty to talk about: the rabbi's death and the world to come, the angels' meeting him at the gates of Paradise, his welcome, and who would await him.

Shmulik knew everything—even what it was like up there. He spoke about everything as if he'd seen it all. Actually, he said, the rabbi did not die. He merely removed himself to another world, a better world where they prepared for him the Feast of Leviathan and the Wild Ox and the Preserved Wine and all the other good things of Paradise. Oh yes, there the rabbi would first begin to taste life. A new life, a happy life in a magnificent Paradise, together with such notables as Abraham, Isaac and Jacob, Joseph, Moses and Aaron, King David, King Solomon and Elijah, Maimonides, the Baal Shem Tov and the Rizhiner Rebbe.

Shmulik described them all as if they stood in life before him. Father Abraham with a white beard; Isaac, tall and thin; Jacob, ailing and bent; Joseph—handsome; Moses—short of stature but with a wide forehead; Aaron, tall and holding an almond staff; King David with his violin; Elijah—a poor Jew; Maimonides—well dressed, a curly beard; the Baal Shem Tov—a simple Jew with a plain wooden staff; the Rizhiner Rebbe—a handsome man wearing a silk gaberdine.

Hearing this made Sholom long to see those men; he yearned to be with them in Paradise, even if only to taste a tiny piece of the Leviathan and the Wild Ox and have a drop of the Preserved Wine. The two friends really envied the rabbi, who was now living the good life; they forgot that he had just been lowered into a dark and narrow grave and covered with sticky black earth patted down with wooden shovels, and that Shmulik himself had just said the Kaddish for him. For the rabbi was childless—may you and all other Jews be spared the like.

7. Shmulik Vanishes

*David and Jonathan Are Parted Forever—The Secret of the Treasure—
A Friend Lost*

 During the week the rebbitsin sat shiva for the rabbi, Shmulik the Orphan wandered around town all by himself like someone twice orphaned. The only thing he looked forward to was evening, when the children were dismissed from cheder and he'd see his friend Sholom, who had drawn even closer to him since the rabbi died. David and Jonathan, the beloved friends, had a feeling that they would soon have to part. They didn't know how this would happen and didn't want to know. That's why they spent every evening together.

Fortunately, it was summer and there were no evening lessons. The two boys could meet in Nochem Vevik's garden and spend two or three hours talking under the pear tree. Or they could wander to the outskirts of town, far beyond the mills, hoping that the gentile boys wouldn't attack them or set the dogs on the "dirty Yids."

Out there the two friends could talk to their hearts' content. And there was plenty to talk about. One thing interested them: What next? What would happen if Shmulik went away? For Shmulik had heard that the rebbitsin's sister had invited her and that she was preparing to move to the far-off Kherson province. If the rebbitsin went, Shmulik too would have to go. What would he do here all alone? He didn't even have a place to put his head.

Naturally, he wasn't going for a long time and, in any case, the move would not be permanent. Once he got there he'd start studying Kabbala. And as soon as he discovered the secret he'd return at once to Voronko and would set to work—to find the treasure. He would fast for forty days, recite forty psalms every day, and on the forty-first day, when no one saw him, he would count to forty times forty while standing on one leg for exactly forty minutes by his watch . . .

"Do you have a watch?"

"I don't have one now, but I'll have one then."

"Where will you get it?"

"Where will I get it? I'll steal it. What do you care?"

Sholom looked into his friend's eyes. He was afraid he might have insulted him; Shmulik would be angry. But Shmulik wasn't the sort of friend to let a word upset him. He didn't stop telling stories about what would happen when the two friends grew up, what they would accomplish in this village, and how happy they would make the Jews of Voronko. The tales flowed like pure oil, they bubbled out of him like fine honey. On that warm, summery, enchanted night the two boys did not want to part. But they had to go home to sleep; otherwise they would be punished. They bade each other good-bye.

"See you tomorrow."

But one tomorrow followed another—and no Shmulik. Where was he? He had picked himself up and gone off somewhere to the Kherson province with the rabbi's widow. When? How? Without even saying good-bye?

Stunned and forlorn, Sholom remained alone, lonely as a stone. His best, dearest, most beloved friend was gone. The whole world darkened. What good was the world if Shmulik was gone! What good was life without Shmulik! And the forsaken and lonely friend felt a queer tightness in his throat. Something tickled his nose and clamped his heart. He hid in a distant corner and cried his eyes out.

What do you think? Is he alive somewhere, this extraordinary Shmulik with the dreamy eyes and charming speech which flowed like pure oil and bubbled out of him like fine honey? Where was he now? What was he doing? Was he an itinerant preacher? A rabbi or teacher? Merchant, shopkeeper or broker? Or was he a pauper, down at the heels? Perhaps he had sailed to the golden land, America, where he was making a living. Or perhaps he is already resting where all of us will be one hundred years from now, and is providing a feast for the worms.

If anyone has any news of Shmulik, if anyone has heard of him—please let me know.

8. Meir Medvedevker

A New Friend Who Can Sing—Cheder Rascals Put on a Show— A Barefoot Scamp Becomes a Star

 Sholom didn't have to worry or complain too long about the loss of his bosom chum. God soon sent a replacement for Shmulik and gave him a new friend.

This is how it happened. Since the old rabbi had died and the village had been left without a rabbi, Nochem Rabinowitz cast aside all his business affairs and traveled to Rakitne, where a rabbi named Chaim Medvedevker had won far-reaching fame. When Sholom's father brought this rabbi to Voronko, the village rejoiced. Not only was he a great scholar, pious and blessed with a good voice—but since he was a great pauper to boot, he also taught the older children in the Talmud Torah.

Nevertheless, Reb Zorechl the teacher wasn't deprived of his livelihood, God forbid. How could you simply cut a man off from his source of income? Reb Zorechl, then, stayed on as a teacher of Bible and handwriting—namely, Yiddish and Russian, German, French and Latin, which neither the children nor the teacher could make heads or tails of. The new rabbi taught Talmud. And though Sholom was still a stubborn mule and refused to grow, he was put into the highest grade anyway. For when the rabbi tested him on a page of Pentateuch and Rashi's Commentary, he pinched Sholom's cheek with satisfaction and said, "You're some devil!" Then he turned to Sholom's father. "It would be a sin to let this scalawag study only Bible. He should be introduced to Talmud. Don't worry, it won't hurt him."

Naturally, Father was elated. Although the "devil" wasn't enthusiastic about studying Talmud, he was proud as a peacock to be in an older class, and he strutted about with his nose in the air.

Reb Chaim Medvedevker didn't make the move from Rakitne

alone; he brought two sons. One, Avreml, was already married. He had a protruding Adam's apple, an excellent voice, and led prayers beautifully; the other, Meirl, also had a nice voice and a protruding Adam's apple, but when it came to studying he had a wooden head. Nothing sank in. He not only had a thick head but he was a rascal as well. He and Sholom quickly became friends. But don't dismiss Meirl so lightly. He had a wonderful attribute. He sang songs—and what songs they were! But there was one drawback—he had the temperament of a true artist. He hated to sing for nothing. If you wanted to hear him sing, you had to pay. A penny for a song. If you were broke, an apple would do. In a pinch, half an apple, a couple of plums, a candy—but never for nothing. In return, however, he sang songs so sweetly and with such depth of feeling that you forgot artists like Caruso, Chaliapin, Sobinov and Sirota, and all the other singers in the world.

> I go out on a Vilna street
> And hear wailing, "Vey! Oy vey!"
> How they weep, alack aday!

All the children listened openmouthed, touched to the quick. But Meirl wasn't moved by his song at all. He also had a way with cantorial pieces. Once, the teacher—his father, Reb Chaim—stepped out of the classroom for a moment. Meirl jumped up, faced the wall, and draped a tablecloth over his shoulders like a prayer shawl. Then he put his finger to his throat like a seasoned cantor and quickly sang "God our King who sits on the throne of mercy" from the Penitential Service, and concluded with "He called in the na-ame of . . ."

Just then the rabbi entered. "What's this? Pulling cantorial pranks? Come here, you apostate, and stretch out on the bench like this."

And the "execution" began.

Meirl Medvedevker not only excelled in singing. He had another obsession: play-acting, masquerading, pretending to be someone else. He performed roles in *The Sale of Joseph*, *The Exodus from Egypt*, *The Ten Plagues*, *Moses and the Ten Commandments* and many other plays.

Once he dressed up as a robber. He held a big stick in his hand and thrust the rebbitsin's meat cleaver into the rabbi's sash around his waist. He was barefoot, with trouser cuffs rolled up, and his eyes blazed like a cutthroat's. Sholom played the role of a hunchbacked pauper. He stuffed a pillow into his back, turned his cap inside out, and went begging for alms. But he lost his way in a forest. (The children were the trees.) And Sholom the pauper, leaning on his stick, walked among the trees, looked for the path, and bumped smack into—Meir the Robber. The robber pulled the cleaver out of his sash and sang a song which ended:

"Give me money . . . give me money."

But with tears in his eyes, Sholom the pauper begged for mercy, if not for himself then at least for his wife and children. She'd become a widow and the children orphans. At which Meir the Robber grabbed the pauper by the throat and threw him to the ground. Just then the rabbi came in and the commotion began.

"As for him"—he pointed to his own son—"that scoundrel, that apostate, that anti-Semite, there's nothing to talk about. But you, Nochem Rabinowitz's son, how can you compare yourself to that heretic?"

Evidently Reb Chaim had prophetic gifts. Many years later Meir Medvedevker—by then known as the singer Medvedyev—converted. Nevertheless, it must be said that he fulfilled the mitzva of honoring his father like the finest Jew, in the nicest way. He bought his poor old father a house in Rakitne, showered him with gold, visited him every summer, and brought gifts for the entire family. Reb Chaim the rabbi, who wasn't aware of the trick his son had pulled in order to earn the title "Artist of the Imperial Theater," had a happy old age. But let's return to Meirl's childhood, when he still hadn't the faintest idea that someday he'd be known as Michael Yefimovitch Medvedyev and would take the world by storm.

9. *Another Friend Lost*

Nabbing Pears and Getting Smacked—Learning to Steal—Tisha B'Av in the Priest's Garden—The Execution

 It's no surprise that the two boys, Meir Medvedevker and Sholom Nochem Vevik's, grew fond of each other and became bosom friends. Their souls found a common bond, and they had a premonition of future success. This feeling was not entirely illusory. Twenty years later, when the two met (it happened in Byelotserkov, in the Kiev province, as we shall see later), one was the famous entertainer Medvedyev, and the other was writing sketches for the *Di Yiddishe Folksblatt* signed Sholom Aleichem.

Now back to their childhood again, when one was still called Meirl Medvedevker and the other Sholom Nochem Vevik's, and they still strolled barefoot through the Voronko streets like all other well-to-do kids. To tell the absolute truth, neither of them had any great desire for the Torah study that Reb Chaim Medvedevker tried to instill in them, nor for the piety he sought to implant. Their interests lay elsewhere. For instance, picking green gooseberries, shaking pears or plums from a tree, even in one's own garden, was more fun than languishing over a page of Talmud, reciting a psalm, or praying with the devotion that the rabbi demanded of his students.

"The Talmud isn't a goat—it won't run away. God will forgive us for not praying. As for the psalms—let the old Jews sit and recite them," Meirl told Sholom. He taught him how to climb the tallest tree before you could say "Shema Yisroel," and how to jump and catch hold of a cherry tree branch so that the cherries popped right into your mouth. Then your lips turned black and your fingertips bore witness that you'd been picking cherries. But how bad could it get? So you get smacked—big deal!

Getting beaten in Hebrew school was so routine the cheder boys felt neither humiliation nor pain. "So what if you get a few whacks from the teacher? They'll heal by the time you marry." Only an older student who was already engaged would feel embarrassed. Anyway, only one thing scared him—that his fiancée might find out. And not so much his fiancée as all her girlfriends—for they would taunt her: "Your future husband got a licking on his you-know-what."

But this didn't bother Meir, for he wasn't engaged, and he led his friend Sholom away from the straight and narrow path. Meir taught him how to skimp on prayers and how to sneak carob, candies, honey cakes and other goodies from right under his mother's nose in the shop. This wasn't stealing, God forbid, but taking. For that one wasn't punished in the other world.

Maybe everything would have gone smoothly if misfortune hadn't struck Meirl. He climbed a fence into the priest's garden and stuffed his shirt full of pears. The priest's daughter happened to be at the window—and noticed. The priest then ran out with his dog and caught Meirl. The dog tore his pants and the priest snatched his cap and sent him to the winds.

Perhaps even this wouldn't have been so tragic if it hadn't happened on Tisha B'Av. Think of it! All Jews were in their stocking feet, crying and bemoaning the destruction of the Holy Temple, while he, the rabbi's sonny boy, was traipsing about bareheaded and with torn trousers!

In our era of pogroms, the poor boy's punishment is not fit to be described. But that's not the main point. What's important is that Nochem Vevik's withdrew Sholom from the cheder and, following his example, other fathers did the same. Unfortunately, Reb Chaim was left without pupils. Since his wages as a rabbi and cantor did not suffice, he had to pack up and move back to Rakitne. And so once more the village was without a rabbi.

But don't worry—this state of affairs didn't last too long. Nochem Vevik's brought in a new rabbi from Barishpoli, a young man named Shmuel Eli. He was learned, sang well and, to top it off, played chess, for which you really have to be a brain! But Shmuel Eli had one flaw: he was a bit of an intriguer and a flatterer, and liked to talk to young women when no one was looking.

And that's how our hero lost his second friend.

10. Sirko

A Smart, Courteous Dog—Compassion for Living Creatures— Metamorphosis of a Man—A Devoted Friend

The name alone tells you that Sirko was no man but a dog, a plain mutt with gray hide. I say a plain mutt, but must add at once that he wasn't that plain, as we'll soon see. But first some details. Namely, how does a Jew come to have a dog? Here's the story.

When Nochem Vevik's moved from town to the village and took over the local post office and the courtyard with everything in it, he found a dog in the yard. Although a young pup, Sirko was quite smart—he already recognized his new masters. Moreover, he had respect for Jews. He didn't snap like other hounds who went into a mad frenzy whenever they saw a Jew in a long gaberdine passing by.

Naturally, Sirko had no contact at all with his new masters; he didn't even get a whiff of the inside of the house. Perhaps from the outset he'd been taught with a smack on the head that a dog wasn't allowed near a Jewish home.

He couldn't set foot in the kitchen either. Once, on a Friday afternoon, one-eyed Frume the Maid showed him his place by scalding him with a pailful of boiling water. But she did this good-naturedly and even laughed.

Oh, that Frume! That girl had the heart of a Tartar. She couldn't tolerate cat or dog. One day, with tears in his eyes, Sholom just about managed to save the cat, which Frume had tied to a leg of the table and was beating so mercilessly with a broomstick that the hapless creature's cries could be heard for miles.

"Frume, darling, sweetheart, what are you doing? Have pity on living creatures! God will punish you. Hit me instead, hit me but not the cat," Sholom pleaded and presented his back to the despotic maid. Realizing she'd been too brutal with the cat, she poured a pitcher of cold water over her, barely reviving the half-dead creature.

And why do you think Frume had done this? There was absolutely no reason for it. Frume presumed that "the nibbler" (Frume called the cat by no other name) had nabbed something, for she found the cat licking herself. "Why is she licking herself all of a sudden?" Frume was suspicious of everyone. A cat was obviously a nibbler; a dog—a devil; a gentile—a thief; a child—a pig. And so on down the line. But let's return to Sirko.

After being driven so miserably from the house and the kitchen, any other dog would have kissed the place good-bye. But Sirko wasn't that sort. Even on pain of death he wouldn't leave the courtyard. Here he was born and here he'd give up the ghost. Especially since he had wonderful protectors here: the owner's children. They liked him despite Frume's efforts at humiliating him. The life Sirko led would have made any dog happy. The children brought him the best of everything in their pockets—in secret, naturally, so no one would see or even guess, for it would have been disastrous for both sides. Sirko knew the time for breakfast, lunch and supper, and eagerly awaited his ration of goodies. He already knew whose, and which, pocket to sniff—and there he would poke his nose. A clever dog!

Listen to the tricks the children taught him. They would put a clean bone or a piece of bread on the tip of his nose and tell him in Russian (a dog is usually addressed in a gentile language): "Don't touch it!" And Sirko would patiently wait until he heard the order "Eat!" and then he would leap and snatch the treat.

Winter nights, when the children went to cheder, Sirko had no patience to wait for his friends. Every night around nine he materialized under the cheder window. He scratched the frosty panes with his paws, signaling it was time to close the holy texts and go home to eat supper. The teacher thought of Sirko as a clock. "No doubt about it, your dog is a metamorphosed creature," he said as he dismissed his pupils. They took their greased paper lanterns and happily made their way home, singing the Russian army marching song:

> One two three four
> We're going home
> Right through that door!
> Five six seven eight
> It's time to leave
> By the front gate!

Sirko bounded ahead gaily, frisking and rolling in the snow—just for the crusts of bread and dry bones from supper. A diligent dog!

Often, when he felt gloomy and despondent—scolded at home, reprimanded at cheder—Sholom would go behind the trees in the back of the garden, on the other side of the fence. There, on a pile of rubbish, he would sit down with his faithful Sirko, who would stick out his chin and look right into Sholom's eyes like a human being.

What is he looking at? What thoughts run through his head? Does he indeed understand everything like a man? Does he have a soul like, forgive the comparison, a human being? Then Sholom thought of his teacher's remark: "The dog is a metamorphosed creature." He recalled what King Solomon said in Ecclesiastes: "There is no difference between man and beast." But if there's no difference, why is he a dog and I a human being? Sholom mused as he looked at the dog with combined compassion and respect—the dog also looked at him as at his equal. A dog who was a friend! A dear, devoted friend— Sirko!

11. Sirko's Tragedy

A Terrible Accusation—The Fate of an Innocent Dog—Bitter Tears

That Sirko was a wise dog is no exaggeration; he knew who loved him more than anyone else. No wonder then that Sirko was closer to Sholom than to any of the other children. He formed a silent bond of friendship with him, loved him, would do anything for him—he was ready to sacrifice himself for his friend and master.

But since he was mute, and had no words to express his affection, Sirko displayed it in canine fashion by jumping and yelping and rolling on the ground. A word from his master sufficed for him. As soon as he said, "Back to your place!" Sirko would lie down, quiet as a pussycat, and watch his master with one eye.

A quiet love reigned between dog and master. The latter couldn't imagine what would happen if Sirko were gone. What do you mean, gone? How could that be? Was Sirko a person who would pick up and leave and forget to say farewell? No matter how often the gentiles tried to inveigle Sirko into their part of the village, the following morning he'd return, tongue out and panting. He would throw himself on the ground, then leap up to his master's neck, yelping and licking his collar. One could have sworn there were tears in his eyes.

But still—still the day came, that dark and gloomy day when dear, devoted Sirko went away forever, and in such an unjust, terrible and tragic manner.

This sad event took place during the summer, in August. There had been a spell of awfully hot weather, no rain at all. People collapsed from the heat. Such heat waves are dangerous for dogs—they go mad.

A rumor spread in town that a dog had gone mad and bitten several other unidentified dogs. Afraid, the villagers took steps to protect the children from the bite of a rabid dog.

They sent all the children to old Trofim the witch doctor. His sharp nails could remove blue pimples from one's tongue without the slightest pain. This wasn't a dangerous operation; but still, having a gentile dig into your mouth with his fingernails and look for blue pimples under your tongue was no pleasure.

Next, the villagers turned their attention to the dogs. From God knows where they brought two dogcatchers armed with thick rope and iron hooks. They soon set to work. In one day these hangmen did away with a score of dogs. They could tell at a glance which dog was mad. Who would have thought they'd also choose the good, wise, well-behaved Sirko?

People said that the dogcatchers were paid per executed dog. Unfortunately, there may have been innocent victims, and Sirko was one of the first.

The children learned of this only later, when they returned from cheder. They revolted, were up in arms. "What do you mean, they got Sirko? How could you let them do such a thing?"

Naturally, the response was a counterrevolution. "Very nice! Cheder lads have nothing else to do but think of dogs!" Then the boys were treated to a torrent of slaps—and for dessert the parents also informed their teacher and asked him not to spare the rod. The teacher listened and didn't spare it.

But all this was nothing compared to Sirko's being destroyed for no reason whatsoever.

Most depressed of all was Sirko's beloved master—the author of this autobiography. For several days he didn't eat and at night he couldn't sleep. He tossed from side to side, sighing and groaning softly, unable to forgive the cruel, nasty people who had absolutely no compassion, no pity for living creatures, no sense of justice. Sholom considered at length the essence of a dog and a man. Why was a dog so loyal to a man, and why was man an executioner? And then recalling Sirko and his kindly, clever eyes, Sholom pressed his face into his pillow and wet it with his bitter tears.

12. The Evil Impulse and the Good Impulse

Pug-Nosed Ozer—An Informer—Many Caretakers—Grandma Mindy's Sabbath Fruit—Preachers of Ethics and Morality

 If perchance the boy forgot that he had once befriended a dog, he got constant reminders: "Sirko sends his regards." No opportunity was lost for a moral discourse—to give Sholom something to remember later. Listening to these lectures was worse than a hiding. There's good reason for the proverb: "A quick slap goes but a harsh word grows." Especially since he was presented with both slaps and words.

Words flew from all sides. Everyone under the sun reprimanded Sholom—and with sweet talk too. You might wonder, why should the shamesh care how the rich man's son prayed? Or why should he mind if the boy looked out the window while everyone else was saying the Silent Devotion? Do you think he didn't have good reason to look out the window? Despite the Silent Devotion, the scene out there was fascinating. One could learn a moral from it. A dog was chasing a cat. All abristle, the cat ran as if shot from a bow, with the dog in hot pursuit. The cat leaped onto a fence—the dog right after her. The cat off the fence—the dog likewise. The cat on the gutter—the dog too. The cat from the gutter to the roof—the dog, stuck. He stopped like an idiot, that son of a dog, and licked his lips as if to say: "Why am I chasing a cat who's not my own kind, and what am I doing on the roof?"

"Is that the proper way for a lad to stand for the Silent Devotion?" Melech the Shamesh seized Sholom by the nape of the neck. "Wait, you little devil, till I tell your father."

Or what concern was it to Ozer, the pug-nosed bathhouse attendant (Ozer had once been a shoemaker; in his tired old age he switched jobs), if Nochem Vevik's little boys slid down the hill on their rumps and tore their trousers? But Ozer happened to see this from the bathhouse and began shouting in his snuffling voice:

"You little bastards! Demons! The devil take your fathers' fathers! Ruining new pants! Ruining things is a sin! I'm going to the cheder right now to tell your teacher!"

Snitching on someone was not only a mitzva—it was a necessity, every Jew's duty, for every Jew had children and no one could predict how his own children would turn out. So they had to be watched and helped—if not with one's hands, then with one's mouth. That's why the children had so many guides and guardians. They heard so much preaching, criticism and moralizing that their ears buzzed incessantly. "Zzh, zzh, zzh—don't do this!" "Zzh, zzh, zzh—don't go there." Everyone droned: parents, sisters, brothers, the teacher, the maid, uncles and aunts, grandma—especially Grandma Mindy, who deserves a few lines.

Grandma Mindy was tall and neat, well-dressed and terribly pious.

Her task was looking after the grandchildren and their religious observances. She straightened out the boys' earlocks with moistened fingers, cleaned and smoothed their clothing, listened to their prayers, Grace After Meals and bedtime Shema Yisroel. That's why all the grandchildren had to come to her on Sabbath and wish her "Gut Shabbes." They sat like millstones on a bench near the wall and waited for her to present them with a none-too-generous portion of fruit, served in a shiny bowl: a little apple, a little peach, a carob, a fig or a few scrawny raisins. All this to the accompaniment of endless moralizing. Her preaching focused on the need to obey parents and good pious people. Be good Jews! God punishes for the slightest infraction—for not praying, for bad thoughts, even for a stain on your gaberdine. This preaching went on and on until the children no longer enjoyed the little apple, the little peach, the carob, the fig or the few scrawny raisins.

But Grandma's moralizing was no comparison to the veritable fount of morality with which the teacher drenched his students that same Sabbath day before the Afternoon Service. His vivid depiction of the good impulse and the evil impulse, Paradise and Hell, the Guardian Angel of the Dead, and the sling in which the wicked were cast from one end of the world to the other drew rivers of tears from everyone's eyes. The teacher saw millions of imps, demons and evil spirits gathered at the children's feet. He saw them under their fingernails. He was certain that each of them was a candidate for hell. Even if a pupil had not sinned, but had prayed and studied and done everything that the good impulse orders one to do, then that boy had submitted to the evil impulse and sinned in his thoughts. If not in his thoughts, then during sleep, dreaming about some forbidden thing.

In brief, there was no hiding from the devil, the evil impulse, except if you stretched out and died. But, as if for spite, you still wanted to live it up—fool around and laugh, nibble on sweets, rush through prayers, think of forbidden things—this was all the doing of the evil impulse, who had plenty of agents to lure the innocent into his net. Whereupon, like a calf, you followed him of your own accord and did everything he ordered. He was lucky, for people obeyed him much more than the good impulse. But all the moral preaching and ethical sermonizing were to no avail. On the contrary, the greater the diligence of the good impulse, the more strenuous the efforts of the evil impulse. I hesitate to say it, but I think if there were no good impulse, the evil impulse would have nothing to do.

13. Theft, Cardplaying and Other Sins

The Children Help Mother for the Fair—Playing Cards in Honor of Hanuka—Berel the Widow's Son Gives Stealing Lessons— A Young Outcast

The evil impulse had Nochem Vevik's children firmly in his cruel grip. The rascals skipped more than half their prayers and told Grandma a whopping lie: that in addition to the regular prayers they had also recited several psalms. As if that weren't enough, they also learned how to steal, sneak food, play cards, and commit other sins. Naturally, all this happened gradually, one misdeed leading to the next, just as the Talmud states: "One transgression leads to another." This is how it happened.

I think I mentioned that the Voronko Jews made their living selling to the peasants, especially during the long-awaited fairs. The Jews scurried about, did business, earned some money. The peasants, meanwhile, did what they had to do: steal. Especially the women. It was impossible to defend yourself adequately against them. If you managed to pull a scarf or a ribbon out of one woman's sleeve, another was nabbing a wax candle or some carob. What could one do? Sholom's mother, Chaya Esther, devised a plan. She placed her children in the shop to guard against theft—and the children devotedly came to her aid. Besides stuffing their pockets full of carob, tobacco, nuts and dried prunes, they also swarmed around the green metal cashbox, and when Mama spoke to a customer they slipped a few coins into their pockets. They took the money to cheder and bought blintzes, cakes, poppy-seed tarts, chick-peas and sunflower seeds—or they gambled it away in cards.

Playing cards was an epidemic in all the cheders. It started at Hanuka and lasted the entire winter. Everyone knows that during Hanuka it's a mitzva to play cards. Of course we don't mean real cards, God forbid. We're talking about imitation cards, Jewish ones. But it's all the same. The same bad habit, the same gambling. On Hanuka the teacher not only ordered his pupils to play cards, he even joined in. What's more, he gladly won all their Hanuka gelt. And losing your money at cards to your teacher was a pleasure and an honor and a joy. In any case, it was preferable to being beaten by him—any rational person will agree with that.

But when Hanuka was over—good-bye holiday and good-bye cards! The teacher gave strict orders: "Be careful. Don't you dare touch a card or even talk about cards. Whoever does takes his life in his hands. It's a whipping for sure."

The teacher had evidently once been a little rascal himself and loved to play cards not only during Hanuka. Otherwise, how would he have suspected the children of this? Nevertheless, his pupils played cards all winter long with greater enthusiasm and higher stakes than during Hanuka. They gambled away their breakfasts and lunches, and whoever had a spare coin lost that too. And when they ran out of money and wanted to gamble, they sought all kinds of ways to get money. Some infiltrated the Rabbi Meir Baal Ha-Nes charity box and with a wax-tipped straw pulled out, one by one, the wept-over pennies that Mama had thrown in every Friday just before lighting the Sabbath candles. They also came up with other bright ideas, like offering to go shopping and pocketing a few coins in change. Some even sidled up to their father's wallet or their mother's pocket at night when everyone was asleep and made off with what they could. All this was done with great trepidation and much risk. And it all went down the drain with gambling at cards.

The problem was when, where, and how they could play without the teacher's knowledge. This was solved by the boys in the higher class: boys like Eli Keyle's, a yellow-haired chap who was already engaged and had a silver watch, and Berel the widow's son, a common boy with thick lips and a set of healthy teeth that could chew through iron. Even then Berel was already sprouting a beard. But it was his own fault, Berel said, because he smoked cigarettes.

"For proof," he said, "start smoking yourself and before long your beard too will begin to grow."

Just for the fun of it, Berel taught many of his classmates to smoke. He not only taught them to smoke, he showed them how to get the raw materials for smoking. More accurately put—he taught them to steal. Naturally, for his tutelage Berel was paid—with tobacco and cigarette paper.

Berel had his own system. Whoever obeyed him and brought him tobacco and cigarette paper—why he was a stout lad, a chum. And whoever was scared and couldn't bring himself to steal was considered a baby, a milksop, a namby-pamby. His name was mud and he was no longer a friend. If he was lucky he also got a few smacks from Berel too. Disputing him or telling grown-ups was out of the question, for it meant informing on yourself—and no one was hero enough for that. That's why everyone acceded to all of Berel's orders, and sank ever deeper into the abyss with him. God knows how low the boys would have sunk had not Berel himself come to a sad end. He brought it on himself, and in an absolutely astonishing way, which his cheder friends were too young and innocent to comprehend. They only knew that one Friday Berel was caught by the bathhouse, where he had broken part of the windowpane and was watching the women bathing.

Oh woe, the commotion in the village! Berel's mother fainted; he was expelled from the cheder and banned from the bes medresh. No child from a proper family dared have any contact with this miserable apostate, a nickname he was given. Much later (after his widowed mother had died), as if to justify that name, Berel converted and vanished from sight.

14. Feigeleh the Witch

Rascals Repent—A Demon Not a Girl—A Tickling Witch

But don't assume that the evil impulse always won out and that the good impulse always lagged behind. Don't forget it was the beginning of the month of Elul. Coming up were Rosh Hashana, the Days of Repentance, Yom Kippur, and the ordinary prayers, fasts and self-flagellation introduced by devoted Jews. Despite the petty thefts, the cardplaying and other youthful transgressions, I can confidently state that the middle brother, Sholom Nochem Vevik's, was truly pious and God-fearing. He often promised himself he'd be better when he got older. God willing, he'd be as good and pious as Grandma Mindy, his teacher, and all good and pious people told him to be.

He often wept as he prayed, pounded his chest for his sins, and distanced himself from his older brothers and all the scamps who persuaded him to be bad. With the approach of the Days of Awe and the season of repentance Sholom became a true penitent.

Being good and pious is quite pleasant. Only someone who has tried to repent can aver that there's nothing better in the world. A penitent is one who is reconciled with God, subdues the evil impulse, and unites with God. Think of it: What could be better than reconciliation? What can be sweeter than victory? And what could be more precious than God? A penitent feels whole and strong; he's clean, fresh and newly born. He can look everyone in the eye. Being a penitent is wonderful.

As Elul commenced and the first shofar sounds were heard, the hero of this autobiography imagined the evil impulse bound in ropes, thrashing on the ground, begging for mercy. Don't trample me so hard, he begged. The good feeling lasted through Rosh Hashana and especially Yom Kippur! Enduring the long fast, feeling hunger and terrible thirst, yet controlling yourself like a grown-up was a delicious sensation. Only an observant or formerly observant Jew can appreciate that sweet and beautiful feeling. There's no joy comparable to that of leaving the bes medresh hungry and exhausted after Yom Kippur, pure of soul and cleansed of all sins. While hurrying home to break the fast you're already tasting the honey cake dipped in strong whiskey, when suddenly— Stop! What's up? The worshipers are reciting the blessing over the moon. "Dear God, we're starved, tired and exhausted! But one thing has nothing to do with the other. Over Your moon we'll recite a blessing."

Oh, how good it is to be a Jew, an observant Jew, a penitent!

But then the evil impulse—blast him!—poked his nose in and ruined everything. This time Satan came in the form of a village girl with curly hair and green eyes. Where did this girl come from? You'll soon hear. Listen!

The Jewish farmers in the surrounding little villages had an old custom of coming to town for the holidays—from Rosh Hashana through Sukkos. Every householder hosted a village couple or, as they were called, "the holiday folk." Nochem Vevik's guest was a distant relative from Hlubokeh named Lifschitz. He was a pious man with the wide forehead of an intellectual even though he wasn't too bright. He also had a pious wife who loved to pray and take snuff. Childless themselves, they took in as a maid a second cousin's cousin named Feigel. The scamps in town called her Feigeleh the Witch because she was a demon, a high-spirited tomboy. She loved to fool around with the boys when no one was looking and tell stories and sing songs, most of them gentile ones.

One bright, warm night during the Intermediary Days of Sukkos, she stole up to the beds where the young boys were sleeping (because of the village Jews, the children slept out in the yard). She sat down, half-naked, and told strange stories as she braided her hair. These weren't Shmulik's kind of tales, but were about demons, sprites and imps who played all kinds of pranks: they turned clothes inside out, moved the furniture around, turned pages of books, broke dishes, pulled pots from the oven, and did other naughty deeds. Then, talking about wizards and witches, Feigeleh said that a witch could torment a hundred people just by tickling them.

"Tickling? What do you mean by tickling?"

"You don't know what tickling is? Here, let me show you how a witch tickles."

And Feigeleh the Witch made a sudden movement with her disheveled hair and showed them how a witch tickled. At first the boys laughed; then they fought back and wrestled with her. They latched onto her tousled hair and pummeled her full force with their fists. Feigeleh made believe she was defending herself but it was apparent she was having fun. She accepted the blows and wanted more. Her face flamed. Her cat-green eyes glittered. By the light of the moon she looked like a real witch. But worst of all was that this witch not only overcame them all, but one by one she hugged them, pressed them to her heart, and kissed them, kissed them right on the lips.

Luckily, it was before Hoshanna Rabba, before one's fate is finally sealed in heaven, and one could ask God not to consider these unwilling kisses with a female too great a sin. For the Almighty Himself was witness that it was not planned but accidental.

Where did this Feigeleh the Witch come from? What kind of creature was she? A demon? A spirit? A transmigrated soul? Or was it Satan himself disguised as a female to make innocent boys sin— to kiss a girl against their will?

15. The Goblin

His Mischief—Caught—A Loose Girl Is Married Off

Feigeleh the Witch's identity was soon revealed. Here's the astonishing turn of events.

That winter, around Hanuka time, Lifschitz came to Voronko from Hlubokeh with the news that a goblin in his house was driving him crazy.

"At first," Lifschitz said, "he was only having fun at our expense. He turned pages of the Talmud, tore Pentateuchs and prayer books, flipped plates in the cupboard, broke pots, threw my tefillin bag and the mizrach decoration into the slops pail, and turned the pictures of Moses Montefiore to the wall. He did this in total silence. Without a sound. Later he emptied all my pockets and turned them inside out. Then he stole coins from my desk drawer and hid my wife's pearls. It's a calamity, I tell you! So I came to ask your advice, kinsman. What should I do, Nochem Vevik's? Report it to the district police? See the rebbe at Talne? Or move out of Hlubokeh?"

Nochem Vevik's heard him out and asked, "Where does your maid sleep? Does she get along with her mistress?"

"First of all," Lifschitz said in a huff, "Feigeleh is a poor relative. My wife wants to marry her off and give her a dowry. For her, living with us is Paradise. And secondly, she sleeps God-knows-where, in the kitchen behind locked doors. She sleeps so soundly there's no waking her!"

"Does she have any friends in the village?" Nochem Vevik's asked again.

This time Lifschitz flared up and yelled:

"Where does she come off having friends in a village full of gentiles? Or are you suggesting that Feigel is the goblin?"

"God forbid!" Nochem Vevik's laughed at his foolish kinsman. He tried to persuade him that neither imps nor goblins exist. But Lifschitz would hear none of this.

"I swear—may I live to hear the Messiah's shofar!—that at night I myself heard the panting of a living creature and the scratching of a fingernail. The next morning I saw the strange footprints of a chicken on the sand floor in the kitchen."

Realizing who he was dealing with, Nochem Vevik's made an abrupt about-face. "Well, it may be a goblin after all. But you know what? I'd like to see him in action. If you don't mind, I'll go back to the village with you. And since I'm going, I want my younger brother, Nissel, to join me. My Nissel," Nochem Vevik's explained, "is bold, gutsy and strong. He once beat up a local policeman, and I hope to God he can overcome the goblin too. Ready to go?"

"With pleasure!" Lifschitz cried enthusiastically. All three then wrapped themselves in bearskins and set out in a large sleigh for the village of Hlubokeh.

The guests arrived at dusk and were given a fine welcome. While eating a hot dairy meal, they discussed the goblin who had wormed his way into the house. Later, when Feigel served them, Nochem talked about a strange Rabinowitz trait.

"We all sleep like logs. We sleep so soundly you can move our beds outside and even shoot off a cannon by the bed. Nevertheless, even though we have money with us, we're not afraid of dybbuks, imps or goblins. But we're not stupid. The money is well hidden in our underwear, which we never take off. And, anyway, we don't believe in dybbuks, imps, goblins, wizards or God-knows-what other creatures! Our enemies concocted them and fools believe in them."

"It would serve you right if the goblin played his tricks on you tonight so you should know how it feels," Lifschitz said innocently.

The men spent the rest of the evening discussing the affair and drinking wine. Then the two Rabinowitz brothers, pretending to be tipsy, went to sleep and put out the light. Soon they began to snore lustily, one louder than the other—a veritable concert of snores.

Around midnight came a scream, the sound of slaps, and odd outcries in Yiddish and Russian. The Lifschitzes woke in a fright, lit the lights and saw the following: Feigeleh the Witch lay in Nochem's hands, bound and kicking, while powerful Nissel struggled with Chvedor the village scribe, who bit and bloodied his hands. But Nissel subdued him and tied him up like a ram.

At daybreak they brought both Feigel and Chvedor to the town elders. They gave them two pitchers of whiskey and came to an agreement. Since Chvedor was the village scribe, he was to admit his guilt and make restitution for everything he had stolen from the Lifschitzes with Feigel's cooperation. In turn, his only punishment would be a beating, at which all would be forgiven. But to Feigel they spoke kindly. Even though she was a demon, debauched, and

worse than an apostate, they would never hand her over to the gentile
authorities. Their only demand was that she tell them where she'd
hidden the pearls and the other items. They promised to take her to
town and find a husband for her at once. She'd have a lavish wedding
like a girl from the best family—klezmers, a new wardrobe and a
feast. No one would know about the incident, no birdie would chirp,
no cock would crow.

And that's exactly what happened. They found her a vigorous
youth, a woman's tailor named Moshe Hersh. The Rabinowitzes
were the hosts and led the bride to the canopy. The entire town was
invited, and the town council too. Bottles of beer and wine galore
were consumed, and a crowd gathered to watch the merry dancing
of Nissel Rabinowitz and the police chief.

After the wedding Feigel changed so radically you couldn't recognize her. As pious as a rebbitsin, she didn't look a man in the eye,
and made believe she never knew Nochem Vevik's children. If someone in town needed help, Feigeleh was among the first to go from
house to house collecting money in a kerchief. Calling her a saintly
woman was an understatement. Nevertheless (for one thing had
nothing to do with the other), her former name, Feigeleh the Witch,
stuck to her forever. Nochem Vevik's little rascals saw to that, led
by the middle son, Sholom, the greatest scamp of all.

16. The Family

Three Brothers—Three Different Types—Uncle Pinny Dances

Sholom's father, Nochem, had two other brothers: Pinny
and the aforementioned Nissel. Amazingly, each brother had
a unique personality and in no way resembled the other two.
The elder, Nochem, combined the traits of a maskil and a Hasid; he
was a philosopher and a prayer leader, a scholar of holy texts and a
thinker, quiet by nature, melancholy and locked into himself.

Uncle Pinny was very pious and wore long ritual fringes. He was
a handsome man with a comely beard and beautiful, laughing eyes.
Naturally vivacious and outgoing, he was deeply involved in communal affairs, and he performed circumcisions—not for money, God
forbid, but for the sake of the mitzva. He was always in a dither,

busy with other people's problems: lawsuits, cases of desertion, conciliation, and the plight of widows, orphans and paupers. And let's not forget that he was a trustee of the bes medresh, the Hasidic prayer room, the burial society, the Mishna class and the Psalms group. I think he preferred all this to doing business at the market or at a fair. It also cost him plenty. But that made the mitzva greater—for if you complained, the mitzva was no longer a mitzva.

For example, once they auctioned off the concession for the local postal service. To avoid high bids and loss of money, the Jews came up with a bright idea. The one who wanted the post office would pay each of his prospective competitors not to ruin his bid. But since the competitors couldn't be completely trusted, the money was put in escrow until after the auction. What place could be more secure for the money than Pinny Vevik's house? The bidder gave Pinny the money and went to the auction. But the bidder pulled a fast one. He pretended to drop out of the bidding, took the money back from Pinny, then returned and thumbed his nose at all of them. Naturally, the competitors informed the authorities. The bidder was caught first; then they turned their attention to the one who had held the money in escrow.

"All right," the authorities said, "tell us all about it."

And poor Pinny Vevik's told them the whole story; nothing but the truth. He was found guilty of defrauding the public coffers. Luckily for him, instead of a jail sentence he was only given a fine.

Do you think this taught him a lesson? Well, you're wrong. He still preferred other people's affairs, communal matters and helping fellow Jews over his own business. Don't even mention giving up a market or a fair to perform a circumcision! That's why he served as a mohel. And marrying off a poor orphan and dancing all night with the poor relatives was certainly a great mitzva that didn't often present itself.

Speaking of dancing, it's amazing that such a pious Jew could dance so well. Where did he learn this? And who was his teacher during those years? He knew all the steps for Hasidic, Cossack and peasant dances.

"Shh, quiet down. Reb Pinny's going to do a Hasidic dance."

"Give him room, folks, Reb Pinny Vevik's is going to do a Cossack dance."

Or:

"Ladies, to the side. Reb Pinny's going to show us a peasant dance."

Everyone moved and gave him room. Amid a throng of onlookers, Uncle Pinny would perform all three dances. It was a sight to behold.

The poorer the wedding, the greater the festivity. That is, the poorer the parents, the more fervently he danced. He danced his heart out, and all for the mitzva of entertaining the bride and groom. He had the agility and grace of the world's greatest dancers, and he amazed everyone with his lamp dance, which he did while holding burning candles, or with his mirror dance. Nowadays tickets would be sold for such performances to great profit. Uncle Pinny threw his gaberdine over his shoulder, rolled up his sleeves, and tucked his cuffs into his boots. As he danced, his feet barely touched the ground and the edges of his ritual fringes flew in the air. Head back, he closed his eyes and his face glowed with spiritual rapture as during prayers. The klezmers played a Jewish tune, everyone clapped in rhythm, the circle kept growing, and the dancer, avoiding the burning candles, was immersed in ever-increasing ecstasy and spiritual rapture. No, this wasn't dancing. It was rather a kind of divine worship, a pure service of God. Again I ask the same question: How did such a pious, God-fearing man achieve such artistry in dance? Where did he learn this? And who could have taught him?

With this digression about dancing, we've neglected to mention the third brother, Nissel Vevik's, whom we'll discuss in the next chapter.

17. Uncle Nissel and Aunt Hodel

Uncle Nissel Celebrates—Held in Esteem by the Police—Trouble with a Wife—Disguised—Off to America—Spark of a Poet

While the two elder brothers, Nochem and Pinny, were Hasidim, the youngest brother, Nissel Vevik's (lately he'd been calling himself Nissel Rabinowitz), had become quite worldly. Quite the fashion plate too: a split in the back of his gaberdine (that was considered dandyish in those days, stylishly German), lacquered boots with buckles, and nearly invisible, tucked-back earlocks. Nissel considered himself a democrat. For instance, like all other prominent Jews, he had a seat in shul by the eastern wall. Nevertheless, he sat way in the back by the stove in the ante-room, held a Pentateuch with Moses Mendelssohn's commentary, and told the simple Jews around him stories about grandees like Moses Montefiore and Rothschild. He also had a fine bass voice and loved to laugh and make others laugh, particularly women and girls. If he wished, he could make them faint with laughter. How he charmed them is hard to say. But at a word of his the shrieks of laughter would begin.

He was an unparalleled reveler! Without him a wedding was a funeral. Nissel Vevik's, or Nissel Rabinowitz, could resurrect the dead and make an entire crowd talk, laugh and dance. The difference between him and Uncle Pinny was that Uncle Pinny danced and Uncle Nissel made others dance. At a celebration everyone drank, sang and danced with him. Foremost was the police chief. When he exchanged hats with Nissel the festivities were under way.

In general, Nissel Rabinowitz was friendly with the police and ran the village imperiously, as though he were a policeman or an official. Moreover, his Russian was perfect—he spoke it like a gentile. Peas-ants and Jews alike respected him. "Let's go to Nissel," they would say. "We'll talk shop and get a drink."

Nissel liked dabbling in communal affairs even more than his brother Pinny. He was always litigating with, or for, someone. He thought he knew all the laws. After all, he spoke Russian so well one couldn't even tell a Jew was speaking, and he had such good connections with the town officials: He slapped the village elder like a dog, drank with the police chief, and kissed the bailiff like a brother.

Although Uncle Nissel was highly esteemed in town, he was disdained by his own wife, Aunt Hodel. (All great men are considered nothings by their wives!) Aunt Hodel was a small, swarthy woman, but this tiny creature cast a pall of fear over her huge husband. He was scared to death of her.

Amazingly enough, tall Uncle Nissel, esteemed by the town of-ficials, fluent in Russian, always so merry and dressed like a cavalier, and so welcome at ladies' homes—this Uncle Nissel somehow didn't mind having a pillow thrown at his head by his short little wife or a wet broom aimed at his pressed gaberdine. She particularly liked to give him the broom on holidays, especially on Simchas Torah for everyone to see. "Let them know the sort of husband his wife has!" But he thought all this a joke. He locked himself in the living room with all the other Jews, uncorked bottles of whiskey, opened all the barrels of sour pickles in the cellar, removed all the food from the stove—made a mess, a pogrom in the house—and then suffered for three weeks in a row at the hands of Aunt Hodel. But it was worth it—they'd had a grand time.

But best of all, Uncle Nissel didn't make a move without Aunt Hodel. He thought her extremely wise, and justified her conduct by saying that she came from Korsun, in the Kiev region, where everyone was cantankerous.

"For this there's only one cure," he said. "Pearls! God willing, when I can afford to buy her a string of large pearls, her character will change completely."

"I have a better medicine," said his elder brother Nochem. He tried to open Uncle Nissel's eyes with a secret whispered into his ear. But Uncle Nissel became terribly agitated.

"God forbid! May the Heavenly Father protect us from such a pass!"

"Listen to me, Nissel. Do what I say, and everything will be fine."

What Father suggested became apparent only much later. Aunt Hodel herself drummed it all over town by vituperating her husband's family: "Those people! Those Rabinowitzes! Beating up a wife is a daily routine. But their hands will wither before they lay a hand on me."

It was an open secret in the village that though he had influence with the town authorities and was universally considered a powerful man, Nissel Rabinowitz had for years led a miserable life with his wife. If only he hadn't been so influential! This actually brought him to ruin; later, however, it made him, his children and grandchildren happy forever. The following story sounds concocted, but I'll tell it the way I heard it.

In a small village near Voronko, I think it was Berezan, the peasants had sentenced a Jew to exile. At a loss what to do, the Jews ran to Nissel Rabinowitz:

"Look, you have influence with the police, you talk Russian and you're chummy with the chief."

Uncle Nissel ran off at once to the police chief. But he couldn't do a thing; it wasn't his department. He'd have to go see the county bailiff. But the latter was, first of all, a new man, and secondly, a Haman. What next? How could you let a Jew be ruined and see his entire family destroyed?

"Wait a minute! Everything will turn out all right!" said Uncle Nissel. Here's what he did. He obtained a complete official uniform, disguised himself as a district police chief, caught a post chaise, and rode into town with bells ringing. He summoned the local elder and his town council and berated them in Russian: "The devil take you, how can you do a thing like this?" He stamped his feet like an inspector general and told them it was against the law. Then he tore the expulsion edict to shreds before their eyes and warned them:

"Before anyone dares to complain about me to the governor, remember that I, your new district police chief, am the governor's uncle on his mother's side. What's more, my wife is related to the Minister of Interior himself."

Who blew the whistle no one knew. But the whole incident—the torn decree and the bluff about the governor and the Interior Minister—floated up like oil on water and Uncle Nissel was arrested and brought to trial. The upshot was that brave Uncle Nissel simply had to flee the country. First he spent some time in Odessa, secured a false passport and then, under a new name, sailed to America— actually Canada. At first he struggled, but within a couple of years he wrote that he was making a living. Then he brought his entire family over. They also wrote that they were making a living. Later they sent beautiful snapshots—they looked like dukes, lords! But not a word about how they made a living or about life in America.

Some thirty years later, in 1905–6,* Sholom himself had to emigrate to America. Once he had safely crossed the sea, he made it his business to get precise information about his uncle. Sholom discovered that although his Uncle Nissel was long dead, he had left a fine reputation and a fortune. His children and grandchildren were, as the Americans had it, "all right."

But to make the portrait of Uncle Nissel complete, one trait must be added: he was a born poet, a poet lost to the world. He loved to sing Yiddish songs of his own composition. In jail he wrote a poem about himself in the form of an alphabetical acrostic and set it to a

---

*Actually, it was toward the end of 1906 when Sholom Aleichem came to the United States. [C.L.]

beautiful, heartrending melody. Among us there were many such lost talents, talents that were never even discovered.

18. Pinneleh Shimmeleh's Goes to Odessa

Shimmeleh Talks More Russian than Yiddish—Tells of Ephrossi's Munificence—Moves to Odessa—His Son Pinneleh Has an Operation—The Last Supper

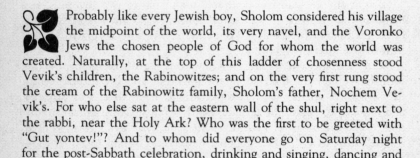 Probably like every Jewish boy, Sholom considered his village the midpoint of the world, its very navel, and the Voronko Jews the chosen people of God for whom the world was created. Naturally, at the top of this ladder of chosenness stood Vevik's children, the Rabinowitzes; and on the very first rung stood the cream of the Rabinowitz family, Sholom's father, Nochem Vevik's. For who else sat at the eastern wall of the shul, right next to the rabbi, near the Holy Ark? Who was the first to be greeted with "Gut yontev!"? And to whom did everyone go on Saturday night for the post-Sabbath celebration, drinking and singing, dancing and reveling till dawn?

There was no finer family than Sholom's. No house was richer. No one was greater than his father. No one was more pious than his Uncle Pinny. No one was merrier than his Uncle Nissel. And looking at his tall father, Nochem Vevik's, in his silk gaberdine with its broad sash and his Napoleonic hat; or at his short mother, Chaya Esther, as her delicate white hands kindled the Sabbath lights in her large, hand-chased silver candlesticks; or looking at tall, neat Grandma Mindy as she spoke to God as to an intimate; or at strong Uncle Nissel speaking Russian like a peasant—seeing all this, Sholom's heart was filled with joy at being born under the golden banner of such a family, where he felt as happy and secure as a prince in a fortress or a royal palace.

But suddenly the pillars of this fortress began to totter. The palace began to cave in, and all the enchantment of a happy village suddenly vanished. The young prince grew aware that Voronko was not the navel of the world, that bigger cities and richer Jews existed. He learned all this from his new friend Pinneleh Shimmeleh's, whom we shall now briefly depict.

Besides the Rabinowitz brothers there was another well-to-do man in town. Shimmeleh was a sturdy fellow with a round belly, a smiling, sympathetic face and an off-center mouth. He wasn't as rich as he was a squanderer. "He doesn't give a damn about a ruble," folks said in town. He spent as much as he had and, when he ran dry, he borrowed, went into debt, and continued to live it up.

Shimmeleh was considered somewhat of a heretic in town because he wore a cape, and rounded and trimmed his beard. But he donated generously to charity, and on a whim invited guests and prepared lavish feasts in midweek. That's the way to live!

Of all the Rabinowitzes, Shimmeleh liked Uncle Nissel best of all. Like him he wore a gaberdine with a slit in the back; his earlocks too were short and tightly curled. He also liked to talk to everyone in Russian: "Son of a bitch, what are you prattling about? Time to pray to God." Because he was left-handed, he had an extraordinary handwriting. (All lefties write beautifully—that's a known fact.) He was home only for the holidays. As soon as a festival ended, he departed—no one knew his destination—and didn't return until the next holiday. He brought back so many presents the entire town was agog and discussed Shimmeleh's gifts for a long time.

Once he came back before Passover and spread the news that he was leaving Voronko. Where to?

"Oh, far away. Very far. Near Odessa. Only cows stay in a hick town like this. The devil take you, if you saw Odessa, you'd know at least what a metropolis is. Go to Ephrossi's office and see all the clerks. The devil take you, you'd wish you and I both had the gold that rolls around there during the course of a day, son of a bitch!"

Naturally, everyone listened to Shimmeleh openmouthed, amazed at Ephrossi's vast business and at the sums of money that passed through daily. But behind his back they made fun both of Shimmeleh and of Ephrossi's business. Leading the mockers was Shmuel Eli, the new rabbi and cantor who had just moved to town from Barishpoli. He was a clever young rascal, as impudent as they come.

"Spit in his eye," he said. "First of all, Shimmeleh's not going anywhere. Secondly, he's not going to Odessa but somewhere closer—to Rzhishtchev. And it's not because we local folks are cows, but simply because he's a debtor. He doesn't even own the hair on his head, ha, ha, ha."

Still, no matter what—whether to Odessa or Rzhishtchev, or whether because the Voronko folk were cows or because he was a debtor—the hair on his head was indeed not his own. Shimmeleh wasn't joking. Right after Passover he began to sell his possessions for half price. Many things he gave away for nothing. He dressed the girls like brides, and ordered short coats from Yisroel the tailor for the boys, in keeping with the style of a great metropolis like Odessa. And to create an even greater furor in Voronko, Shimmeleh ordered his wife, Henye, to prepare a feast—and make cheese dumplings for the entire village.

Naturally, everyone came to the party, and the first to arrive was Shmuel Eli, the rabbi and cantor who had made so much fun of Shimmeleh behind his back. To his face, however, Shmuel Eli now flattered him, much to everyone's disgust.

Children too attended Shimmeleh's festive banquet. But instead of staying in the house with everyone else, they gathered outside next to the covered wagons and watched the family packing. Sholom secluded himself with Shimmeleh's youngest son, his friend Pinneleh, in one of the wagons. They climbed up to the very top, sat down, and discussed the distant journey on which the family was about to embark.

At that time, Pinneleh Shimmeleh's, a lad with a careworn face and big, yearning eyes, was Sholom's closest friend. Sholom liked him because he was aware of everything happening in the world. In addition to the stories about big cities that Pinneleh had heard from his father, he himself had been in the big city of Pereyaslav, and all because of a pea.

Once, while playing, Pinneleh had shoved a dried pea into one ear and tried to take it out of the other. Obviously, the stubborn pea refused to come out of either ear. It began to swell and gave him such headaches that the scamp had to admit the truth. First he got a good beating—"That'll teach you not to put peas in your ear"—and then they tried poking wire and knitting needles and matchsticks into the ear. Finally, they brought him to the big city for an operation.

Concerning this journey to Pereyaslav, Pinneleh had much to say, and this unwittingly made him ten feet tall in the eyes of his friends. No small matter for a youngster to have been in Pereyaslav and actually seen countless houses with tin roofs, sidewalks on every street, white churches, mounds of watermelons and cantaloupes, an infinite number of apples and pears on the ground, soldiers marching in the street, and other such marvels and wonders.

Since then Sholom and Pinneleh had become fast friends, one soul. Pinneleh's departure from Voronko was more of a blow for Sholom than anyone else. Besides envying Pinneleh for going while he remained behind, Sholom found the separation difficult because he liked Pinneleh as much as he'd liked his previous friends.

At their last meeting, before the farewells, the happy Pinneleh, well scrubbed and neatly dressed, put his hands into his pockets and began making fun of Voronko. "What's Voronko? A hick town, a hole, a village. Worse than a village. And the people? Beggars, paupers, down-at-the-heel shnorrers. You dummy, all the people in Voronko, poor and rich, don't even have half of what one Ephrossi in Odessa has."

Then Pinneleh began to brag about himself and his family. Soon their wagons would leave the village so quickly they'd leave a trail of smoke. He spoke of the places they'd see and what they'd do when they came to Odessa. All the big shots in the city would welcome them with freshly baked challas, roast ducks and good cherry brandy. Ephrossi too would be on hand.

"Who's this Ephrossi?" Sholom asked.

"Don't you know Ephrossi?" Pinneleh replied like a grown-up. "He's a relative on my mother's side, a rich man, a millionaire. I told you, dummy, he has more money in one pocket than all the Jews in town have put together. Imagine, he's so rich, when he goes riding he takes a six-horse carriage, and an outrider gallops before him. He's dressed from head to toe in silk and velvet. And he has two winter coats, one bearskin, the other muskrat. He eats only white challa and roast duck all week long and washes it down with the best cherry brandy."

"And what will you do there?" Sholom swallowed his spittle, thinking of the roast duck and the cherry brandy.

"What do you mean, what?" said Pinneleh earnestly. "What do all Jews do in Odessa? What does Ephrossi do? He has granaries full of wheat; my father will have granaries full of wheat. Ephrossi has an office with clerks; my father will have an office with clerks. And money—money will flow into our pockets by the sackful. Odessa? Are you kidding?"

Then Pinneleh described Ephrossi's munificence and the beauty of the city with its three-story brick buildings. "You silly goose! Our village compared to Odessa is like . . . how shall I put it? Like, for instance, a fly compared to a church, or an ant to an elephant."

You could have sworn that Pinneleh himself had been there and seen everything with his own eyes. Sholom stared wide-eyed at him and greedily swallowed everything he said. How terribly he envied him! But there was one thing Sholom couldn't quite grasp and he didn't hesitate to ask his friend.

"Since Odessa is such a marvelous city and Ephrossi the millionaire is your relative, why did you keep it a secret till now? Why didn't you move out there sooner?"

To which Pinneleh responded without further thought:

"You dummy! He's not a close relative like an uncle, a cousin or an in-law, not at all. He's a distant kinsman. Not even a third cousin. It's just that the two of them, Ephrossi and my mother, come from the same town, from Mezhiretchke. My mother's mother came from Mezhiretchke and Ephrossi's father, so they say, also came from Mezhiretchke."

Pinneleh's answer didn't satisfy Sholom. But time passed and the two friends got into such an involved conversation about Odessa, Ephrossi's familial lineage in Mezhiretchke, and other matters, they didn't realize how quickly the morning had passed. The villagers had long since finished eating the cheese dumplings. Cheerful, faces red and shiny, they stood by the wagons saying friendly good-byes to Shimmeleh and his family, kissing and wishing one another well. Doing most of the kissing was Shmuel Eli, the rabbi and cantor. With upper lip curled as if about to laugh, he wished the departing family the best of luck. He asked Shimmeleh to give his regards to all of Odessa and to Ephrossi. "Remember now, don't forget to give him my regards."

"Farewell, you sons of dogs," Shimmeleh told everyone good-humoredly for the last time as he got in the wagon. "So long, and don't think badly of me. With God's will, may you soon pull yourself out of this mudhole—Giddyap!"

"Giddyap!" Pinneleh echoed, standing in the wagon with his hands in his pockets like an adult. He looked fondly and proudly at his friend Sholom—and then the wagons began to move.

When they were gone, leaving behind a smell of horses and a wall of dust, Shmuel Eli held his sides and burst out laughing. He shook as if ten thousand demons were tickling his feet.

"Ha, ha! He's going to Odessa! To Ephrossi, ha, ha, ha!"

At that moment the two-faced Shmuel Eli earned himself a new enemy, a bloody foe: Sholom Nochem Vevik's, who didn't feel at all like laughing. On the contrary, he wanted to cry. First of all, he had lost a friend. Secondly, he was jealous: Pinneleh was traveling. Where to? Far away to Odessa. But above all—and that was most important—the formerly beautiful, charming village of Voronko had somehow become smaller, darker, less significant. Suddenly, all its luster and enchantment were gone. Hurt to the core, Sholom went to cheder with an embittered heart.

P.S. Many years later, it turned out that Shmuel Eli the cantor had not laughed in vain. Shimmeleh and his family did not go to Odessa but to Rzhishtchev, a small village in the Kiev district, not too far from Voronko. So why that charade with Odessa and Ephrossi? That question you'll have to ask of Shimmeleh's children, for he himself is long gone.

19. Change Your Place, Change Your Luck

About to Leave Voronko—Hersel Puts a Dunce Cap on His Partner— Grandma Mindy's Shroud

Sholom didn't know who started it all, but it was Shimmeleh who took the first step. Right after his departure the Voronko householders began talking about moving to bigger towns. "Change your place, change your luck," they said. One mentioned Barishpoli, another Rzhishtchev or Vasilkov, and others spoke of places even farther away.

Nochem Vevik's children heard people whisper that their father too would soon return to the big city of Pereyaslav, from which he had moved when his children were still small. And they concluded with "Change your place, change your luck."

The children thought of Pereyaslav as awfully big, full of mystery and enchantment. "It's a place to make a living," said the grown-ups. The children heard this but didn't understand; still, they felt that Pereyaslav must be a good place. Although they were delighted, they regretted having to leave the village where they had spent their happiest years, the golden era of their childhood.

What would become of the old Voronko shul if all the Jews leave? little Sholom thought. Who would sit in their seats by the eastern wall? And what would become of the hill behind the shul? And the Jewish stores? What would happen with the treasure? Is it possible that so much wealth buried deep in the ground for the Jews for so many years would be lost? Could the whole town simply go under and be forgotten?

As careful as the adults were not to discuss "such things" at home in front of the children, the latter still caught fragmented words and phrases. "Change your place, change your luck." "Business is falling off." The children couldn't quite grasp why one's luck would change if one changed one's place, and how business could fall. But from each remark the children gathered that something was brewing, something was happening.

The constantly quiet, soft-spoken and melancholy Nochem Vevik's became even quieter and sadder. His back was more bent than before. Twice as many wrinkles appeared on his pale forehead. He would lock himself into a room with his younger brother, Uncle Nissel, smoke one cigarette after another, and secretly discuss their plans.

During the past winter the Rabinowitzes had stopped giving the post-Sabbath parties at their house for the entire village. The last Shemini Atzeres and Simchas Torah they had still reveled in the house. Uncle Nissel had exchanged hats with the police chief and even danced with him on the roof. But it was no longer the same merriment and fun. Even Aunt Hodel was even-tempered; she had lost much of her venom. The whole family had become unnerved. Only Grandma Mindy held herself proud as an oak. Clean and neat as before. But her Sabbath fruits weren't quite the same. The apples were somewhat frozen, spoiled and moldy, the nuts stale, and the figs wormy. Grandma Mindy prayed and said Grace After Meals as usual. Like a man, she recited loudly and with gusto from her big prayer book, talking her heart out to the Creator. But her prayers were no longer the same. Something was happening in the family; something secretive was afoot with the Rabinowitzes.

This state of affairs dragged on all winter, until suddenly the blister broke. The truth surfaced like oil on water. The entire village now knew the secret: that Nochem Vevik's partner in the leasehold, a heavyset, red-nosed man (his name was Hershel, but since he lisped everyone called him Hersel S.), had made his partner Nochem utterly destitute. Not only did he rob him blind, but he also stealthily severed Nochem's link with the lease. This prompted an outcry in town.

"Reb Nochem! Speak up! Take him to the rabbi. To a court of law."

But when it came to rabbinic arbitration, Hersel S. simply laughed at them all and expressed himself so vulgarly it would be a disgrace to repeat it.

"What a scoundrel!" Uncle Nissel gestured while smoking a thick cigarette. "I swear, if I won't see that rascal, that charlatan, that crook, that foul-mouthed thief in prison for at least twenty-five years, my name isn't Nissel."

"What do you mean, see him in prison? And where do you get twenty-five years from?" his elder brother Nochem poured cold water on his remarks. He smiled bitterly as he smoked a thick cigarette. "He put a dunce cap on me and now we have to go back to Pereyaslav. Change your place, change your luck."

Now this was straightforward talk which the children understood. But one thing was still unclear. What kind of dunce cap were they talking about? No one dared approach Father to ask him. We had too much respect for Father to go up and ask him, "Father, what kind of dunce cap did they put on you?" The children only saw that Father was flickering, hunched over. Every one of his sighs and groans tore out a piece of your heart.

"You'll stay here and study during the summer. It would be a sin to break up your studies in midterm. But, God willing, for Sukkos we'll send a wagon for you and you'll come and join us."

And so, one bright summer day, as two covered wagons drove up to their house as they once had to Shimmeleh's, Nochem Vevik's broke the news to his children. The family began packing for the journey and saying good-bye to the village. But their departure couldn't be compared to Shimmeleh's. The packing and the farewells weren't the same, nor was there any festive dumplings party. Everyone was immersed in gloom and melancholy. The entire town commiserated with the Rabinowitzes.

"May God help them! People who change their place, change their luck. Poor souls, it's a pity on them!" These remarks were made behind the family's back and the children still didn't understand who was to be pitied.

If anyone was deserving of pity it was Grandma Mindy. In her old age she had to gather her belongings and pack her trunk for the journey. Meanwhile, the children had a chance to peek into it. They saw pressed silk kerchiefs that lay between the pages of her big Siddur, silk holiday dresses, and velvet cloaks that had odd-looking short sleeves and squirrel-tail fringes. Off in a corner was a large bundle of white material. This was Grandma's shroud, which had been prepared ages ago for future use. In case she died, one hundred years later, she wouldn't have to burden any of her children with preparing a shroud. Everyone knew this; still the children plucked up their courage and asked:

"What do you need so much white material for?"

This was asked by none other than the shortest in height and the biggest mischief maker, the author of these memoirs. His grandmother rewarded him with a nice sermon and a promise to tell his father.

"I've had enough of you, you little devil," she said. "Don't think I don't know you imitate me behind my back and mimic the way I pray and say grace!" (Indeed, all this was true.) "I'll tell him everything. Every last bit. I'll get it all off my chest."

But the upshot was—nothing. She didn't even say a word. On the contrary, before she left she kissed every grandchild like a mother, and cried as only a mother can cry. Later, as the wagons were about to move, she called to the children once more.

"Be well, children! God willing, I hope you all live to be at my funeral."

What a wish!

20. The Crowd Disperses

Shmuel Eli Plays Chess—Saying Good-bye—Teary-Eyed Women Make Faces—Restraining Laughter

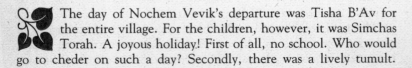 The day of Nochem Vevik's departure was Tisha B'Av for the entire village. For the children, however, it was Simchas Torah. A joyous holiday! First of all, no school. Who would go to cheder on such a day? Secondly, there was a lively tumult.

Members of the family gathered, packed, moved cupboards. You heard the tinkle of glass and the clang of silverware. Then the covered wagons arrived and everyone ate quickly, like on the eve of Passover. The children wondered when they'd get the few pennies they were promised as going-away presents. They still hadn't seen a hint of them. Meanwhile, people were still coming to say good-bye. That is, they came to hear "Stay well," to which they'd respond, "Have a good trip," and then wish their friends lots of good things like health, luck, success and all the best.

The first to arrive was Shmuel Eli the rabbi and cantor, a frequent visitor. Just as a pious Jew doesn't skip a prayer, he didn't skip his daily chess game with Reb Nochem. Playing chess was his pleasure, beating Reb Nochem his greatest joy. Shmuel Eli was a strange man. If he lost, he yelled; if he won, he yelled. But he rarely won. Most often he lost. Losing a game, he'd shout that he'd made a mistake; he didn't move the piece he had wanted to move. Had he made a different move, he would have won, not lost.

Uncle Nissel couldn't stand watching a game like that.

"What are you yelling for?" he would ask Shmuel Eli.

But Father wasn't like that. He listened in silence to Shmuel Eli's raging tirade, smiled demurely into his beard, and continued playing. Seeing them playing, Mama was beside herself.

"Now, an hour before leaving, you sit down to play chess?"

"Just this last time, dear Chaya Esther. You're leaving, everyone is dispersing, no one's remaining. Who will I play chess with?" Shmuel Eli pleaded. The cantor pushed his hat back and set to work. Then he began to seethe and holler. "That's not the move I wanted to make!" Nochem smiled and let him make another move.

But this time the game didn't proceed in the usual fashion. Every few minutes new people came to say good-bye. When a neighbor like Reb Isaac entered, it was only polite to stop the game. True, Reb Isaac had a goatee and a high, thin voice at prayers; still, he was a Lubavitch Hasid and a very honest man. Right after him came Dan, a young man with hair so white it was almost yellow, yellow as flax. Reticent by nature, he usually spoke to no one. But now that Reb Nochem was leaving Voronko, Dan suddenly became talkative.

"I'd move too!" he said, "if I only had where to go. The devil take it! I'd love to sell my business, if I only had a buyer. To the blazes with it!"

Shmuel Eli looked daggers at him but Dan did not let up his torrent of words. The plug was pulled out. He simmered down only when others entered to say good-bye. First the men, then the women. All with long noses and anxious expressions. Some with tears in their eyes. One of the women brought sweets for the children. Bless her, a saint!

The two women who had been married in the Rabinowitz house were in tears. Frume the One-Eyed Maid and Feigeleh the Witch. They cried and blew their noses and made such funny faces that Sholom, the little devil, could no longer restrain himself. Right then and there, behind their backs, he gave such a flawless imitation of their antics that the children burst into raucous laughter. Then the to-do began.

"What are you giggling about?" Mama asked.

Chaya Esther, usually ill-humored, and now in a dither and upset because of the trip, stopped her work and took out all her frustration on the children. "Will you tell me what you're laughing at? What're you so happy about?"

Frume the Maid came to her aid. "I'm ready to swear on the Torah that it's all that little rascal's doing, that brat, that louse, that scamp, that outcast, that no-good guttersnipe."

Of course, she meant no one else but Sholom, who stood there with a perfectly innocent look on his face. No doubt he would have received his comeuppance from his mother, if old Grandma Mindy hadn't intervened and saved him from a certain beating. Seeing that her grandson was in danger, Grandma Mindy called out for everyone to hear:

"Children! There's an old custom that before we leave on a trip, we sit down for at least a minute."

Grandma Mindy sat down on the forlorn sofa, which was too old to be transported and too rickety to be sold. Everyone followed suit. For a while silence reigned. Even a fly could be heard. Then came the final act, the most difficult part—saying good-bye and kissing. Thank God, they survived that too. The wagons were ready. Once more the cry "Be well!" and once more "Have a good trip!" Again all the people wiped their eyes and blew their noses and made all kinds of funny faces.

God Almighty! How can one keep from mimicking the women's expressions, their waggling goiters, and their twisted mouths. They didn't even let you say good-bye properly. Then everyone turned gloomy all of a sudden. The children felt sorry for Father, Mama and Grandma Mindy. Now they were carrying out her old, iron-banded trunk, which contained her shroud. Sholom felt a pinch in his heart, a tug at his soul. He wanted to cry. Especially when he saw a man like Uncle Nissel wiping his eyes when no one was looking. Uncle Nissel crying? How could that be?

Father now called the youngsters in one by one and took some silver coins from his purse. Mama too. And Grandma Mindy had already prepared a paper-wrapped packet of coins for each child. Added up, it came to a hefty sum. With God's help the wagons would soon roll. Now they were moving, the wheels turning. Everyone suddenly pushed forward: "Have a good trip! Good luck!" Grandma Mindy peered out of the wagon, as if she wanted one last look at the place she was leaving forever. Once more, gloom encompassed everyone. The feeling of pity and sympathy flared again for a fleeting moment, then died away. We wanted to count our batch of coins.

After all the tumult and hurly-burly, silence descended. The wagons had departed, leaving a thick cloud of dust, the smell of pitch and a strange emptiness. One by one, the visitors gradually dispersed, shamefacedly, as if they'd been publicly whipped. Uncle Nissel was nowhere to be seen. Shmuel Eli the cantor stayed the longest. He watched the far-off wagons, protecting his eyes from the sunlight, which wasn't really that strong. Then, with a bitter smile, he said to himself: "Everyone's dispersing like worms."

And he spat.

21. Gergeleh Ganev

Moshe the Slaughterer—A Saintly Man—Gergeleh—The Art of Swiping Apples

The children, of course, weren't just abandoned in the village. Father looked for someone to be a teacher, guide and guardian rolled into one; a person who would teach, feed, and care for the children. Soon Father found just the man he was looking for—Moshe the Slaughterer, the old Voronko ritual slaughterer's son, a talented and proficient young man, well versed in Bible and Talmud.

Moshe was unique, a gentle soul, a gem of a human being. His only flaw was his frail health. Also, he was too good, too soft. He tried a new direction in teaching—not with slaps, but with warm soft-spoken words. Not accustomed to such treatment, the children deceived their teacher left and right, and led him to the bathhouse, so to speak. They neither prayed nor studied. Later, when Moshe was already quite ill with consumption and lay in bed, the kids roamed around freely, idling about and befriending Gergeleh Ganev, a young, barefoot orphan with devilish eyes and a harelip. This vagabond's real name was Gershon. But he said his mother, Sarah Feige the Cook, had lengthened it to Gergeleh. "My stepfather, Joseph Meir the Woodchopper, added the name 'ganev' on his own, even though I hadn't taken a thing from anyone yet. If not for that nickname maybe I'd never have become a thief. Now to spite them all, I *will* become one, if only there were something to swipe."

Thus boasted Gergeleh Ganev with a serious, grown-up air to Sholom, who looked openmouthed at this lad with the clever eyes and harelip. They had become friends in Moshe the Slaughterer's cheder. All week long Moshe was a teacher; on Thursdays he slaughtered the chickens, geese and ducks that the women and girls brought to him. With them was a boy with a harelip—Gergeleh—holding a chicken that his mother the cook had sent to be slaughtered for the Sabbath. While waiting with the women for Moshe, Gergeleh entertained the crowd. That is, he made such strange faces and gestures and pulled such mad antics that the entire group of women split their sides laughing and affably called him names like "ganev," "apostate" and "loon."

"Now here's someone after my own heart!" Sholom said and made friends with him. In secret, of course, so no one would know. For a child from a good family could have gotten into trouble for befriending a cook's son who was a ganev besides.

But there was a certain joy in chumming with a boy one could only meet at dusk, between the Afternoon and Evening Services, and exchange a few quick words, pull a couple of tricks, run up the hill, and so on. There was a special pleasure in slipping him a penny, a candy, or just a piece of bread, without anyone noticing. Gergeleh happily took everything, not as charity, God forbid, and without even saying thank you. He took it with both hands like a debt due him, ordered more for tomorrow, and suggested how other things could be gotten (rather, stolen) for him. Gergeleh didn't do this vulgarly, but with great finesse. For instance, within a short time this same Gergeleh taught his friends how to get free apples and pears in the marketplace. Not from other people's gardens, God forbid! For what child of a decent family would dare climb over a fence like a goy and jump into someone else's garden where a guard who could break your bones stood with a chained dog that could kill a man? Gergeleh Ganev playfully taught them how to get as many free apples as they wished and not even violate the commandment "Thou shalt not steal." How? Listen and you'll find out—and you decide if it can be considered stealing.

Summertime. Apples and pears have just ripened. Women sat in the marketplace at dusk displaying their wares on little tables or on the ground, discussing this year's bumper fruit crop. Then they talked about the drought. A dry spell brought dust, and dust brought lots of fleas. The husbands were in shul for evening prayers. Now was the best time. The gang set to work to get free apples. They were all barefoot, armed with sticks tipped with hook-shaped nails. Then they began running. That was called the "post chaise." One boy was the horse and the other held the reins, prodding the horse, whooping and whistling and shouting "Giddyap!" Approaching the pile of fruit, Gergeleh ordered "Sticks down!" at which the gang activated their hooked sticks. Since the running had created a cloud of dust, no one noticed the few apples or pears rolling away. Then the kids broke into a run once more and Gergeleh and the other rascals dropped to the ground to nab the runaway fruits, which they either stuffed into their pockets or popped into their mouths. What a lark! And the fun of it outstripped the joy of stealing or the value of the apples.

In general, Gergeleh was a merry boy, even though everyone under the sun laced into him. For who would stand up and protect a poor orphan? And a ganev to boot? The shamesh of the shul once caught him with someone else's Siddur; and Ruda Basye, who baked bagels and dumplings, shook half a cake from his bosom. Breaking the bones of a scamp like that was a mitzva! Gergeleh also had a mouth like a fishwife's. He found fault with everyone and gave everyone a nickname. Since he himself was free as the wind and had nothing to lose, he loved to stick out his bare foot like a poker and make everyone trip and fall flat on his face. It made no difference to him if it was the rabbi himself, the rebbitsin or the slaughterer's wife—plop, and down you went.

Little Sholom loved this. In time he grew so fond of Gergeleh that he hid in his pocket huge slices of bread he had taken from the slaughterer's wife's table, may God forgive him that theft. Sometimes he even swiped a lump of sugar from the sugar box as well. Although Gergeleh loved sugar, he liked tobacco more—he was dying for a smoke. But where could Sholom get tobacco if the teacher was ill and didn't smoke and his father was away? Gergeleh gave him an idea: visit Uncle Nissel more often—he always smoked a superior brand.

Excellent advice. Uncle Nissel had a generous heart. His tobacco pouch stood on the cornice under the mirror, open and readily accessible. Little Sholom often climbed up there. He put his hand in, took a handful of tobacco and stuffed it into his pocket. Once, unfortunately, Aunt Hodel saw him (and it had to be she who caught him!). Then the sky came crashing down. Sholom thought it was the end of the world. No punishment was good enough for him. Not even the four Biblical death penalties. The scoundrel hoped for a quick, severe sentence. But God performed a miracle. A stroke of luck. That is, a terrible tragedy. Suddenly, someone ran to Uncle Nissel and told him to hurry; Moshe the Slaughterer was dying, the entire village was there. He was near his end . . .

This was a new blow for the little criminal, perhaps even greater than the first one. No other teacher was more beloved than Moshe the Slaughterer. He was an angel, not a teacher. Only when the pallbearers lifted the black-draped coffin onto their shoulders and carried him to the cemetery did Nochem Vevik's children remember what a brilliant teacher he had been and how little they had appreciated him. And then the tears gushed out of them. They mourned their young teacher Moshe like a brother.

Sholom wept the hottest tears. He felt he had betrayed his teacher; he was an out-and-out sinner. First of all, Moshe had considered him the best and most honest student. In reality, Sholom could barely read the weekly Torah portion by Thursday. Swaying, singing and gesturing, he only pretended that he knew it. He had deceived him. And how often he'd skipped most of his prayers. Indeed, he never recited the Evening Service at all, but ran around with Gergeleh Ganev, teasing the priest's dog through the fence or swiping apples in the market. Here, in this world, the teacher was unaware of all this; he never would have believed it of Sholom. But there, in the other world, he knew everything—everything.

22. Meir Velvel the Coachman and His Horses

*Uncle Nissel—The Gang—Meir Velvel's Three-Horse Wagon—
The Coachman's Story*

 At the end of summer—it was still quite warm, but smells of September were in the air—a wagon drawn by three horses arrived from Pereyaslav. The coachman, a talkative chap named Meir Velvel, unbuttoned his jacket and from the recesses of some pocket pulled out a letter written by Father to his brother Nissel Rabinowitz. It said that, in addition to the wagon, the children were being sent three pairs of boots and enough food—biscuits, hard-boiled eggs and pears—for the two-day journey. Besides, there was an extra gift from Grandma Mindy, a warm blanket and an old shawl for the children in case of cold or rain.

The coachman was instructed to take the children the next morning after prayers. He was to spend the first night in Barishpoli, and then, God willing, they could arrive at their new home in Pereyaslav late the next afternoon.

Where can one find the nuances to depict the children's joy when they heard the letter and were given the three pairs of boots? What should they rejoice over first? The new boots? Or the two-day trip in a covered wagon drawn by three horses? Or their arrival the day after tomorrow in the big city of Pereyaslav?

"Come, you rascals, you scamps, you scoundrels. Sit down and try on the boots," Uncle Nissel ordered, cuffing the three boys on the nose or on the ear.

Uncle Nissel loved children: his own and others' were all the same to him. That's why a slap from him wasn't a punishment but a pleasure, even if your ear smarted for half an hour. If you like someone, even a slap is a gift. And the children loved him because he was practically the only one in the family who never punished the children, preached to them or kept an eye on them to see that they prayed or studied. On the contrary, in tandem with the pack of rascals, he was a rascal himself. He loved to laugh and play pranks. With them he put a healthy dose of snuff into the nose of an old man who had fallen asleep in shul and then trumpeted "God bless you!" when the man woke up sneezing and coughing. And on Simchas Torah he was more of a devil than anyone else. He himself gave Gedalya the Drunkard liquor, then helped the children bind him like a calf, lock him in a room, and tie his hand to a long rope attached to a bell. When Gedalya sobered up and woke he would unwittingly begin to ring the bell as if there were a fire and the entire village would gather in a tumult and commotion: "What's burning? Where's the fire?"

Naturally, it wasn't easy to part with an uncle like this. When the children said farewell, he consoled them and gave them a whack on the shoulder.

"Don't worry. It's nothing. We'll see each other. I won't be here too long either." It was as if his heart had intuited it—as the reader knows from previous chapters.

The boys felt good in their new boots, which fit well. Then they explored the wagon and got to know the three horses and the coachman who would take them to the big city.

The wagon was like any other. It was covered with patched canvas and padded down with hay and rushes, which seemed soft and comfortable. How comfortable it really was the children discovered the next day, when not one of their bones was whole. So much for the wagon. The horses too deserve a brief treatment, each one separately. For each had as much in common with the other as a Bar Mitzva to horseradish. This was a Jewish troika.

We'll start with the middle horse, Smarty. No one knew why he was called that. Frankly, he wasn't overly bright. But one must admit he was rich in years. This was apparent from his old face, runny eyes, scraggly tail, and bones that jutted from his formerly ample rear. Nevertheless, despite his age, almost the entire weight of the wagon lay on him, because the other two nags only pretended to pull.

The other two horses also had nicknames. One was called Dancer because of his hopping gait. All four legs were constantly doing a jig, but each leg danced to its own tune. They never got together. That's why nothing good came of his dancing. First off, he only bothered Smarty. Moreover, he made the wagon rattle so that the passengers' very souls were shaken. But Meir Velvel settled accounts with him: "Boy, are you going to dance!" he warned Dancer, and brought the point home with his whip or with the wooden handle. The coachman took him to task and constantly beat him during the journey. But to no avail. Dancer, unimpressed, did not stop dancing. On the contrary, it was worse when he was whipped. He responded with his two hind legs, as if to say: "If you want, here's more!" He was a short horse, shorter than Smarty and with a much cleverer face. But no matter. Perhaps Meir Velvel didn't exaggerate when he boasted that Dancer had once been a famous stallion, but ever since someone had cast an evil spell on his legs, he'd become impossible. So the horse came into Meir Velvel's possession, and from that time he'd been teaching him a thing or two with his whip.

That's why Meir Velvel paid scant attention to the third horse, a short, chunky, hairy-legged mare. Only rarely, just for the sake of it, did he give her the taste of the whip. Meir Velvel called her Privileged Character because of her fine lineage. She had once belonged to a priest, the coachman said. How did she end up with him? It was a long story, and he couldn't provide all the details.

"First of all, it happened too long ago, so how can I remember everything? Secondly, even then I didn't get the story straight. But I do remember"—here Meir Velvel smiled—"that this privileged character was stolen. It wasn't me who stole her, God forbid! Others stole her and I bought her for next to nothing. But when I bought her I didn't know—may I not know from anguish and grief!—that she was stolen merchandise. For if I'd known she was stolen, and from a priest to boot, I wouldn't have touched her with a ten-foot pole, even if they showered me with gold." An earnest expression now came over Meir Velvel's face. "Yes, even if they showered me with gold. Not because I'm such a saint, afraid to go near a stolen horse. What do I care if the next fellow is a thief? If you're a thief, they'll roast you in the world to come. I wouldn't have bought her for another reason. I hate cops like pork. I don't want to get involved with them. For proof, let me tell you about some trouble I once had—a misfortune, a false accusation. My competitors, coachmen who are my enemies, set out to trip me up. Yankel Bulgatch had a hand in it, may he fry in hell."

And here Meir Velvel began another story, then another, and another, from all of which one might easily suspect that Meir Velvel was indeed quite deeply involved with horse thieves and the police.

Still, his chattiness was a good attribute, for with his nine measures of talk he entertained the children during the journey from Voronko to Barishpoli, and from Barishpoli to Pereyaslav. His mouth didn't stop for a minute. The children learned his life story, from his boyhood, when he served as assistant to Yankel Bulgatch, to the time he married and became an independent coachman, whereupon Yankel Bulgatch persecuted and tried to undermine him. "But he can go to hell, for all I care," Meir Velvel snapped, then began to talk about his wife. "Once, she was young and beautiful. I was head over heels in love with her. I almost croaked for love of her, that's what a beauty she was. Today, if I were young again, I wouldn't even give her a second look. But then I was still a young tyke."

The kids didn't quite understand the word "tyke." But when Meir Velvel, continuing the story of his life, told them that his wife gave birth to a little tyke less than a year after their wedding, had another little tyke a year later, and kept on delivering one little tyke after another—the kids realized what "tyke" meant.

When he finished his own story, Meir Velvel the Coachman discussed Yankel Bulgatch and other coachmen, calling each one by name and recounting the name and number of each one's horses, and whether they were prime steeds or just tottering skin and bones.

Done with coachmen, Meir Velvel turned to horse dealers, gypsies, thieves and "prophets." According to him, the difference between a thief and a "prophet" was that the thief led a horse out of the stable while the "prophet" showed the owner where to find the stolen horse. That's why you had to make common cause with the "prophets" more than with the thieves. The things the children learned from Meir Velvel in two days they couldn't have learned elsewhere in two years. Now that we know the coachman, his covered wagon and his three horses, let's turn back to Voronko for a while and see how Sholom bade good-bye to his little village before leaving it forever.

23. Farewell, Voronko

Saying Good-bye to the Village—Daydreams of the Treasure—
A Silly Incident with Frume the Maid

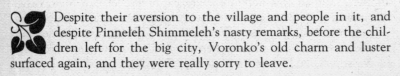 Despite their aversion to the village and people in it, and despite Pinneleh Shimmeleh's nasty remarks, before the children left for the big city, Voronko's old charm and luster surfaced again, and they were really sorry to leave.

Sholom bade good-bye to the village as if it were a living thing, a dear, devoted friend. He began with the courtyard, saying good-bye to each tree in the garden, which already belonged to someone else, and concluded with the hill in back of the shul and the meadow on the far side of town. Here he had played with his best friends, beginning with Shmulik the Orphan and ending with Gergeleh Ganev.

Sholom made a special stop at the spot where, according to Shmulik, the treasure was almost certainly hidden. He stood alone, in holy silence, as if enchanted. His head buzzed with thoughts. What would happen to the treasure if a goy found it, God forbid, and not a Jew? And was it possible that a goy would indeed find it? Only Shmulik would know. Where was Shmulik now? Would Sholom ever meet him again? And what would happen if they met? First they'd probably return briefly to Voronko to see the old familiar places where they spent the best years of their childhood. Then they'd buckle down to get the treasure. First one boy would fast for forty days and then the other. When the period of fasting and psalm-saying was done, they'd begin to look for the treasure. Once they found it, they would divide it equally. What a glorious day that would be! Of course, Sholom's father would get the lion's share. Uncle Nissel would also get a goodly portion, followed by Uncle Pinny and the rest of the clan. They'd also leave a big part in town for the Jews of Voronko. Moshe the Slaughterer's wife, the poor widow, would get such a large sum she'd no longer talk of getting married again. That would spare her the long journey to Chvastev to her poor relatives who could hardly make ends meet. And though they didn't deserve it, the two pious ladies, Frume the Maid and Feigeleh the Witch, would also get a large share, beyond their husbands' wildest dreams. And old Ruda Basye, who baked bagels, dumplings and cakes, and supported her family with her swollen hands, would be able to retire in her old age. And Melech the Shamesh and Gedalya the Drunkard—why should they be left out? And Shmuel Eli the cantor, who complained that Voronko was too small for him—he had a good voice and would be able to outsing the world's greatest cantors if only he had sheet music—would be provided with music. That left only Gergeleh Ganev. What could be done with the boy to make him stop stealing? First, his mother should stop being a cook and his stepfather the woodchopper should be urged to buy his own house. Line his pockets with money and tell him explicitly it's for his stepson

Gergeleh, and counsel him to stop beating him and calling him a ganev.

During these musings, Gergeleh Ganev materialized. Barefoot as always, and in tatters.

"What are you doing here?"

"What about you?"

They spoke a while and then, about to part, Sholom told Gergeleh he was leaving.

"I know, I heard, I even saw the covered wagon and the three horses."

"You saw them? Well, what do you say?"

"About what?"

"The horses."

"What should I say? They're horses."

"And how do you like the covered wagon?"

"It's just a wagon."

Since Gergeleh wasn't in a good mood, Sholom tried to cheer him up.

"You know, I just was thinking of you when you showed up."

"Really? What were you thinking of?"

"I was thinking . . . I was thinking of you in connection with the treasure."

"What treasure?"

Suddenly Sholom felt ill. Should he or shouldn't he tell him?

"What treasure?" Gergeleh asked again.

There was no way out—he'd have to tell him. And Sholom told him the whole story.

Now Gergeleh was curious. "Where is this treasure?"

Sholom now felt worse. Should he or shouldn't he tell him?

A flame flickered in Gergeleh's eyes. "Afraid to tell me, huh? You think I'll go dig it up?"

Now Sholom regretted he had begun. He began talking to Gergeleh the way Pinneleh Shimmeleh's had spoken to him, looking down his nose at his friend.

"Dummy, even if I tell you, you still won't be able to get there, because for that you have to know Kabbala. That's number one. And number two, you have to fast forty days and on the forty-first day—"

"And on the forty-first day you're an ass," Gergeleh interrupted him and looked down at Sholom's boots, which he apparently liked.

"New ones?"

Sholom felt ashamed. He had brand-new boots while Gergeleh was barefoot.

"If you like," he told Gergeleh, "come with me to Uncle Nissel's and I'll give you something . . ."

"A present? Sure!" Gergeleh was delighted, and both boys hurried to Uncle Nissel's house. There they encountered a group of good friends and acquaintances. Having heard that a wagon had come for Nochem Vevik's children, they ran over to say good-bye and send regards to the Rabinowitzes.

Among the visitors were the two saints, Frume the Maid and Feigeleh the Witch, without their husbands. They said their husbands would come later to say good-bye. Everyone eyed the children with respect. After all, they were traveling to the big city, to Pereyaslav. The visitors even spoke to them differently, advising them how to travel and where to spend the night in Barishpoli. Uncle Nissel snapped his middle finger at the children's noses as was his wont, and asked the rascals:

"Will you drop me a line once in a while?"

"What a question! We'll write every week. Twice a week. Every day."

Shmuel Eli the cantor asked the children to convey his special regards to their father. "Tell him that since he left I haven't even played chess once, because Voronko is a wilderness."

Aunt Hodel suddenly became so sugar-sweet you could have put her in a cake. She said she couldn't understand how children could be sent on their way hungry. And what kind of nourishment were biscuits, hard-boiled eggs and pears for two whole days? They would starve! So she began packing whatever she could for the journey: a small crock of goose fat, a little jar of sugared fruit preserves, probably from last summer, and prune jam so sour that you saw stars with the first spoonful.

While Aunt Hodel was packing food for the trip and the children were busy saying good-bye, a small tragedy was being played out between Frume the Maid and Gergeleh Ganev. Seeing Gergeleh, Frume glared at him with her blind eye and asked Feigeleh:

"What's that ganev doing here?"

An awful scandal could have ensued had Sholom not taken his

friend by the hand and led him out into the courtyard (on a day such as this everything was permitted, even palling around with Gergeleh Ganev).

"I told you I'll give you a present . . . Here!"

Sholom, pleased with his generosity, took his old boots from under his coat and gave them to Gergeleh. But the boy had evidently expected another sort of gift, not an old pair of boots. And besides, he was incensed at blind Frume's remark, and vexed that his friend wouldn't tell him where the treasure was buried. What's more, he was in a bad mood that day to begin with. So he took the boots from Sholom's hands but immediately threw them away in anger, then ran from the courtyard in his bare feet and vanished from sight.

It was a silly incident—but how much aggravation it caused. Gergeleh's flight embittered Sholom's farewells to his village and poisoned all the joy of his first big, beautiful long trip. Try as he did to blot out the image of his humiliated friend, it spitefully returned to haunt him. The scene repeated itself in his mind's eye and crimped his heart. "You've humiliated and shamed a poor friend."

The wagon had already passed the market, the stores, the little houses, the Jewish cemetery and, forgive the proximity, the gentile graveyard. It had crossed the little bridge and passed the meadow— good-bye, Voronko! At that moment Sholom felt a strange tightness in his throat, and a warm wave of compassion for the little village flowed through him, as if the village had become an orphan. This feeling and his resentment at Gergeleh's flight softened his heart and made his eyes wet. Turning his head so that his brothers would not see, Sholom wiped away a tear and said a last farewell to the village. "So long, Voronko, good-bye . . . good-bye."

24. *The Trip*

The Trip in Meir Velvel's Wagon—Philosophical Thoughts—The First Stop—Barishpoli—An Inn Full of Noses—Sleeping on the Ground— Farewell Forever, Voronko

 Only someone who has grown up in a village and leaves it for the first time to embark on a journey into the big wide world will understand the children's happy feelings and delight during their first wonderful trip. At first they couldn't find their place in the wagon. They leaned sideways, as Father did during the Seder, put their hands in their pockets and stretched out, or stood and held on to the hoops of the covered wagon. But Meir Velvel the Coachman did not tolerate this. And although he was in cahoots with the children throughout the trip and told them stories about coachmen, this didn't stop him from promising them that if they tore a piece of the canvas he'd tear their guts out. Then, having said this, he whipped his horses and continued on his way.

If you remember the sensation of traveling for the first time, you know how quickly the road flies, how the ground disappears beneath the wheels and the horses' legs, and how everything glides before your eyes. You recall the smell of late-summer grass, the branch of a lone tree caught in the wagon roof, and the feeling of fresh air entering your nostrils and then gently stroking your throat. What a pleasure! You feel so elated you want to sing. You feel absolutely marvelous.

After passing all the village houses, the bridge, the meadow and the cemetery, the wagon flew farther and farther until the children saw tall "living corpses" who moved their hands up and down, up and down. At first they were scared, but when they looked more closely they saw they were only windmills. Soon they too disappeared and only sky and fields, fields and sky, were seen, and the youngsters felt like jumping off the wagon, or better yet flying out and swimming to that infinite blueness. Unwittingly, Sholom began to think how small is man and how great is the One who has created this big, beautiful world. Lulled by these thoughts, he dozed off. Suddenly, a huge wagon drawn by big-horned oxen appeared. A tall, barefoot peasant in a floppy hat walked alongside. Meir Velvel greeted him in Yiddish interwoven with Russian: "Greetings and salutations! May the good Lord bless you! May your stomach swell and your pants fall down!"

The peasant didn't know if the Jew was blessing or cursing him. He stood therefore a while, confused, then nodded, mumbled thanks under his breath, and continued on his way. The children burst into laughter. During that entire first day of the trip Meir Velvel had not even smiled. Now he turned to the children and said with feigned innocence, "What are you laughing at, you rascals?" And so passed the first day of the delightful, end-of-summer journey.

How beautiful were the last days of summer! Some fields were bare, some plowed. The wheat had been cut. Here and there one could see a flower, an ear of corn, a blossom. Unripe cantaloupes and watermelons lay in the peasant gardens. The long squash on the ground absorbed the earth's juices, and the tall sunflowers, so proud and high, showed their rich yellow caps. The whole world was still full of ants, buzzing, humming flies, and leaping grasshoppers and butterflies that flitted gaily in the air. The smell of the field seeped into your nose. The world around seemed so huge and the sky above an endless dome. Once again Sholom thought that people are much too small for this large world and that only God, whose glory fills the earth, is commensurate with this universe.

"Off the wagon, rascals, we've arrived in Barishpoli. We're spending the night here, and tomorrow, God willing, we'll move on."

Barishpoli was a new town. Better yet, a new village, a big village. The same houses as in Voronko. The people too were the same, but with different noses. Coincidence or not, but to the boys' astonishment the innkeeper, his wife and their four grown daughters all had long noses. And to top it off, the maid had the longest nose of all. When the coachman told the innkeeper who the little fellows were, the long-nosed landlord gave them a warm welcome and told the long-nosed maid to put up the samovar. Then he winked to his long-nosed wife to prepare a bite to eat and ordered his long-nosed barefoot daughters to put on their shoes.

A little later the travelers made themselves quite at home with these barefoot girls. Terribly curious, the girls asked the boys, "Where do you come from and where are you going? What are your names and how do you like Barishpoli?" They wanted to know everything, even how old they were. Then all of them, the boys and the girls, tasted the sour prune jam which Aunt Hodel had packed for them, and the shrieks of laughter resounded to the sky.

Then they played blindman's buff, a game where a blindfolded youngster has to tag whomever he can. Excited by the game, whenever one of the girls tagged one of the boys, she hugged him so tightly to her chest he almost passed out.

At night the guests were bedded down on the floor strewn with hay. Lest they feel slighted, the long-nosed mistress showed the boys that her daughters also slept on the floor in the other corner of the same room. "And despite this they seem to grow very nicely, thank you," she added and blew her long nose. The boys would gladly have taken that spot but they were ashamed to undress in front of the girls. But the girls unabashedly threw off their jackets. Barefoot and bare-necked, wearing only dresses, they undid their hair and exchanged queer glances, looked at the boys, and laughed without stop.

"Be quiet!" the innkeeper shouted and extinguished the hanging lamp. But in the dark, suppressed laughter and the rustle of hay was heard from both sides of the room. Not for long, though, for the healthy, innocent sleep of the young overtook them and closed the children's healthy, innocent eyes.

The Morning Service blessings chanted by the innkeeper in the traditional melody informed the children that it was daylight and time to be on their way to Pereyaslav. That last word sent a hot flush through them and filled their hearts with joy. Meir Velvel the Coachman, his face shining like a saint's, put his tefillin away. Then he went out to harness the horses, haranguing Smarty and Dancer and Privileged Character in his own juicy idiom; but the choicest sermon was reserved for Dancer. "Don't dance when there's no music!"

The sunlight seemed to coat the entire courtyard with gold; gems and diamonds sparkled all around. Even the refuse that had piled up during the summer, perhaps even two summers, was decked with gold. Let's not forget the rooster and his hens who were pecking at the refuse heap. They looked like pure gold, feathers and all. Their cackling was like a balm. Their manner of scratching the ground with their feet was utterly enchanting. And when that yellow rooster climbed up on the heap, shut his little eyes and let loose a mile-long cantorial cockadoodle-doo, the boys felt the beauty of the world and the greatness of the Creator. They had an urge to sing praises to Him. Not to stand up and pray, God forbid, like the innkeeper or Meir Velvel; no, the children weren't too crazy about that. But deep in their hearts they did want to thank and glorify God.

"Into the wagon, rascals, we've still got another day of riding ahead of us." Meir Velvel rushed them, paid for the hay and oats, and said good-bye to the innkeepers. The boys too said nice good-byes to the long-nosed family and climbed into the wagon. As soon as the rattling wagon rolled out of Barishpoli and entered once more the wide world of fields and gardens, sand, forests and endless sky, the boys were enveloped by a new sense of sweet freshness and well-being. But by now there was already *too* much sky. By now the children were bored, less with the sky than with the riding. Actually not so much with the riding as with the coachman and his stories. And besides, their heads pounded, they felt dizzy, and their sides hurt from being shaken up and bounced around. And the noise of the wheels! They thought it would go on forever and never stop. They wanted to get off the wagon; they yearned for the ground. They longed for home, for their village, Voronko. The hero of this autobiography hid in a corner of the wagon, sighed lightly, and in his heart bade farewell again and again to Voronko, whispering out of his brothers' earshot:

"So long, Voronko. Good-bye . . . good-bye!"

25. *The New Home*

The Metropolis of Pereyaslav—A Chill Meeting—Pawning the Silver—Father's Worries

On the second afternoon of the journey—after two days of being shaken, rattled and jounced—full of dust and ears ringing with the coachman's yarns, the young travelers sensed they were almost home. In the darkness they saw lights glimmering in distant houses—sure sign of a nearby town. Then the wheels clattered on cobblestones and the wagon shook more than ever before. Now they were really in town, in the big city of Pereyaslav. Meir Velvel's wagon rolled tumultuously into a dark courtyard where a smoky lantern and a little hay broom—traditional signs of an inn—hung on a gate.

The children were astonished and embarrassed that their parents were now innkeepers. What? Their father, Nochem, would now host guests? And their mother, Chaya Esther, would cook supper for them? And their grandmother Mindy would serve them? They couldn't imagine a greater comedown or humiliation. And the dreamer Sholom, who had always imagined better times and thought constantly of the treasure, grieved in silence. He wept secretly and longed desperately for life in beloved little Voronko. He couldn't understand why the grown-ups had said, "Change your place, change your luck." This was some change-place-change-luck! It was a lot of humbug!

"Off, rascals, we've arrived," Meir Velvel announced, after stopping his horses near the porch with a long "Whoaaaa!"

Broken, sore and hungry, the boys jumped off the wagon one by one and began straightening up. The door opened. On the dark porch figures recognizable by their voices began to appear. The first was tall and wide—Grandma Mindy. She craned her old head and said, "Oh, thank God. They've arrived." The second figure was short and brisk—Mama, Chaya Esther. "Have they arrived?" she asked. "Yes, they've arrived," came the voice of the third tall and thin figure. That was Father, Reb Nochem Vevik's, now known as Reb Nochem Rabinowitz. (In the big city, grandfather's name—Vevik—was retired from use.)

The reunion was not the one the children had expected. Of course, everyone exchanged kisses, but they were cold ones. Then the parents asked them, "What's doing?" And since there wasn't much to say, they replied, "Nothing." The first to remember that the children might want to eat was Grandma Mindy.

"Are you hungry?" she asked.

Some question, hungry! "Of course."

"Will you have something to eat?"

"Sure we will."

"Did you say your afternoon and evening prayers?"

"What a question!"

Mama rushed to the kitchen to prepare some food, while Father tested the children's progress in Torah studies. Indeed, they had advanced. But why was everyone pestering them when they wanted to inspect their new home?

The children looked around to see where they were. They saw a big, gloomy, rather foolish-looking house with lots of little rooms separated by thin partitions. These were the guest rooms—but there wasn't even one guest. There was a large room in the middle of the house with all the red Voronko furniture: the round three-legged table, the old veneered sofa with its tattered upholstery, the round veneered mirror with its two carved upraised hands, like a kohen's during the priestly blessing, and the glass cupboard with the multicolored Passover dishes, the silver Hanuka lamp and the old silver spice box shaped like an apple on a leafed branch. Neither the gilded wine cups and goblets nor the silverware was anywhere in sight. Where were they? Much later the children learned that their parents had pawned them with a Pereyaslav grandee along with Mama's pearls and jewelry, which they were never able to redeem.

When Mama served a none-too-festive supper—warmed-over kasha, beans and day-old bread—Grandma Mindy said, "Go wash your hands." Mama herself sliced a piece of bread for each child—*that* had never happened before. A miserly trait! Meanwhile, Father, sitting off to a side, did not stop testing them in Bible. He seemed pleased with the boys' knowledge, especially the middle one's. Sholom knew the material inside out and could recite entire chapters of Isaiah by heart.

"Enough, let them go to sleep!" Mama said. She took the leftover bread from the table and locked it in the cupboard. That too had never been done in Voronko. A disgusting practice!

Whether because of the long trip and their broken bones, or because of the cool reunion and beggarly reception—the new home the boys had dreamed of didn't have the expected and desired charm. Their high hopes crushed, they were happy when their parents told them to say the bedtime Shema and go to sleep.

Lying on a straw-filled sack on the floor, the hero of this autobiography couldn't fall asleep for the longest time. With the other children, he was in a large, unfurnished and dark anteroom that connected the living room and the kitchen. All kinds of thoughts tumbled in his head, questions upon questions. Why was it so dark and gloomy here? Why was everyone so worried? What had happened to Mama to make her so terribly stingy? Why had Father become so hunched over, depressed, and so much older-looking? It made your heart heavy just looking at his yellow, wrinkled face. Was it because of the "business is bad" remarks Sholom had heard in Voronko? Is this what they meant when they said, "Change your place, change your luck"? Oh, if only he could have taken with him just a tiny part of the treasure hidden in Voronko!

Recalling the treasure, Sholom remembered his friend Shmulik the Orphan and his wonderful tales about hoards of gold and silver, the diamonds and gems found in the earthly Paradise, and the treasure that lay hidden in the hill behind the Voronko shul from Chmielnicki's times. Then Sholom began to dream about treasures, gold and silver, diamonds and gems. He saw his dear friend Shmulik's charming face, his gleaming, slicked-down hair. He thought he heard Shmulik's soft, hoarse voice talking sweetly, like an old man, consoling him with kind words:

"Don't you worry, dear Sholom. Here's a present for you—one of the two stones. Choose the one you like, either Yoshfe or Kadkod."

Sholom was confused. He had forgotten which was better. As he stood there musing, Gergeleh Ganev leaped toward him, grabbed both stones and vanished. And Pinneleh Shimmeleh's—what was *he* doing here? Hands in his pockets, he shook with laughter.

"Why are you laughing, Pinneleh?"

"Because of your Aunt Hodel and her prune jam. Ha, ha, ha."

"Wake up, dunderheads! Look, look! It's impossible to wake them. This mess has to be cleaned up, supper has to be prepared, and they're sleeping, still in dreamland!" Mama complained. Short and brisk, Mama was in a dither because she had to do all the housework herself.

"Nu, nu, and prayers?" Grandma Mindy seconded her. She held her big Siddur and turned one page after another, praying with devotion.

"After prayers you'll go say hello to the family. And you'll begin cheder, God willing, after the holidays," said Father, in a voice softer than the others'. Despite the warm weather, he wore a queer-looking robe lined with cat fur. Bent over and careworn, he inhaled the smoke of a thick cigarette and sighed so deeply it rent your heart. He seemed to have aged and become smaller. Sholom wanted to dash out of the house as soon as possible to inspect the town and get to know the relatives.

26. *The Big Town*

Getting to Know the Family—Aunt Hannah and Her Children—Eli and Avreml Test Sholom in Bible—Uncle Pinny Tests Him in Calligraphy

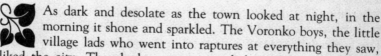 As dark and desolate as the town looked at night, in the morning it shone and sparkled. The Voronko boys, the little village lads who went into raptures at everything they saw, liked the city. They had never seen such long, broad streets with wooden sidewalks; houses roofed with tin; windows with green, blue and red shutters, and brick shops with iron doors. The market, the churches and, forgive the proximity, the shuls and bes medreshes, even the people—everything was so big and beautiful, so clean and festive! No, Pinneleh Shimmeleh's had not exaggerated when he told wonders about this great city. The children's feet seemed to glide

like wheels over the wooden sidewalks as they accompanied Father
to visit the family. Only their respect for him kept them from stopping
every minute to marvel at the sights. As usual, Father led the way
and the children tagged along.

Entering a large courtyard, they passed through a large and bright
glass corridor into a luxurious mansion. It had waxed floors, soft
couches and chairs, wall-length mirrors, carved cupboards, glass
chandeliers, and brass lamps on the walls.

Aunt Hannah's house, a royal palace, was a strange place. There
was no father (Aunt Hannah was a widow), and the children didn't
obey their mother, their teacher, or anyone else. Anarchy writ small.
Everyone did as he pleased. They continually bickered and called
each other names. They laughed uproariously and spoke all at once.
The racket made your head spin.

Aunt Hannah, a tall, imposing woman, could have been a grande
dame, the kind who takes snuff from a golden box picturing an old-
fashioned prince in a powdered wig and silk stockings. Aunt Hannah
had once been a beauty, as was apparent from her stunning daughters.
As soon as the children came in, the tumult and hollering began.

"Is that them? Is that him, the Bible expert? Come over here,
don't be shy. Look, just look at him blushing, ha, ha, ha."

Father evidently couldn't keep from boasting about his son's
knowledge of Bible. Therefore, on the spot they crowned him with
the title: the Bible expert.

"Pour the Bible expert a glass of tea. Fetch him an apple and a
pear. Give the Bible expert a taste of our Pereyaslav fruits."

"Listen, you know what? Let's call in Eli and Avreml to test him."

Eli and Avreml, young men with nice beards who lived right next
door, were summoned. (They were Aunt Hannah's relatives on her
husband's side.) Their father, Isaac Yenkel, once rich, was now
constantly suing the government. He wore an earring in his left ear,
had a handsome round beard, and didn't look at or speak to anyone.
The constant deprecating smirk on his face seemed to say: Why
should I talk to you if you're all a bunch of asses?

The two youths at once began testing the Voronko lad and heard
him recite entire chapters of the Bible by heart. Why deny it? Sholom
passed with flying colors. Not only did he cite chapter and verse for
every word he was asked, he also told them where all other words
with that same root appeared. Father beamed with joy, literally puffed

up with pride. His face shone. The wrinkles on his forehead disappeared; he seemed to straighten up and become a new man.

"In that case, let's give the Bible expert another apple, another pear, another nut, and lots of sweets," Aunt Hannah's beauties ordered. The name "Bible expert" stuck to him for a long time, not only among kin; in shul too the little scamps called him nothing but "the Voronko Bible expert." Even the adults, down to the last one, tugged at his ear and said: "Tell me, you little Bible expert, where is this verse from?"

The Bible expert liked Aunt Hannah's house and Aunt Hannah's boys, Pinny and Moche, two little rascals whom Sholom quickly befriended. He fancied that no finer or richer home existed in Pereyaslav or anywhere else on earth. Who ever heard of apples taken out of a barrel, nuts from a sack, and candies from a large bag?

Uncle Pinny's house was entirely different. It was a Jewish home with a sukka, lots of sacred texts, a complete set of the Talmud, a silver Hanuka lamp, and a long Havdala candle. No comparison to Aunt Hannah's house. His was a religious home. Everyone was observant. The children took after Uncle Pinny. His sons wore long, ankle-length gaberdines and knee-length ritual fringes. The daughters' kerchiefs were set modestly over their foreheads; they didn't look a strange man in the eye. Seeing a stranger, they turned beet red and giggled at length. Their mother, Aunt Tema, had white eyebrows. She too was very pious. She sat by her mother, who looked exactly like her. One couldn't tell who was the mother and who the daughter if not for the slight trembling of the mother's head which seemed to say: No, no, no.

At Uncle Pinny's house Father didn't boast about his Bible expert. Here they weren't so keen on Bible. Who studied Bible here? Bible was for heretics. Still, he couldn't refrain from boasting about his children's handwriting.

"My children's handwriting," said Nochem, "is world-famous. Take this little one, for instance." He pointed to the Bible expert. "He has an extraordinary hand. A master calligrapher!"

"In that case, let's have some pen and ink," Uncle Pinny ordered and rolled up his sleeves, as if ready for work. "As soon as I see pen and ink we'll test this calligrapher's handwriting. But now! Right this minute!"

Uncle Pinny's order was the command of a stern general, and all the children, boys and girls together, scrambled hastily to find pen and ink.

"A piece of paper!" the general ordered once more. But a sheet of paper was nowhere to be found.

"Listen! You know what? He can write here on the flyleaf of my little Siddur," suggested Uncle Pinny's younger son, Isaac, a strange-looking boy with a pointy head and a long nose.

"Write!" Father ordered the Bible expert.

"What should I write?"

"Whatever you like."

The Bible expert or, rather, the master calligrapher, dipped his pen into ink, thought a while, and for the life of him couldn't think of anything to write. Uncle Pinny's family no doubt thought Sholom could write only when no one was looking. But then Sholom remembered something that used to be inscribed in every Jewish book in those days. He rolled up his sleeves and dipped pen into ink a second time. A few minutes later he wrote in the holy tongue:

"Even though the sages have forbidden us to write in sacred books, making a sign is allowed."

Following this preface he added:

"This Siddur belongs. To whom does it belong? It belongs to the one to whom it belongs. But to whom does it belong? He who bought it. Who bought it? He who bought it bought it. But who bought it? He who paid for it. Who paid for it? Whoever paid for it paid for it. But who paid for it? The rich man. Who is a rich man? He who is a rich man is a rich man. But who is a rich man? The renowned young Isaac, son of the noted rich man Pinchas Rabinowitz of the city of Pereyaslav."

The furor this caused is hard to describe both from the standpoint of the Hebrew vocabulary and the calligraphy. But the latter took the day. The scribe did his best not to shame his father, God forbid. He diligently did his utmost. Sweating like a beaver, he chose the most beautiful pearl-tiny letters that had to be read with a magnifying glass, and drew upon all his penmanship skills learned from his teacher in Voronko. There Reb Zorechl had trained an entire generation of calligraphers who dispersed throughout the world and almost all of whom excel to this day with their consummate hand.

27. Between Terms

Arnold of Pidvorke—New Friends—Germiza the Teacher and Torah Reader—The Voronko Rascals Display Their Talent

 Do you know what "between terms" means? It's the equivalent of vacation, holiday, time off. But for the cheder lad none of these words has the impact of "between terms."

A child returning home for vacation from a secular primary school or gymnasium has had plenty of free time; he was satiated with fun, frolic and running around. He had time and enough for mischief with his friends all year long. No doubt he had fooled around more than he had studied. But the Jewish cheder lad worked himself to the bone all year, poor thing. He sat in the classroom till late at night studying, studying and more studying. Then suddenly—between-terms time! No classes for one and a half months, from around mid-August to the end of September. Could there be a better vacation? What's more, this was the time of the Jewish festivals: the Days of Awe, Rosh Hashana and Yom Kippur, Sukkos and Simchas Torah. And added to this was the new home in the big city of Pereyaslav.

First the children had to look at the town, which they had hardly seen. Besides visiting Aunt Hannah and Uncle Pinny, and attending the Big Shul, the Old Bes Medresh, and the Cold Shul where Tsali the cantor prayed, the Voronko children had scarcely been anywhere. There were many streets and places to explore, such as the Altitze and Trubelye rivers and the long bridge. And let's not forget the suburb, Pidvorke—where Arnold lived—which was a separate town, but still connected to Pereyaslav.

Arnold of Pidvorke often visited Nochem Rabinowitz to chat and speak of Maimonides, Judah Halevi's *Kuzari*, Spinoza, Moses Mendelssohn and other great men whose names Sholom couldn't remember. Except one whose queer name—Draper—had etched itself into his memory. Father thought highly of Arnold. "An extremely erudite man. If he weren't Jewish he could be a prosecuting attorney." Sholom couldn't understand why he should be a prosecuting attorney, and why a Jew couldn't be one. He knew only one thing about anti-Semitism: dogs. From personal experience. In Voronko the peasant boys had sicked their hounds on him. They knocked him over, bit him, and left permanent scars.

During the course of his later studies Sholom was very much indebted to Arnold, and we shall meet him again later. Meanwhile, it was between terms and the eve of a holiday. Time to make new friends and meet new boys.

Among the town notables Moshele Isaac Bigdor's led the list. Scrubbed and neat, this yellow-haired chap in an alpaca gaberdine was so conceited it was beneath his dignity even to talk to himself. And Moshele had good reason. First of all, his father, Isaac Bigdor, owned a private house with a white porch. What's more, it contained countless clocks and watches. At noon, the chiming split your eardrums. Isaac Bigdor himself had the eyes of a bandit and was suing everyone under the sun. All the boys in shul were afraid of his gaze.

Next on the list was Zyama Koretsky, a slightly stoop-shouldered scamp of the first order. He wasn't friends with everyone and not everyone was friends with him because his father, a lawyer in Petersburg with a trimmed beard and pince-nez, had modern tendencies. Zyama taught all the children to swim and to skate on ice, and many other things that Jewish children didn't know.

Next came Israel Benditsky's pale and tender little boy; thick-lipped Chaitl Ruderman, the teacher's son; Avreml Zolotushkin, swarthy as an Arab; the neatly groomed Merperts; and the Lipskys with their shiny boots. To them you needed a special privilege to talk, for no one else wore such highly polished boots in midweek. Then came the Kanaver children, devils one and all, who played with dogs and tortured cats. But Sholom didn't want to associate with any of them.

He preferred making friends with boys like Motl Sribne, a chap with long earlocks who played the violin, or Eli Dodi's, a vivacious lad who never stopped laughing. They prayed side by side in shul, shared one Machzor, and got into mischief together. They imitated Rafael the shamesh squinting and auctioning off the Torah honors: "Eighteen guilders for kohen!" and Vove Koretsky's nasal whistle. They mimicked Benny Kanaver taking snuff, Isaac Bigdor's shrug, and Sholom Wilensky's habit of stroking his beard and clearing his nose. Thank God, there were plenty of people to imitate. The way Germiza the teacher read the Torah, for example. Sholom studied him for two Sabbaths in a row. Germiza the pockmarked teacher shook one leg, contorted his face, bared his yellow teeth, stretched his long neck, moved his pointy nose up and down, and concluded the Torah reading with an odd, quavering, guttural voice: "See, I have set before you this day life and good and death and evil." You could have died laughing.

Everyone who heard Sholom imitating Germiza reading the Torah swore he had him down pat. But when Germiza learned that Sholom was mimicking him he was annoyed. He went and told Nochem Rabinowitz the whole story.

"I heard it said you have a little boy who is imitating the way I read the Torah."

This created a bit of a stir. Nochem promised he would investigate as soon as the children came home. When they returned, Father pounced on them. He guessed it must be Sholom's doing.

"Come here, Sholom. How do you imitate Germiza's Torah reading?"

"How do I imitate him? Like this."

And Sholom perkily shook a leg, contorted his face like Germiza, bared his teeth, stretched his neck, pointed his nose up and down, and sang out in an odd, quavering, guttural voice: "See, I have set before you this day life . . ."

Never before had Sholom seen his father laugh the way he laughed that day. He could hardly catch his breath. When he had finished laughing and coughing, he wiped his eyes and told all the children:

"You see what between-terms vacation is causing. You don't have a thing to do and your minds are on the devil-knows-what, like imitating Germiza reading the Torah." (Here Father couldn't control himself and hid his laugh in his scarf.) "God willing, right after Sukkos, I'll take you to a teacher and you'll start going to cheder. No more vacation."

Since vacation would soon be over, the children would have to start having fun right and proper. So they began to take advantage of their freedom in the best possible fashion. They weren't choosy, but played with any brat, made friends with everyone, and whooped it up like recruits before the draft. The Voronko boys showed the Pereyaslav boys that though they came from a village, they still knew many things that the big-city fellows didn't know. For instance, they weren't aware that any name could be set to a rhyme. Like Abie baby, Pinny skinny, little Gitl, Leibl table, Idl fiddle, Feigl bagel, and so on for any name you chose.

The big-city fellows also didn't know how to speak zyx, the backward language. For instance, "a hcnup ni eht eson" meant "a punch in the nose." Or "og ylf a etik!" meant "go fly a kite!" *Zyx* was great fun. Sholom could have spoken it for an hour with his eyes closed. With *zyx* you could talk about anyone, even to his face, and he'd never know what was going on.

And furthermore, what was wrong with these Pereyaslav boys who let a priest go by without a nasty crack, as if he were a plain man in the street? But the Voronko boys weren't such dummies. They wouldn't let a priest go scot-free. No matter how many children there were, they'd all stand behind the priest and chant a ditty:

> Your head is shaven,
> Devil's haven.
> I'll take some bread,
> But you drop dead.
> I'll be merry,
> But you we'll bury.
> I'll take a sleigh,
> But you eat hay!

The Pereyaslav boys said that singing such songs in the presence of a priest was forbidden in the city. It could lead to big trouble. Some news! Afraid of a priest! True, it was bad luck if a priest crossed your path. But being scared? Pereyaslav was indeed a big, beautiful city—no denying that—but between terms was much more fun in Voronko. So thought the Voronko boys; still, they wished that their days of vacation in Pereyaslav would stretch on endlessly.

28. Teachers

Reb Aaron Chodorover—One Teacher after Another—Monish—
Playing Cards in Cheder

Vacation time wasn't over yet, the holidays were still far off, but Nochem Rabinowitz was already negotiating for a teacher. There were several to choose from. First, the previously mentioned Germiza, who read the Torah so beautifully. Then Reb Aaron Chodorover, who was an excellent teacher but loved to tell his pupils tall tales of long ago. One was about his strong, fearless grandfather. One winter night as his grandfather drove a sleigh through a forest, hungry wolves appeared and gave chase. At which his grandfather jumped off the sleigh, grabbed each wolf, reached deep into his mouth until he caught his tail, then turned him inside out.

In another story his grandfather saved the entire town from disaster. One Sunday at a fair, after the peasants got good and drunk, they began beating Jews. The grandfather, who was in the middle of his prayers, cast off his tallis and tefillin and seized the biggest peasant, Ivan Poperilla. He grabbed both his legs and used Ivan as a club to beat the heads of the other goyim. The peasants fell like flies. When the grandfather had brought down every last one of them, he released Ivan and told him: "Now you can go home, and I can go back to my prayers."

Besides being strong, his grandfather was also terribly scatterbrained. When he fell into a reverie, said Reb Aaron Chodorover, it could be dangerous. Once, he walked around his house lost in thought, pacing back and forth. Before he knew it, he was standing on the table.

After Reb Aaron Chodorover, one instructor followed another: Reb Joshua, Reb Meir Hersh, Reb Yakir Simcha, the Koidenover teacher, and Fat Mendl. But each one had his flaw. If he knew Talmud, he was weak in Bible. If he mastered the Bible, he didn't know Talmud. Fat Mendl might have been the best if his flaw hadn't been the whip. Children trembled at the mention of Fat Mendl's name. Monish didn't spare the rod either. But Fat Mendl could kill you. On the other hand, he knew how to teach. Father promised the children that, God willing, he would hire one of the two.

Now that a teacher was secured, they turned their attention to penmanship. But with whom would they study? They had already mastered the art of writing Yiddish and Hebrew with the Voronko teacher, Reb Zorechl. But what about Russian? A good friend, Arnold of Pidvorke, suggested that the children be enrolled in the state-run Jewish school. Tuition was cheap and it was a good place to learn. But as soon as Grandma Mindy heard of this she swore that her children would remain Jews as long as she lived. No use arguing! Then discussions began about the teachers. Noah Bussel was a good instructor, but he was a son-in-law of a coachman. Itzi the scribe, who taught letter writing, had a fine hand but his Russian was shaky. Abraham the scribe, Itzi's brother, was weak on both scores. What was to be done? That left Monish, who had all the excellent attributes: he knew Bible, grammar, Talmud, and wrote Russian magnificently. True, he didn't know what he was writing and what's more wrote ungrammatically, but that didn't matter. The children were too young to know Russian grammar anyway. They should rather first learn Hebrew grammar. And what about Monish slapping his students? If they did their work he wouldn't hit them. Would a teacher strike his pupils for no reason? Indeed, the children later testified to the truth of this. Monish considered slapping and hitting despicable. He had an extra bone in this thumb which, when he poked it into your ribs, back, or temple, made you see your great-grandfather in the world to come.

Sholom diligently avoided this bone. He succeeded perhaps because he was among those who knew the required page of Talmud by Thursday, or at least pretended to. Bible, well that goes without saying! He was also good at calligraphy. As for mischief—that's when Sholom felt the teacher's thumb bone, which he hasn't forgotten to this day. But not for this reason was Nochem Rabinowitz dissatisfied with Monish. His flaw was that he hadn't the faintest notion about Hebrew grammar.

"Reb Monish, why don't you study Hebrew grammar with the children?" Father asked.

"Big deal, grammar-shmammar." Monish gave a derisive snicker. This upset Father terribly. At the end of the term he transferred the children to a new teacher.

The new man had such a mastery of grammar, he knew the best textbook by heart. Still, he had his fault too. He loved to dabble in communal affairs. He had something to do every day. If not a wedding, then a bris; if not a bris, a Redemption of the First Born party, a Bar Mitzva, a divorce, or cases of abandonment, arbitration or conciliation. Whether this was bane or boon depends on your point of view. The children considered him an angel, and his cheder Paradise. You could play any game you wanted, even cards. Not the Voronko card games. Feh! Real card games, the sort that prisoners played. The cards themselves were like jailbirds' cards—black, greasy and thick. Despite this, the children gambled away all their breakfasts and lunches. If they got their hands on a penny or two, that too was invested in cards.

All the money was won by the older boys, like Zyama Koretsky, who's been mentioned before. He introduced his young friends to all kinds of sweet temptations. His three principles were: (1) disobey parents, (2) hate teachers, (3) have no fear of God.

The bigger fellows always liked to tease and mock the younger boys once they had pocketed their money. This was something real cardplayers did not do. Nevertheless, don't assume it was easy for them. They suffered plenty too. First, the rebbitsin had to be bribed not to tell her husband that the boys were playing cards. Second, the teacher had a son, Feivel, who was called Lips because of his thick lips. Lips had to be pampered and flattered and paid off with a breakfast or a snack, but mostly with nuts. Lips loved to crack walnuts. The way he cracked nuts made you sick to your stomach. Especially with someone else's money. But what could the boys do? Would it be better if Lips snitched to his father that the pupils were playing cards?

Neither the teachers nor the studies gave Nochem Rabinowitz any satisfaction. He tested the children every Sabbath and shook his head with a sigh. He was most concerned about the middle son, the Bible expert. He evidently expected much more from him. "What's going to be?" Father asked. "What'll be the end of it? Before you know it, you'll be Bar Mitzva and you won't even be able to deliver a simple Talmud discourse." Father then began to look for a qualified Talmud teacher—he looked and looked till he found one.

29. The Talmud Teacher

*Moshe David Ruderman the Talmud Teacher—
His Son Shimon at the Brink of Apostasy—What the Town Did—
Uncle Pinny Angry*

The teacher was a dark-browed, asthmatic, hunched-over Litvak named Moshe David Ruderman. Not only was he a noted Bible and Talmud scholar but he knew Hebrew grammar too. In other words, he had all the fine attributes. What's more, he was pious, truly religious. Who could have known that this man too would have a flaw? And what a flaw it was! His failing was that his son was enrolled in the secular district school. Only two Jewish boys in all of Pereyaslav studied there. One was Moshe David Ruderman's son, Shimon, who early on began to grow a beard. The other was the lawyer Tamarkin's boy, Chaim. Short and thickset, with small eyes and a hooked nose, he wore his shirt over his trousers like a peasant, played ball with the gentile boys, prayed in shul only on Yom Kippur, and secretly smoked thick cigarettes.

These were the pioneers, the first swallows, so to speak, of the Haskala movement in Pereyaslav. At school, they were the only two Jews among hundreds of peasant lads. At first the latter looked at these little Yids as if they were a curiosity, from another world. Then they laid them down on the school courtyard and smeared their lips with lard. Then they became friends, brothers, one soul. In those days the peasant boys were still—ah, woe!—free of prejudice, and knew nothing about anti-Jewish incitements; the venom of anti-Semitism hadn't touched them yet. As soon as they threw the Yid to the ground, smeared his lips with lard and broke his bones, he became a comrade in arms like everyone else, despite his Jewish name.

Transferring Nochem Rabinowitz's children to Moshe David Ruderman wasn't an easy task. When Uncle Pinny learned that his brother had engaged a teacher whose son studied at the district school, he left no stone unturned. Pinny argued that that school was but one step away from conversion.

"Why?"

"Just like that. Just wait and see."

And that's exactly what happened. Evidently it was destined that this time Uncle Pinny's prophecy come true. Here's the story:

One Sabbath the news spread that Shimon Ruderman and Chaim Tamarkin were at the brink of apostasy. Naturally, no one believed this. "Where? What? How? The things a town can dream up!" But as the folk saying goes, if church bells chime, it's a holiday. That very Sabbath people scurried about as if their houses were on fire. Everyone in town ran to the monastery. What had happened?

"I'll make the story short and sweet. Want to see a sight? Go to the monastery and look up toward the roof. The two boys from the district school are standing there bareheaded and eating bread smeared with lard for everyone to see."

The scare was so great that no one thought of asking: How can you see all the way up there, to the top of the monastery, and know what the bread is smeared with? Lard or butter, perhaps even honey? But everyone was in a dither. The community was up in arms.

"Tamarkin's sonny boy doesn't surprise us. His father, old Tamarkin, is a pork gobbler. He's always involved in lawsuits and
petitions. Folks say that his little Chaim was already a goy in his
mother's belly! But Moshe David Ruderman? He's a God-fearing
man, a teacher. The finest in town. How can we let something like
this come to pass?"

It turned out that some Jews had already known it would happen.
How? By a logical conjecture that one cannot treat a child too
harshly.

"If you send your children to the district school, it's as if you've
made up your mind they're going to become goyim," respectable
householders concluded. "So you can't expect them to wear ritual
fringes. And if they skip an Afternoon Service once in a while, you
just have to keep quiet and not break a cane over their heads or beat
them like a dog . . ."

A meeting was then called to decide on a course of action. How
could two Jewish boys be saved from apostasy? The townspeople did
everything they could; they tried influence, they stirred up the local
authorities. Naturally, Uncle Pinny worked harder than anyone else.
With rolled-up sleeves and disheveled beard, he ran around all day,
perspiring, not eating or drinking, until—thank God, the affair was
resolved. The two boys were taken from the monastery.

The upshot was that one of them, Chaim Tamarkin, actually
converted a couple of years later. Shimon Ruderman was sent to the
rabbinical school in Zhitomir on a government stipend to study to
be a crown rabbi. With God's help, he not only graduated but became
a crown rabbi in Luben, a town near Pereyaslav.

"Well, Nochem? Who was right?" Uncle Pinny crowed. "Now,
please God, will you take your children from this teacher?"

Pinny was delighted. First of all, he had saved two Jewish boys
from apostasy. Second, his brother's children would no longer study
with a teacher who knew Hebrew grammar and had a son in the
district school. Third, his prediction that a child who studied in a
public school is ripe for conversion had come true.

But this time Uncle Pinny was terribly mistaken. His brother
Nochem was stubborn and absolutely refused to look for another
teacher.

"I have nothing against Moshe David Ruderman. Hasn't the teacher
had enough heartache and humiliation? It just wouldn't be right to
also deprive him of his livelihood in midterm."

Uncle Pinny heard his brother out with a bitter smile, as if to say: "I wish I were lying, but you're leading your children down a crooked path." Then he stood, kissed the mezuza, and left the house in a rage.

30. The Old-Fashioned Cheder

*A Portrait—The Students Help the Teacher and His Wife—The
Teacher Makes a Blessing—His Preaching Prompts New Sins*

 No, Father did not take the children away from the discredited but skillful teacher Ruderman. On the contrary, they stayed with him for a second and even a third term. Everyone was satisfied: the teacher with his pupils, the pupils with their teacher, and Father with both.

Happiest of course were the pupils. God had sent them a teacher who did not hit them. He didn't lift a finger. He didn't even know what hitting meant. Except once in a while when a boy vexed him terribly, or didn't want to pray, or had such a thick skull that even if you pummeled him nothing would penetrate—then Ruderman lost his patience. He laid the boy down on the bench and quickly smacked him with his velvet skullcap a couple of times. But that was it. Now back to your seat.

Another nice thing about Ruderman was his machine that ground grits. The device had a wheel and a handle; on top of it lay a bag of buckwheat. When the wheel turned, the buckwheat grains slowly made their way to the box and then to the grinding stone, which slowly ground them, discarded the chaff, and made grits of the buckwheat.

Naturally, the ingenuity of the machine lay in turning the handle. The quicker you turned, the more grits were ground. Almost all the children wanted to work the handle. Everyone wanted to help Reb Moshe David, who, unfortunately, could not make a living from teaching alone. He had to take on side jobs: he ground buckwheat and his wife baked honey cake. You'd think there was nothing to do when baking honey cake, right? Wrong! There was plenty to do. And the children gave a hand there too. Less for baking, actually, than for slapping. Honey-cake dough made of rye flour had to be slapped and punched for a long time until it became elastic. And who could slap better than cheder children? There were so many volunteers for dough slapping that the children first slapped each other for the privilege of slapping the dough. Everyone wanted to be first.

Don't wonder that the cheder youngsters ground buckwheat and slapped dough. They had done much grubbier work for Reb Zorechl and other Voronko teachers, like smearing loam on the earthen floor in honor of the Sabbath, taking out the slops, bringing water from the well, and drawing lots for tending the baby. Don't even mention taking a chicken to the ritual slaughterer! Helping the teacher's wife flick chicken feathers was a great honor! Anything was better than studying. *That* was worst of all.

Now let's describe an old-fashioned cheder so future generations interested in Jewish life in the blessed Pale of long ago may have a clear picture of it.

The cheder was in a rickety little peasant house with a thatched roof. Sometimes it tilted to one side; sometimes it didn't even have a roof, as if it were hatless. It had one window, at most two. The broken pane was stuffed either with paper or with a little pillow. On Sabbaths and holidays its earthen floor was sprinkled with sand. Much of the room was taken up by the oven, the stove and the sleeping area atop the stove, which was reserved for the teacher. His children slept near the oven and his wife near the wall in a bed bolstered almost up to the ceiling with countless cushions and pillows. On the bed you sometimes found a sheet of noodles on a white cloth, biscuits and bagels (if the teacher's wife was baking), or occasionally a child (if it was very ill).

Under the oven was a chicken coop where hens were raised, usually for sale. By the slanting, bulging wall stood a cupboard for bread, pitchers and little pots. Above the cupboard were stored the metal kitchenware, a sieve, a broom, a grater, and other such implements. Near the front entrance stood pokers and shovels, a huge slops pail always full, a wooden tub that leaked, and a constantly wet towel. In the middle of the room—a long table and two long benches. That was the cheder, the one-room schoolhouse, where the teacher taught his pupils. Everyone, teacher and students, shouted. The rebbitsin's children, who played on top of the stove, yelled too. Their mother, busy in the kitchen, shouted at them for yelling. The hens in the coop clucked. This prompted the cat to jump down from the stove and calmly slink into the coop and scare the hens, the devil take her!

That was the old Voronko cheder. But the one in the big city of Pereyaslav wasn't any better. Like his Voronko counterpart, the Pereyaslav teacher taught his charges wearing a cotton-wadded coat and a velvet skullcap in winter, and ritual fringes over a broad-sleeved shirt in summer. After his nap in the winter, he drank an herb tea made of linden blossoms; in summer, he sipped cold water from a wooden pitcher, which he strained through one of his broad sleeves. Before drinking he devoutly intoned the blessing and all his students sang out Amen. If a child brought in a fruit, the teacher recited the appropriate blessing over it and the children said Amen. If someone brought in a green cucumber, the teacher peeled it, said the blessing, and the pupils answered Amen.

As long as you didn't have to study, it was all worthwhile. The children were sick of studying. They studied all day long. Wintertime they studied late into the night. They got up at dawn and studied. They even had lessons on Sabbath mornings; even if they didn't study, they had to sit in cheder all afternoon and listen to the teacher's sermon.

The teacher's moral and ethical chastisement was a rich fantasy worthy of *A Thousand and One Nights*. His remarks made the children see the world to come; they got a taste of punishment in store for sinners in their graves; they heard how Dumah, the Angel of Death, comes on tiptoe, opens your stomach, removes your guts, slaps them across your face, and asks: "Wicked sinner, what's your name?" Then the teacher told how two angels of destruction, who torture the dead in hell, take you and toss you like a ball from one end of the world to the other. And if you ever told a lie, they hang you by the tongue on a hook where you dangle like a hunk of meat in a butcher shop. And if you forgot to wash your hands upon waking, two demons pluck out your fingernails with pliers. And if you trimmed your nails on a Friday and accidentally left a paring on the ground, you're doomed to return to earth to look for it.

All this for minor misdeeds. And what about major transgressions? Like skipping sections of prayers? Omitting an Afternoon Service? Not saying the bedtime Shema? Harboring an evil thought? Dreaming and daydreaming? For these there was no compassion in the other world. Absolutely none. Repentance, prayer and charity were efficacious only here, in this world. *There*, in the other world, it was already too late. Finished.

"There you're on a par with all the other wicked. There you head straight for the eternal flames, into the boiling cauldron, right into hell, you rascals, right into hell!"

Thus the teacher concluded his Sabbath sermon. The children hearkened and wept; they repented, beat their breasts in contrition, and silently promised henceforth to be good and pious. But no sooner had the teacher and the children risen from the table than the entire sermon was forgotten. The other world, hell, the angels of destruction, all vanished like a passing shadow, a flitting dream. Once more the children committed sins and misdemeanors. They skipped sections of prayers, they omitted an Afternoon Service, they didn't say their bedtime Shema. Who gave thought to washing hands or praying when the sun was shining outside and shadows slanting on the walls winked and beckoned: "Come on outside, fellows, come outside! It's beautiful outdoors. The little bridge is but a hop-skip away. One step more and you're on the other side where the brook flows and water gurgles. There green grass and yellow flowers grow, birds fly and grasshoppers leap." And the light green meadow begged you to stretch out on the soft, aromatic earth. But just then either Father or Mama, and older brother or sister, came along and asked: "Have you said your prayers already? Get back to cheder, you little devil, back to cheder with you!"

31. *The Bar Mitzva*

Success—A Gallery of Characters—Mama's Tears

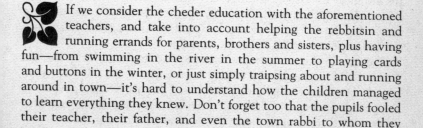 If we consider the cheder education with the aforementioned teachers, and take into account helping the rebbitsin and running errands for parents, brothers and sisters, plus having fun—from swimming in the river in the summer to playing cards and buttons in the winter, or just simply traipsing about and running around in town—it's hard to understand how the children managed to learn everything they knew. Don't forget too that the pupils fooled their teacher, their father, and even the town rabbi to whom they

were taken to be tested. Where did Sholom get the raw material to hoodwink an entire town of Jews who had gathered to celebrate his Bar Mitzva? Nochem Rabinowitz's little boy distinctly remembers that he didn't understand a word of the Talmud discourse prepared for him for his day of celebration. Nevertheless, the town was abuzz with his Bar Mitzva. Fathers were envious and mothers wished they had such children.

It was truly a festive occasion. A magnificent holiday. Many people had a hand in the celebration, under the leadership of Grandma Mindy, who looked like a real commander in her Sabbath dress and head covering. She decided who would and who would not be invited, who would sit at the head table, which plates would be used, and which wines and liquors would be served. She quarreled with and fumed at everyone; she didn't even spare the Bar Mitzva boy. "Behave like a grown-up! Don't bite your nails, at least when people are around! Don't laugh and don't make the other children laugh!" In other words, don't be a rascal.

"Thank God we've lived to celebrate your Bar Mitzva. So it's high time you started behaving," Grandma Mindy contended. She spit on her fingers and straightened out the last bit of earlock over which she'd struggled with her son Nochem. For Nochem Rabinowitz had long wanted to snip off the earlocks, but Grandma Mindy had refused.

"When I die and my eyes don't see it," she replied, "*then* you can make goyim out of your children. But as long as I'm alive, I'd like to see at least a little sign of Jewishness on their faces."

In addition to the entire family, a large crowd had been invited to come straight from shul to the Bar Mitzva party. Among the guests, of course, was Sholom's teacher, Moshe David Ruderman, wearing his Sabbath gaberdine and his faded velvet skullcap that lay on his head like a pancake. But the teacher made himself small and kept his distance. Ever since the near apostasy of his son, Ruderman had become greatly dispirited. He hardly touched the wine or the culinary treats, but sat off in a corner, hunched over, coughing softly into the broad sleeves of his Sabbath gaberdine.

Then came the moment for the speech. The Bar Mitzva lad had to stand and display his knowledge for the guests. At this Ruderman stirred. His back straightened; he raised his thick black eyebrows and pierced Sholom with his glance. Then his moving thumb prompted Sholom with the prepared text like a conductor's baton.

The Bar Mitzva boy almost fainted with fright. His throat was parched; everything swayed before his eyes. He seemed to be walking on ice. In a minute the ice would crack—and he and all the guests would sink. But gradually, aided by the teacher's glance and his thumb movements, Shólom felt increasing confidence. He began to stride forward as though walking on an iron bridge and felt a warmth in all his limbs. The discourse was delivered like a song.

While speaking (along with his teacher, Sholom too moved his thumb), the Bar Mitzva boy surveyed the guests. He noted their expressions and didn't skip a face. There was Isaac Bigdor, who always hitched up his shoulders and was watching with his bandit's eyes. There was old Joshua Sribne—folks claimed he was already one hundred years old. His tongue moved like a bell clapper in his mouth, for he had no teeth. His son Berke, quite old himself, listened with closed eyes and tilted head. There was fat, broad-beamed Asher Neides, whom everyone called Uncle Asher. His silk gaberdine was bursting at the seams and he was gray as a dove. There was Yossi Fruchstein with his large false teeth, glinting spectacles and wispy beard. He was a heretic who played chess with Nochem Rabinowitz and read secular books like *The Mysteries of Paris* and *Paths of the World.*

Next to Yossi stood his younger brother Michael, a clever rascal, a freethinker who even ordered the gentile girl to put out the light on Sabbath. He thought highly of Jews like Moshe Brenner and Benny Kanaver, who, as everyone knew, purposely moved their heads during a haircut when they were younger so the barber would snip off their earlocks. Israel Benditsky was also invited. He used to be called Israel the Klezmer, but now he already had his own house, bought a seat by the eastern wall in shul, and grew a neat, long, shiny black beard. Even though he occasionally consented to perform at a prestigious wedding, no one dared call him a klezmer, not even behind his back. Indeed, he was a distinguished-looking man and behaved like a householder. When he laughed, he displayed all his small, white gap teeth. Even squinty-eyed Rafael the shamesh didn't pass up Sholom's Bar Mitzva. He stood bent over, totally absorbed in Sholom's discourse. Looking at his thin face and hooked nose, Sholom thought that any minute Rafael would pound the table and call out in his Sabbath manner: "Eighteen guilder for kohen!"

Sholom took in everyone and everything. All the faces looked festive—above all, Uncle Pinny's. He sat up front, next to the Bar Mitzva boy's father, wearing his silk Sabbath gaberdine, a broad silk sash and a blue velvet hat. Uncle Pinny inspected Sholom from head to toe and smiled into his beard, as if to say: "Well, that little rascal certainly knows a thing or two. That's perfectly evident. But does he pray every day? Does he wash his hands upon awakening? Does he say the bedtime Shema? Does he refrain from carrying on the Sabbath? I have my doubts."

But Nochem's face beamed like the sun. Everyone could see he was the happiest man on earth. Head high, lips moving as he followed his son's remarks, he looked at the guests, his brother Pinny, Ruderman, the Bar Mitzva boy, and Sholom's mother.

And Mama, little Chaya Esther, wearing her silk Sabbath kerchief, stood modestly off to a side, unnoticed among the other women. Spellbound, she sighed softly and cracked her knuckles. Two tears, sparkling like two diamonds, caught the sun's rays as they rolled down her young, happy, but already wrinkled face.

What kind of tears were they? Tears of joy? Pleasure? Pride? Or tears bemoaning the hard times? Or perhaps her mother's heart was telling her that this Bar Mitzva lad whose voice rang out so beautifully would soon, very soon, be saying Kaddish for her?

Who knows why a mother cries?

BOOK TWO

32. The Young Man

*His Brother Hershel Is Engaged—An Examination Plus Prompter—
A Tefillin Bag, a Watch and a Bride*

 "God be praised, you're a young man now. No longer a child, a rascal, a devil. Time to behave like a God-fearing Jew, for time doesn't stand still. In fact, in no time you'll be engaged."

This was Moshe David Ruderman's little sermon to Sholom on the morning after his Bar Mitzva. His teacher, assisting him with his tefillin, tied the leather thongs so tight on Sholom's left hand that his fingers swelled and turned blue. The large tefillin on his head kept sliding down between his eyes or off to a side. Sholom tried hard to stand straight, keep his balance and not look at the rascals who watched with curiosity as the Bar Mitzva boy prayed with tefillin for the first time.

Frankly, if it were not for these little scalawags, Sholom would have prayed with heartfelt devotion. He liked the tefillin ceremony. He liked the prayer that began "I have betrothed thee unto me for life . . ." He liked the smell of the fresh leather straps. He liked people telling him he was already a young man. He liked being counted for a minyan; it meant he was equal to other Jews, a man among men. Even Rafael the squinty-eyed shamesh looked at him differently, with concealed respect. And his friends, of course, envied him. Sholom remembered how he had envied his elder brother Hershel at his Bar Mitzva. Actually, not as much the Bar Mitzva as the engagement which soon followed. Hershel's fiancée had given Hershel a tallis bag as a gift, and his future father-in-law a silver watch. Both the betrothal and the fate of the watch deserve to be recalled in brief.

Hershel was a remarkable Bar Mitzva boy, neat and handsome. He loved dressing up, but he had no head for studies and no great desire to learn. Nevertheless, since he came from a prominent family—he was Nochem Rabinowitz's son—he was introduced to the daughters of the finest families.

One day, a distinguished-looking, black-bearded man (a relative, it turned out) arrived from Vasilkov. He didn't come alone, but brought with him an examiner, a young man with a little yellow beard. Smart, bright, expert in Bible and fluent in Hebrew—but a bit of a nudnik, a pest who wormed his way into your marrow. First, the examiner began showing off how much *he* knew. He straightaway got into a long argument with the fiancé's teacher about Hebrew grammar. Whatever the teacher said, the young examiner contradicted. Then he grabbed the teacher by the elbow and demanded:

"Tell me, in the verse from Ecclesiastes, 'Dead flies makes the ointment of the perfumer fetid and putrid,' why is the verb 'makes' singular and not plural?"

To which the teacher replied: "And you tell me why the verse in Ecclesiastes, 'Remember your Creators,' is plural and not singular?"

But the examiner outflanked the teacher by countering:

"If you don't mind, tell me where the following verse appears? 'They went from nation to nation.' "

Thrown off balance, the teacher answered sheepishly:

"It's from the prayer, 'Give thanks unto God . . .' "

This answer did not satisfy the young examiner. "And where does *that* phrase come from?"

The teacher became even more confused. "Well, it's probably somewhere in the Psalms."

The yellow-bearded examiner burst out laughing. "No offense, teacher, but it's not *somewhere* in the Psalms. It appears once in the Psalms and, if you'll forgive me for saying so, it's also found in Chronicles . . ."

This was a deathblow for the teacher. Drops of perspiration formed on his forehead. He was finished off. "He's a foxy one!" the teacher later told the children as he wiped his brow with the tail of his gaberdine. "If he starts testing Hershel, he's through. The match will be called off." And since the teacher was an interested party to the match—well, not so much to the match itself as to the commission to be derived therefrom—he had a bright idea, and whispered it into the ear of the fiancé's little brother. He told Sholom to hide behind the large veneered sofa, upon which he seated Hershel. Then the parents sat around the semicircular gimpy table, and the young examiner started taking the fiancé to task. Meanwhile, Mama was setting the table, bringing honey cake and whiskey, confident that the test would go well.

"All right, my fine young fellow, how about telling me where this line appears: 'The complacent regard calamity with contempt.' "

"In the Book of Job," came the whisper from behind the sofa.

"It's in Job," Hershel sang out, loud as a demon.

"Right you are, it's in Job! Now where in the Bible do you find a rare form of the word 'thought'?" the examiner continued.

" 'On that day his thoughts perish.' It's in the Psalms," whispered the prompter from behind the sofa, and Hershel repeated it word for word.

"Well, it looks like we're finished with the Bible, doesn't it?" the examiner remarked and glanced at the table where Chaya Esther busied herself with the honey cake and preserves. "So why don't we dip into Hebrew grammar? What kind of verb is 'they perished'? What aspect is it in? Which person? Number? Tense?"

Little Sholom answered softly behind the sofa and the fiancé repeated every word. "The verb is intransitive, in the simple aspect, third person plural past." And then he conjugated the verb from first-person singular to third-person plural.

"Enough, enough, enough!" the examiner cried out in delight. He rubbed his hands, looked at the set table, and turned to the beaming father of the bride-to-be.

"Mazel tov! You can see for yourself that the young man is adept at everything. Now we can have a bite, right?"

Were Hershel's parents aware of this little ploy, or did it involve only the teacher and the fiancé? And was the examiner too perhaps in on the ruse as well? It's hard to say. In any case, both sides were pleased; neither side was fooled, God forbid.

Now let's turn to the story of the watch. Naturally, after the examination, Mama immediately went to see the bride, a clever girl whom Mama liked. The family prepared an engagement feast, wrote the betrothal contract, broke plates as was the custom, and the future father-in-law gave the fiancé a silver watch.

Hershel spent hours gazing at his gift. It was a mitzva to ask him the time. He guarded that watch like the apple of his eye. When he went to sleep he couldn't find a spot safe enough for it. Before leaving for shul on the Sabbath, he sought a hiding place in all the dresser and cabinet drawers. He was scared to death that his watch might be stolen, God forbid.

Then one day Hershel, who loved neatness and cleanliness, got the bright idea of dressing up in his suit. In those days, a fine tricot that stained easily and absorbed tons of dirt was in fashion. He hung the suit on the porch and began to beat the dust out with his flexible cane. He swung with all his might, completely forgetting all about the watch hidden in a pocket. Of course, the watch was demolished—it became a heap of broken bits of silver, porcelain, glass and lots of tiny wheels. Seeing this, the fiancé let out a wail and burst into tears. No consolation helped, not even promises to buy him a new watch. It tore your heart out looking at Hershel.

The Bar Mitzva boy Sholom also considered himself a young man now. He longed for three things: a tefillin bag like the one his brother had, a watch, and a fiancée. The fiancée appeared to Sholom in the guise of a princess, one of the beauties that his friend Shmulik the Orphan talked so much about. Sholom saw her so clearly he often dreamed of her. In fact, after his Bar Mitzva, he once saw her in real life and immediately fell in love, as we shall see in the next chapter.

33. *First Love*

Rosa Berger, the Shulamite of the Song of Songs—Chaim Fruchstein—Dangerous Rival—Squeaky Boots and French—Playing the Fiddle—Sweet Dreams

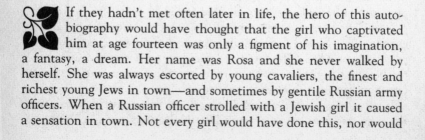 If they hadn't met often later in life, the hero of this autobiography would have thought that the girl who captivated him at age fourteen was only a figment of his imagination, a fantasy, a dream. Her name was Rosa and she never walked by herself. She was always escorted by young cavaliers, the finest and richest young Jews in town—and sometimes by gentile Russian army officers. When a Russian officer strolled with a Jewish girl it caused a sensation in town. Not every girl would have done this, nor would

the town have forgiven every girl. But Rosa was an exception. She was forgiven, for she was Rosa, the only girl in town who played piano; the only girl in town who spoke French. She talked and laughed with gusto—an incomparable girl!

Moreover, she stemmed from a distinguished family. Her father was one of the richest and most prominent men in town, a Jewish aristocrat. When he was younger, folks said, he was smooth-shaven. Now, already old and gray, he grew a beard, wore glasses, and had pouches under his eyes. His daughter inherited this feature, but it blended well with her beautiful blue eyes, arched, silky eyebrows, Greek-Jewish nose, alabaster face, and small but majestically proportioned figure, which dazzled the dreamy cheder lad, Sholom Nochem Vevik's. One glance from her lovely Shulamite eyes and the innocent Bar Mitzva boy was struck with the holy fire of love.

Yes, the Shulamite from the Song of Songs. Only she had such divine eyes. Only she could penetrate your soul with a sweet, loving look. And I guarantee you that she looked at Sholom only once— perhaps twice. And then only in passing, accompanied by an entire troop of escorts, among whom was one fortunate soul named Chaim Fruchstein, Yossi Fruchstein's only son. He had a long nose sprinkled with red pimples, surprisingly large teeth, and was rather short-legged. But he dressed like a dandy: high-heeled lacquered boots that squeaked when he walked, and a vest as white as newly fallen snow. His hair was parted precisely in the middle, and he bathed with an aromatic perfume that made its presence felt for a mile.

He was the most fortunate of Rosa's cavaliers. The town considered him her fiancé because he was rich Yossi Fruchstein's son, and rich men always made suitable matches with one another. Besides, he was the only youth in Pereyaslav who spoke French. Since they both spoke French, what match could be more appropriate? Another thing: she played piano, and he, violin. When they played duets, Sholom would forget about everything and listen all night outside her window.

Sholom often stood under Rosa's open window on a summer evening, listening to the divine tones which Rosa's beautiful fingers drew out of the shiny grand piano and the sweet melodies which the short-legged Chaim Fruchstein coaxed out of his violin. Ah, what emotions ran through Sholom then! He felt pleasure and grief; he blessed and cursed at the same time. He enjoyed the divine music and grieved that not he but someone else was playing with Rosa. As he blessed the hands that brought angelic sounds out of dead wood, he cursed the day that he was born to Nochem Rabinowitz and not Yossi Fruchstein, and the fact that Chaim Fruchstein was a rich man's son while he, Sholom, had misery and hardship. Not only was he unable to convince his parents to get him high-heeled lacquered boots that squeaked, but his own boots were frayed, the heels lopsided and the soles worn down. If he requested lacquered boots they would ask him: "What for?" And if he told them he wanted boots that squeaked the only thing he'd get would be slaps.

How wonderful it would be if he had a treasure. The kind Shmulik the Orphan talked about. But it was nonsense! There was no treasure. That is, there was a treasure in Voronko but it was hard to find. It was deeply buried. When it was found, it disappeared and concealed itself even deeper. And the miserable Sholom cursed the day he was born into the Rabinowitz family of fine lineage, and not into the Fruchsteins. He began to hate the pimply, big-nosed, short-legged Chaim Fruchstein more than anyone else. He hated him with a passion because God had blessed him with squeaky boots, French, and musical talent.

Once, as Sholom stood outside listening to the divine tones and angelic music that emanated from the room, the wretched youth promised himself and swore by the light of the moon and the stars that henceforth he would learn to play the violin like the lucky Chaim Fruchstein. With his playing he'd put all the Chaim Fruchsteins in his side pocket. He would also learn to speak French like Chaim Fruchstein. God willing, he'd soon be on a par with him and perhaps even surpass him. And only then would he come to Rosa's house and tell her in the language of the Song of Songs: "Return, return O Shulamite . . . Turn to me for a moment and listen to me playing the violin." When Shulamite-Rosa would hear him running his bow over the thinnest strings, she'd ask in amazement:

"Where did you learn this?"

"I taught myself," Sholom would reply.

Chaim Fruchstein would stand there, astonished and envious of Sholom. If Chaim would tell her something in French, Sholom would interrupt, also in French. "Watch what you're saying, Reb Chaim, because I understand every word."

At which Chaim would be thunderstruck and Shulamite-Rosa would ask Sholom:

"You speak French too? Where did you learn French?"

"I taught myself," Sholom would reply.

And then Shulamite-Rosa would stand and take Sholom by the hand. "Come," she'd say. And the two of them would leave, he and Rosa, for a stroll on the Pereyaslav sidewalks, both talking French, while the entire troop of cavaliers, including the short-legged Chaim Fruchstein, would follow. Everyone in town would point a finger and ask: "Who is that happy couple?"

"Don't you know who that is?" would be the answer. "That's Rosa and her chosen one."

"Who is her chosen one?"

"The Voronko Bible expert and master calligrapher, Sholom Nochem Vevik's, Sholom Rabinowitz."

Sholom hears all this but pretends he hasn't. He continues walking hand in hand with the lovely Rosa. She gazes at him with her beautiful blue eyes and laughs. He feels her small warm hand in his and hears his heart beating: tick-tock, tick-tock. Down below, his boots seem to talk of their own accord: squeak, squeak, squeak. This amazes him. Playing the violin and talking French—well, that he has taught himself. He worked and slaved until he learned them. But the boots—how did they get that squeak? Did they teach themselves? But perhaps it's his imagination. And Sholom presses hard with both feet, presses with all his might, and gets a jab from his elder brother, with whom he shared a bed.

"Why are you kicking like a colt?"

Sholom woke. Was it all a dream? Again and again he replayed the scene in his mind. And he didn't stop daydreaming. Reality and dream, fantasy and reality fused. And so the days passed, so many he lost track of them, until a visitor came to Pereyaslav, a horrible visitor, a plague. Like a hurricane it turned everything upside down and devastated many homes, including Nochem Rabinowitz's. Sholom's love for the beautiful Shulamite-Rosa vanished like a dream, a fantasy, a bygone day.

The visitor—cholera.

34. Cholera

*The Epidemic—The Masseurs—Grandma Mindy Takes Charge—
She Cries at Graves, Prays, Works with Doctors—
Uncle Pinny Forbids Tears*

It began almost frivolously right after Passover. But later, sometime after Shevuos, when the fruit ripened and green gooseberries were cheap, almost free, it became quite serious. Words like "epidemic" and "cholera" were bandied about more frequently. People spat when they said the word, and a pall of fear fell over the town.

Naturally, only the adults were terror-stricken. For the youngsters it was rather festive. Grown-ups carefully watched the children's diet. They felt their foreheads morning and night and checked their tongues. Finally, the cheders were disbanded until, God willing, the epidemic was over. But the epidemic was in no rush, and the cholera raged.

But the town didn't sit on its hands either—it did everything possible. First off they began a treatment called "rubbing." A group of masseurs was quickly formed to massage anyone who didn't feel well. Indeed, these rubdowns saved many people. Among the masseurs were the town's most distinguished citizens. The city was divided into districts, and each district had its own group of masseurs. Sholom looked at them with great awe and respect and considered them brave and heroic men. It was obvious that they feared neither cholera nor death. They encouraged one another, bantered cheerfully, drank "L'chayim," and hoped that the Almighty would have compassion and rout the plague.

Of course the Rabinowitzes were also among the volunteers. At night, when Father returned from his district, he reported who had been massaged and who hadn't. Everyone gathered around him admiringly and listened eagerly and anxiously to his account. But Mama cracked her knuckles nervously, looked at her gang of children, and said:

"Let's hope he doesn't bring the cholera into the house, God forbid."

"Cholera isn't the sort of sickness that's transported," Father replied with a smile. "Whoever it's destined for gets it right at home."

Evidently it was destined for Mama, diminutive Chaya Esther. One fine morning she woke and told her mother-in-law, Grandma Mindy, about her strange dream.

"I dreamed it was Friday night and I was lighting the candles. Suddenly Frume Sara the silversmith's wife, the one who just died last week of the illness, came into the room. She puffed up her cheeks and blew out my Sabbath candles . . ."

Hearing this strange dream, Grandma Mindy laughed and of course interpreted it favorably. But the two women were obviously terror-stricken. Then Mama lay down and asked for a mirror. She looked into it and told Grandma Mindy:

"Mother-in-law, it's bad! Look at my fingernails."

To be sure, Grandma Mindy laughed it off and wished all such bad dreams on her enemies' heads. But secretly she sent the older boys to look for Father and bring him back from his massaging rounds. And without waiting for Father, Grandma Mindy placed large water-filled pots into the oven and tried to help the ailing woman by herself. She did everything humanly possible and also sent for Doctor Ko-zatchkovsky, the best physician in town.

Kozatchkovsky, a stout and red-faced gentile, was so healthy that the Jews said he would die on his feet. Despite his reputation, Grandma Mindy also brought in Yenkel the Medic. Since he was a Jew, it was easier to talk to him. True, Yenkel was only a medic; nevertheless, he wore a cape like a doctor, and wrote prescriptions like a doctor, and read Latin like a doctor, and charged fees like a doctor. When a coin was placed in his hand, he seemed unwilling to take it; still, he felt the size of the coin in his pocket and always knew just how much he had been given. Because if it was too small, he simply asked for another one. But he did this tactfully, with a smile, while stroking his long hair and adjusting his glasses.

After chasing the little ones out, Grandma closed herself into her small room with Yenkel the Medic. She whispered at length with him until Father returned. Father was frightened to death; nevertheless, Grandma Mindy laced into him and reprimanded him with a vengeance. It was funny seeing Father attempting to justify himself before her.

If you didn't see Grandma Mindy during those days you've never seen anything magnificent. A Jewish commander, a woman field marshal. Her dark green silk kerchief, adorned with silver apples, was knotted in back of her head, and the sleeves of her chocolate-colored dress were rolled up. With the black rep apron over her dress, her meticulously washed hands, and wrinkled, stern old visage, she looked as if she were lording it over a wedding and not bustling about her seriously ill daughter-in-law, who was fighting for her life. It seemed that it wasn't Mama struggling with death; rather it was Grandma Mindy struggling for her, waging a war with the Angel of Death, who rustled his gossamer black wings. He made his presence felt but had not yet appeared. The children didn't know what was happening but instinctively sensed something awesome and mysterious. Grandma Mindy's face seemed to say:

"Death wants to take the children's mother, but with God's help I will not permit it."

When Grandma said she wouldn't permit it, trust her. Once, Doctor Kozatchkovsky visited Mama, who was by then critically ill—this was obvious from the doctor's red face, which had turned even redder. Grandma Mindy summoned all the children and lined them up by size (the eldest, with a beard, was already on his own, while the youngest was a girl scarcely one year old). When the doctor emerged from the sickroom, she fell on his feet, kissed his hands and introduced him to the troop:

"Look, see, dear man, how many little mites, how many orphans the sick woman will leave if, God forbid, let's not even mention it! By all that's just, have pity, dear man, on these little mites, on these innocent lambs."

These remarks could have melted a heart of stone. They even moved Doctor Kozatchkovsky, who spread his hands and said:

"What can I do? I'm doing everything possible." Then he raised his index finger. "He's the one you have to talk to." In other words, to God. Thanks a lot for the advice, dear doctor. When it came to God, Grandma didn't need him as a middleman. She knew the way to God without his help. She had already been to shul and hired a man to say psalms continuously for twenty-four hours. She had been to the cemetery and prayed that her ancestors intercede for Mama. A mother like Chaya Esther should not make her son a widower and her grandchildren orphans, she pleaded. A saintly woman like Nochem's wife should not die. "No, dear Father in heaven, you are a good God, you won't do such a thing."

But nothing helped. Indeed, God is a good God, but little Chaya Esther never rose from her bed. She died on a Sabbath morning while Jews were still in shul.

Dead? After their teacher Moshe the Slaughterer's death this was the second death that the youngsters felt more than they understood. Their anguish was great. True, their mother had not been as gentle or affable as other mothers. Yes, she would often hit, slap, and jab them. "That'll teach you that children aren't supposed to be gluttons and ask for more! That'll teach you that children aren't supposed to bare their teeth and whinny." Meaning that children weren't supposed to laugh. But the children *did* laugh, for how could one refrain when one felt like laughing? But such laughter cost them dearly. They paid for it with tweaked ears and swollen cheeks—Mama's small but strong hands made their presence felt.

Now, however, the children forgot all this. They forgot her slaps and jabs, her cuffs and punches, and remembered how Mama would put her hand into her pocket and look for a penny for every child. How on the first of the month she would feed them cabbage and honey as a remedy against worms. How Mama would not leave the bedside of a sick child. How Mama's small hand would touch his forehead, take his pulse, stroke his little cheeks. How Mama would sew new clothes for the children before each holiday. How Mama would wash their hair on Fridays. How Mama would laugh during the Seder when the four cups of wine made the children tipsy. The children recalled these and many other incidents as they lay with their faces pressed into pillows and cried their hearts out.

But their weeping increased tenfold when they heard Father crying—who ever heard of a father crying?—and Grandma Mindy sobbing, lamenting, and arguing with God, keening with a melody as if she were reading a prayer: "Why didn't you take me instead, and not a young branch, a mother of so many tiny mites, may no harm befall them?"

Comparing the children to mites at that sad moment made the children smile. Why mites? But suddenly the door opened and like a whirlwind Uncle Pinny and his two sons stormed into the room directly from the Old Shul (that's where Uncle Pinny prayed) with a hearty "Gut Shabbes!" Seeing everyone weeping and wailing, he began to shout and vent his anger at Father and Grandma Mindy:

"What's going on here? Weeping on the Sabbath? Bandits! Cutthroats! What are you doing? Are you crazy or insane? Have you forgotten today is Sabbath and it's forbidden to weep? Nochem, what are you doing? It's forbidden; it's Sabbath! No matter what, Sabbath takes precedence!"

Meanwhile, our uncle himself went off to a side and pretended to blow his nose. Pinny glanced at the place where Mama lay covered with a black cloth. He quickly wiped his eyes so no one would see him crying. But it was obvious, for his voice broke and he spoke more softly:

"Listen to me, Nochem. Enough. You're taking too much upon yourself. Nu, enough! You're not allowed to . . . It's Sab—"

Uncle Pinny couldn't finish the word "Sabbath," for the tears he had swallowed now choked him. He could no longer control himself. He sat down at the table, put his head on his left side, as if saying the weekday morning Supplication Prayer, and began sobbing like a child. "Chaya Esther," he moaned weakly, "Chaya Esther."

35. *Sitting Shiva*

Father Studies the Book of Job—Matches—The Children to Bohuslav

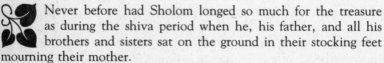 Never before had Sholom longed so much for the treasure as during the shiva period when he, his father, and all his brothers and sisters sat on the ground in their stocking feet mourning their mother.

Ah, if I only had that treasure buried in the village now, he thought. Even just part of it. I could put it to such good use . . . Grandma Mindy would stop crying and complaining and arguing with God, reproving Him for His error in taking the daughter-in-law first and not her . . . Father would stop sighing and groaning and asking why he still lived and what was he without Chaya Esther . . . And the children, where would they be now? Surely with the rest of the children by the river, swimming, fishing, or just running around. It was awfully hot, a heat wave. Sour cherries and currants were dirt cheap and the fragrance of green cucumbers, their skin still prickly, was already in the air. Soon he'd see the fragrant yellow cantaloupes and the sugar-sweet, fiery red watermelons with their crisp texture. Ah, the treasure, the treasure!

Sholom's thoughts took wing and lifted him to another world, a world of fantasies and dreams—sweet, beautiful dreams. He imagined he suddenly found the treasure with all its riches, gems and precious stones, gold and silver, gold sovereigns, diamonds and rubies.

"Sholom, where did you suddenly get these riches?" his surprised father asked.

"I can't tell you, Father, because as soon as I start to talk the riches will disappear."

Sholom was in seventh heaven at rescuing Father from want; however, he felt awful that his mother wasn't there.

"It wasn't fated," said Grandma Mindy. "All her young years she suffered raising the children; now when the time has come to really live, she died."

"Ay, ay, ay, what's to be done?" Father sighed. "What should we do now?" And the little dreamer came down from that happy world of fantasies to the desolate world of tears and woe, where people talked of flour for baking challa or money for shopping, of guests that didn't come to the inn, and of scant livelihood. But these conversations were cut short by Father's sigh and groan: "Ay, ay, ay, what's to be done? What should we do now?"

"What do you mean, what's to be done?" Uncle Pinny assailed him on the final day of mourning. "You'll do what all Jews do. With God's help, you'll marry."

Marry? Father marry? And we'll have a new mother? What will she be like? thought Sholom. The children watched for Father's reaction. But he didn't want to hear of it.

"Marry?" he said. "I should marry? After a wife like Chaya Esther I should marry? And it's you, my own brother, who's suggesting this? Who knew her as well as you?"

Father's tears choked him. He couldn't say another word. Uncle Pinny fell silent.

"It's time for the Afternoon Service," Uncle Pinny said. All the mourners, Father and his sons, rose from the floor and stood to pray. All six sons, among them a grown young man with a little yellow beard (his name was Eliyahu), rapped out a Kaddish—it was a pleasure to hear it. The family members looked with pride at the Kaddish sayers. The women onlookers were envious.

"If she doesn't go straight to heaven having such Kaddish sayers, then it's the end of the world," said a freckle-faced relative named

Bluma. Bluma was married, but she had left her children and mute husband to help out in the house and to cook for the family and tend the children. The children couldn't complain of neglect. On the contrary, since Mama had died more attention had been focused on them—they'd become orphans.

There were even some festive moments during the shiva. First, and above all else, they didn't attend cheder. Secondly, they were served rare treats: sweet tea and challa. Relatives touched their foreheads and bellies and inquired about their stomachs. All of a sudden they had gotten "stomachs." And wasn't it something to share a blanket with Father on the floor and see him wrinkle his broad forehead as he perused the Book of Job? The children heard men and women come and go; new visitors arrived constantly to console the mourners. Their behavior was odd. They said neither hello when they entered nor good-bye when they left. They blinked strangely and muttered, "Mourners . . . Zion and Jerusalem."

For the little devil, Sholom, these visitors were a treasure trove of incomparable character types and scenes that begged to be written down. First was Uncle Pinny with his two sons, Yisrolik and Itzl, in their long gaberdines. Uncle Pinny rolled up his sleeves and talked, but the boys were silent. He discussed a point in Jewish law. When do the seven days of mourning actually end? In the morning or at night? Uncle Pinny rose, promising that he would consult a couple of sacred texts at home to learn precisely. Meanwhile, he didn't say good-bye, but with his sons mumbled something quickly about Zion and Jerusalem—and then vanished! Then came Aunt Hannah and her daughters. They began screaming at Father. "Enough! Enough! Enough already! Enough crying for your wife! You're not going to bring her back to life!" Before Hannah left she said, "You can suffocate in this room." She took some snuff from a little silver box and shouted, "At least open one little window or you'll choke in here, for goodness' sake!"

Then came Aunt Tema's mother; she was toothless, her head trembled, her face smiled, but her eyes cried. She unburdened her heart and told us big news: "We're all going to die."

So much for relatives. Then came strangers. All kinds of people, those who believed unequivocally in God and in the world to come, and those who did not believe in God and in the world to come. Arnold of Pidvorke, for example, made fun of everything. For him divine justice did not exist.

"It's explicitly written in the Bible," Arnold argued, "that man has no superiority over beast."

What he said about God and the Messiah was hair-raising. He had a smooth and glib solution for everything. Only he said good-bye when he left. Which didn't mean a thing, for he didn't believe in anything. Still, Sholom was curious what would happen to this Arnold if he dropped dead all of a sudden. "When I die you can cremate me and scatter my ashes to the winds. I couldn't care less!" said Arnold. But he got a vicious tongue-lashing from Grandma Mindy:

"Let your enemies talk like that!"

But Arnold wasn't moved. He just laughed and said good-bye. Then big-toothed Yossi Fruchstein came and scolded Father for crying so much. "I never expected such behavior from you." Dodi Isaac Bigdor's said the very same thing. He swore by everything holy that if such a tragedy happened to him he'd throw, ha, ha, ha, some coins into the Rabbi Meir Baal Ha-Nes charity box. When Dodi left, everyone burst out laughing, for everyone knew that Dodi's wife, Feige Perl, was some godsend. Thank God they could laugh once at least. Father was still reading Job, but he no longer wept as much as during the first days. And he no longer flared up at Uncle Pinny for suggesting marriage again. He kept sighing and groaning, "What are we going to do with the children?"

"What will you do with the children?" Uncle Pinny stroked his beard. "Let the older ones continue studying and send the younger ones to their grandfather in Bohuslav."

He was referring to Mama's parents, Grandfather Moshe Yossi and Grandmother Gitl, whom the children had never seen. They had only heard that in a far-off town named Bohuslav they had grandparents who were supposedly well fixed; in fact, quite rich. So that's where they would be sent. Now that at least was a plan. The trip itself would be fun, and so would a new town. And what about getting to know grandparents you've never seen? But one decision still had to be made. Who, according to Uncle Pinny, were the older children and who the younger? No doubt a Bar Mitzva boy, though he was still knee-high to a puppy, would be considered part of the older group. This question so intrigued the Bar Mitzva boy he almost forgot his mother, for whom he was saying Kaddish every morning and evening, his father, who sighed and groaned constantly, and the treasure for which he longed so passionately. Now he was drawn to something else: the journey, the new big city, Bohuslav, and Grandfather Moshe Yossi and Grandmother Gitl on Mama's side, who rumor had it were so rich, so very rich.

36. By the Dnieper

The Trip to Bohuslav—Shimon Wolf the Silent Coachman—Waiting for the Ferry—The Coachman Prays by the Riverside—Sweet Devotions

One day at summer's end, before the High Holy Days, a wagon rolled up to the porch. The smaller children—four boys and two girls, including Sholom the Bar Mitzva boy—were placed in it. They were given two shirts each, food for a couple of days, and a letter to their grandparents; they were also warned a dozen times to be careful crossing the Dnieper on the ferry.

Crossing the Dnieper! And on a ferry too! None of the children had ever seen a ferry and hadn't the faintest notion what it was. But while musing that it couldn't be too bad, they completely forgot that their mother had died. In fact, they forgot everything and thought only of the trip, the Dnieper, the ferry. But others reminded them. There was Grandma Mindy, who repeatedly told them not to forget and not to omit one Kaddish for their mother. Grandma stroked their faces with cold, smooth fingers and kissed their cheeks. She bade good-bye to them forever. "Only God knows when I'll have the joy of seeing you again . . ." And as her heart had foretold, when the children returned home from Bohuslav, Grandma Mindy had already joined Mama. Their graves were side by side. Father was saying Kaddish for *his* mother along with his children who were saying it for *their* mother. That year of the cholera was a year of Kaddish. Multitudes of Kaddish sayers. The entire shul was saying Kaddish.

Look how different people are. Meir Velvel the Coachman, who had brought the children from Voronko to Pereyaslav, was sparkling, vivacious and talkative, but Shimon Wolf the Coachman, who was bringing the children from Pereyaslav to Bohuslav, was careworn, sleepy and tight-lipped. Poke him with a pole, shoot him with a cannon, he still wouldn't utter a word. He'd only say: "Get in" or "Get off." The children were dying to know when they would come to the Dnieper. When would they cross it on a ferry? What *was* a ferry? But you could do nothing with Shimon Wolf. He refused to talk. He sat on the coachbox like a scarecrow, whipped the horses, clucked at them with his thick lips, and from time to time uttered the same words: "Giddyap, you plague, the plague take you!" Or "Giddyap, carcasses, may you turn to glue!" At other times he whispered to himself and chanted softly, reciting psalms by heart.

Just as there are all kinds of people with different personalities, there are also—forgive the proximity—all kinds of horses. Shimon Wolf's horses were sleepy like their master. Always sneezing too. They sneezed throughout the entire trip. They sneezed and snorted, they thrashed their tails and dragged their feet. They seemed to be trudging like this since time began. Only God knew if they would ever shlep themselves to a civilized place. All one saw was sky, earth and sand. Endless stretches of sand. And as if that wasn't enough, sometimes the horses just stopped dead in their tracks. Shimon Wolf then descended from the wagon, sang out in his reedy voice a line from the Psalms, "Happy are they who trust in Him." Then he snapped, "Get off!" The children jumped down. What was up? Nothing. The horses couldn't pull the wagon through the sandy terrain. They would have to go on foot for a while. Well, that was no tragedy. If they had to walk, they would walk. Anyway, walking was more fun. Only the youngest orphan, a little one-year-old girl, cried because she didn't want to stay in the wagon by herself. So she had to be carried, which wasn't such great fun. Luckily, the walk wasn't too long.

Soon the road was passable again and Shimon Wolf ordered, "Get in!" The children climbed up and stretched their legs. When they reached another section of deep swampy sand, he said again, "Get off!" and once more, "Get in!" But wait! What was that gleaming out there in the distance? What was sparkling like glass and shining like silver in the sun? Was that the Dnieper shimmering and glittering? The children could hardly sit still in the wagon. But as if for spite, the wagon slogged along. Before coming to the Dnieper they had to pass through a large expanse of knee-deep, thick yellow sand. Slowly, step by step, the horses dragged their feet, hardly able to pull them out of the sand. The wheels cut deeply into the muck and the wagon groaned. The Dnieper came closer and closer, with all its breadth and beauty. Yes, that was the Dnieper! It shone, reflected the sun, and smiled to the young visitors who came to greet the old river for the first time. "Hello, Grandpa, how are you?"

On the riverbanks grew tall, green, yellow-dappled reeds. The reflection of their long, sharp, pointy leaves in the water gave the Dnieper a special charm. Silence all around.

The river was as long and wide as a sea. The water flowed quietly on its way to somewhere. Where to? That was a mystery. The blue sky and the sun that had not yet set were mirrored in the water. The sky was clear. The water transparent. The sand was perfect. The air pure. All was still. A divine stillness. Spacious. A divine spaciousness. It recalled the verse in the Psalms: "The space of God."

Prrr! With a cry a bird flew out of the reeds. Like an arrow it cut through the pure, still air, and then zigzagged and soared far, far away. Soon, however, it changed its mind, returned in zigzag fashion and disappeared once more into the yellow-green reeds. You suddenly had the urge to fly out of the wagon like that bird and glide over the water, or at least undress and jump naked into the water and splash and swim and keep on swimming.

"Get off!" Shimon Wolf ordered. He too jumped down, stuck his whip into his belt, cupped his hands to his mouth, bent his head back, and let out a strange, resonant cry that seemed to come from a broken barrel:

"Fe-ee-eee-eeee-rrrr-y!"

Evidently the ferry was a living thing located on the other side, and it had to be summoned. The children climbed off the wagon, stretched their cramped limbs, and stood next to the coachman to help him call the ferry. Like him they cupped their hands to their mouths, bent their heads back, and yelled:

"Fe-ee-eee-eeee-rrrr-y!"

Then they burst out laughing and didn't know why. They laughed for no reason. They laughed because they felt good. Because they were young and healthy and because they were at the Dnieper. And because soon they would be on a ferry crossing the Dnieper. How lucky they were! Now the sun was bidding the day good-bye. The last, bright golden rays were reflected in the silvery water. Now the children stopped laughing. They didn't feel like laughing anymore. It was too quiet here at the banks of the Dnieper. A holy silence. The air had turned cool; the water gave off a strange smell. It hummed, gurgled, ran. Shimon Wolf the Coachman tied a scarf around his gaberdine, put his whip away, and faced east. He shut his eyes like a pious Jew and began to sway and chant the Afternoon Service in his reedy voice.

Shimon Wolf's prayer out in the open, under the colorful sky, by the banks of the old, beautiful, redolent Dnieper blended with the humming and gurgling of the water and put the happy young travelers in a different mood. They also wanted to pray. This was their *first* voluntary Afternoon Service, the first they weren't forced to say. Never before had they wanted to pray as they did now at dusk, under the open sky, by the banks of the Dnieper, close to God. They skipped some of the passages pertaining to incense offerings—but so what? While on the road, they could do without it. So they began with "Happy are they who dwell in Your house." After singing the psalm, all four boys faced east, shut their eyes, and swayed like the coachman as they recited the Silent Devotion: "The great, mighty and revered God." These attributes could be seen here, at dusk, under the domed sky, by the banks of the Dnieper. Never before had praying been so sweet and grand.

37. On the Ferry

*A Chance Encounter—Esau the Apostate—Recognition—
A Silent Parting*

Before the little traveling orphans had finished the Silent Devotion, they saw on the glistening water a far-off black clump that kept changing colors with the setting sun. This clump increased in size, dipped and disappeared, then resurfaced once more. Then they heard a strange noise: the sound of wheels turning and the groaning of a stretched rope. The boys quickly concluded the Afternoon Service and ran to the shore. There, secured to a wooden pole, was a thick rope that stretched across the river. The approaching clump kept growing and soon became a large wooden creature that resembled a house floating on the water. On top of it was a revolving wheel, by whose power this lumbering thing moved slowly but surely on the water. Finally, the creature drew close enough to be inspected from all sides. The children then realized that it wasn't a creature or a living thing but a kind of ship, a barge that held wagons, horses and men. So this was the long-awaited ferry that would take them across the Dnieper. Now they breathed easier. Now they could relax and sit on the sand until the ferry arrived and docked. For the ferry advanced at a snail's pace; in fact, it scarcely moved. The sun was much quicker. At the edge of the sky a moment ago, it now descended, as if on a downhill course. As it set, it sank and disappeared on the other side of the river, leaving a broad red stripe in its wake. The breeze turned colder. Meanwhile, the children had sat down on the sand. The eldest held the youngest, the one-year-old girl, in his arms. The baby was asleep.

The ferry docked. One by one, the people, wagons and horses quietly alighted; no one said a word. Shimon Wolf the Coachman boarded. He too was quiet, as if by common consent speaking was forbidden. First, he led his horses and wagon aboard and didn't even wish upon them the usual cholera. Then he gestured to the youngsters to follow. A moment later, the ferry, guided by only one man, who bore down with all his weight on the thick rope, began to move so smoothly it hardly made a sound. It wasn't the ferry but rather the Dnieper that seemed to be moving, facing about like a Jew who turns to welcome the Sabbath Queen during Friday night prayers or takes three steps back at the end of the Silent Devotion. Now one could first see how large and beautiful was the river. Beautiful and majestic. They rode and rode and were still far from the other shore.

The sun had set on the other side of the river. A red moon rose which then turned white, pale white, silvery. One by one, like Sabbath lights, stars glowed in the deep sky. At night the Dnieper took on a different hue and shape, as if it had been wrapped in a dark cloak. A fresh, silent chill wafted from the river, a light, even chill. Thousands of thoughts passed through Sholom's mind: the night, the sky, the stars reflected in the calm water. Every star was a person's soul. The ferry was so powerful, he mused, yet it was controlled by just one gentile. One hand on the rope, another turning the wheel—and the ferry moved.

Sholom wanted to observe the ferryman from close up, to watch him work the rope and guide the ferry. He approached and saw that he wore a coat of coarse cloth, big boots and a fur cap. He constantly bore down with all his might on the thick rope cable. The ferryman worked hard; his shoulders moved up and down, up and down. His bones seemed to creak. Esau, Sholom thought. The work of Esau. Only a goy could do work like that. How could a Jew do such rough work? The Torah said of Esau: "And thou shalt work for thy brother."

And Sholom thanked God that he was a descendant of Jacob, not Esau.

Nevertheless, his heart grieved at seeing how hard the young man, Esau's grandson, had to work. He's too young to be a ferryman, too young to be an Esau. But after staring at the peasant's face Sholom gave a start. The face was familiar; so were the eyes. Persistent, he went closer, stood almost in front of the ferryman and saw—it wasn't a youth at all, but a youngster with a coarse sooty face and coarse sooty hands. He had Jewish eyes, but gentile hands. Sholom recalled the verse: "The hands are the hands of Esau." But why did he look so familiar? Where did he know him from?

Sholom searched his memory and remembered one of his friends from Voronko. Berel the widow's son, a swarthy boy with large, thick teeth. Could it be he? No, it couldn't. Sholom was only imagining it. But God Almighty! Indeed, it *was* he! And the boy, seeing that he was being observed, pulled his cap lower over his eyes and cast a sidelong glance at the passenger staring at him. Then their eyes met in the darkness—and they recognized each other.

This unexpected meeting prompted a host of thoughts. Berel a goy? Can a Jew be a goy? Sholom recalled that even then people were saying that Berel had converted. Not for nothing had Berel been described as a spiteful apostate back in those days. Sholom wanted to approach, introduce himself, but something stopped him. On the one hand, he felt strange, distant and cold; on the other, he pitied the Jew who had become a gentile. Why had he done it? To be able to wear a coarse coat, a big shaggy cap, and become a hired hand, the ferry owner's apprentice? But the hired hand himself was not moved. He didn't even turn. Evidently, he couldn't look his friend in the eye, but stared down into the water, as if seeing something there. Berel the goy wrapped his coat tightly around himself, pulled the cap down even farther over his forehead, spit on his hands, and took to his task with renewed energy, leaning on the thick rope with all his might. The rope groaned. The wheel turned. The ferry slid forward. They had arrived.

"Get in!" the taciturn coachman ordered as soon as he moved his wagon off the ferry. He whipped his horses, showered them with nicknames like "cholera" and "carcass" and drove away, leaving behind the Dnieper, the ferry and the ferry owner's apprentice, who had once been a Jewish child, poor thing, our Father Jacob's grandson. And today? Ah woe . . . woe!

38. In the Bohuslav Market

Arriving at Bohuslav at the Fair—Which Moshe Yossi?—To the Rescue

It was already daylight when the little travelers entered Bohuslav, exhausted, hungry and sleepy. From the other side of the forest a bright warm sun was rising. The first site they passed was a huge cemetery; it had many tottering, half-sunken huts and old tombstones with faded epitaphs. Judging by this imposing cemetery, one would have thought that Boshuslav was a grand metropolis. From the cemetery they went straight to the town market, a fairground where everything was jumbled: gentiles, horses, cows, pigs, gypsies, wagons, wheels, horse collars, and all kinds of Jews selling everything. Jews with hides, Jews with hats, Jews with cloth; they offered rolls, egg bagels, cookies, apple cider. Jews sold everything under the sun. And women too! Women with baskets, women with apples, women with chickens, women with fried fish, and just plain women. And squeals and screams and rattles galore. Horses, cows and pigs added to the din. And beggars sang and played lyres— the noise was deafening. The dust was so thick you could hardly see your neighbor. The smells were enough to choke you.

The troop had come at a good time—a market day. The coachman slowly threaded his way through the crowds, wishing the town and its market eighteen doses of the plague as usual, until he drove to the center of town. The town center resembled the cemetery: the same tottering, sunken huts, with a sprinkling of new houses which looked out of place, like rich relatives at a poor man's wedding. Here the real confusion began.

Shimon Wolf the Coachman knew he had been hired to bring the youngsters to their grandparents in Bohuslav. He had been told their names but—to the blazes with it!—he'd forgotten them. Shimon Wolf swore that as he lived and breathed he had known them during the journey, but as soon as he entered that fairground the names just popped out of his head. "A plague," he muttered, but did not specify upon whom.

Meanwhile, one Jew approached, followed by another and yet another, then two more and three more, then women of all sorts, women with baskets and women without baskets, and the tumult reached a crescendo. Everyone talked at once and passed on the news to all the others: a coachman had brought some children to town.

"From where?"

"From the other side of the Dnieper."

"From Rzhishtchev?"

"Why from Rzhishtchev? Why not Kaniev?"

"Not from Rzhishtchev or Kaniev, but from Pereyaslav."

"Where to?"

"You can see for yourself where. He didn't bring them to Yehupetz but to Bohuslav."

"To which family?"

"Listen, if we knew which family, we'd be in good shape. The coachman says he's brought them to their grandfather."

"Which one?"

"Listen, if we knew which one, we'd be in good shape."

"Quiet! You know what? Let's ask the children their grandfather's name. They probably know."

"Why should they know?"

"Why *shouldn't* they know?"

Finally, a man who sold bagels and wore a cap with a cracked visor elbowed his way through the crowd.

"Let me through. I'll ask them. Children! What's your grandfather's name?"

Although they were totally confused by the yelling and tumult, the children remembered that their grandfather's name was Moshe Yossi.

"Yes, it's Moshe Yossi!"

"Are you sure it's Moshe Yossi?"

"Yes, we're sure."

Now everyone knew that their grandfather's name was Moshe Yossi. The next question was—which Moshe Yossi? There were several Moshe Yossis. Moshe Yossi the Carpenter, Moshe Yossi the Tinsmith, Moshe Yossi Leah Dvossi's, and Moshe Yossi Hamarnik. But ask them an easier question!

"Ssh, you know what? What's your father's name?" asked another man, not the bagel seller, but one who wore ritual fringes—he was no doubt from the bes medresh.

"His name is Nochem," the children answered.

Hearing this the man with the ritual fringes pushed everyone else away and began cross-examining the children.

"You say your father is called Nochem. Is his family name Rabinowitz?"

"Rabinowitz."

"And your mother's name is Chaya Esther?"

"Chaya Esther."

"And she died?"

"Died."

"Of cholera?"

"Of cholera."

"Then why don't you say so?"

The man turned to the crowd, his face beaming.

"In that case, ask me and I'll tell you exactly. Their grandfather is Moshe Yossi Hamarnik, their grandmother is Gitl, Moshe Yossi's wife. Their grandfather Moshe Yossi knows that his daughter died of cholera, but his wife Gitl hasn't been told yet. They don't want to tell her for she's old and crippled, poor soul."

The man then turned to the children, his face still beaming.

"Get off the wagon, children, and we'll show you where your grandfather lives. We can't ride there, the street's too narrow. Maybe from the other side. But then we won't be able to turn the wagon around. What do you think, Motl? Can it be done?"

This remark was addressed to a young man with a bent nose. Motl pushed the hat back on his head and said:

"Why not?"

"Why? Y is a crooked letter. Have you forgotten that Hershke Itzi Lyabe's is building a barn on the other side?"

Motl didn't budge.

"So what if he's building a barn on the other side?"

"What do you mean so what? He's piled up lumber."

"Piled up lumber? Good for him!" said Motl.

"It's impossible to talk to a lumbering idiot."

The calmer Motl was, the more incensed the other man with the ritual fringes and beaming face became. Finally, he lost control, spit at Motl and called him a blockhead and a dummy. He took the children by the hand and said, "Come with me. I'll take you. We'll have to walk." He left the marketplace with the little orphans, and led them to their grandfather Moshe Yossi and their grandmother Gitl.

39. A Fine Welcome

*The Crippled Grandmother Gitl—Grandfather Moshe Yossi with the
Bulbous Nose and Thick Eyebrows—Uncle Itzi and Aunt Sossi*

 The Pereyaslav orphans imagined that their grandfather's
house would be a palace. They pictured Grandfather Moshe
Yossi as a patriarch in a silken gaberdine. After all, people
said he was enormously wealthy. But the palace turned out to be a
rather plain little house, although it did have a glass-enclosed porch.
The beaming man accompanied the children to the house, told them,
"Here's where your grandfather Moshe Yossi lives," and then disappeared. He didn't want to be present when they met. The children
walked through the glass-enclosed porch and opened the door. On
a wooden bed, they saw someone but couldn't tell if it was human.
It was a strange creature that looked like a woman without legs and
with twisted hands. At first the children wanted to turn back, but
the creature stared at them with her shiny red eyes and asked pleas-
antly:

"Who are you, children?"

The voice had an intimate and familiar ring.

"Good morning," the children replied. "We're from Pereyaslav."
Hearing the word "Pereyaslav" and seeing a group of children, among
them a baby girl not yet one year old, the old woman immediately
grasped the tragedy.

"Ah, woe is me! Woe is me! My Chaya Esther is dead!" she cried,
wringing her twisted hands and beating her head. "Moshe Yossi?
Moshe Yossi? Where are you? Come here, Moshe Yossi!"

A short old man in tallis and tefillin ran in from a side room. He
had an odd fleshy face, a broad bulbous nose, and big bushy eyebrows.
He was dressed in rags and worn-out shoes. Was this Grandfather
Moshe Yossi? Was this the man who was so enormously wealthy?

First off, Grandfather Moshe Yossi yelled at the children. He
scolded them and waved a warning finger. Since he was in the middle
of prayers and couldn't interrupt them to converse, he talked to the
children in the holy tongue:

"Ee, o, nu! Bandits! Murderers!" And to his wife he also said in
Hebrew, his voice trembling: "I know. My daughter. God has given
and God has taken."

By this he meant to say that he knew his daughter had died, and that the God who had brought her to this earth had taken her away. But this did not calm the old woman, who continued to weep and moan and beat her head and wail: "Chaya Esther! My Chaya Esther is dead!" She kept this up until some people entered. One, a man with very long earlocks (the children had never seen such long ones in Pereyaslav), was their mother's only brother, Uncle Itzi. Then a woman with a flushed face ran in, her sleeves rolled up, holding a ladle: Aunt Sossi, his wife. At her side was their only child, a little girl with red cheeks and tiny lips, a pretty but shy girl named Chava Liba. Other men and women came running too, consoling Grandmother Gitl: Since her daughter was already dead, what good were tears? What the earth covered is lost forever. Afterward, the young newcomers were lectured not to barge into a house all of a sudden and immediately blurt out bad news. Of course the children knew—and God was their witness—that they hadn't even said a word.

Meanwhile, Grandfather Moshe Yossi had taken off his tallis and tefillin and began rebuking the children. "Why didn't you first come to me? If you had any manners, you should have seen me first and talked it over calmly with me. Then I would have gradually broken the news to your grandmother, slowly prepared her. Not slam-bang, the way you did it! That's what wild beasts do, not human beings!"

Evidently, Grandmother Gitl couldn't tolerate this and despite the tragedy she pounced upon Grandfather:

"You old fool! What have you got against the poor children? It's not their fault. How should they have known you're stretching out on your furs and praying? Some fine welcome. Come here, my children, come to me. What are your names?"

One by one, she bade the children approach and asked each of them his name. She stroked and kissed them and wet them with her salty tears. Now she was no longer crying for her daughter but for the forlorn little orphans.

"I knew my Chaya Esther was dead, as sure as it's daylight all over the world. Because for several nights now she's come to me in a dream and asked me about her children and wanted to know how I liked them. Let's give them something to eat. Moshe Yossi, why are you standing there like a golem? Don't you see, you old fool, that the children are faint with hunger? They didn't sleep all night long. Ah, woe is me! Main thing is he preaches at them. Some nice grandfather! Some fine welcome!"

40. *Among Sheepskins*

Grandfather's Bookkeeping—His Preaching, Books and Charity—
When the Messiah Comes—Grandfather's Ecstasy

Right after the children had prayed and eaten breakfast Grandfather Moshe Yossi tested them in Talmud. The exam took place in his private room, where no man dared set foot. No one dared and no one could—for there was no place to turn around.

The room was scarcely bigger than a chicken coop. This coop housed Grandfather, his books—the entire Talmud with commentaries and volumes of Kabbala—and a trove of pawned items: silver spoons, trays, Havdala spice boxes and Hanuka menorahs, copper pans, samovars, Jewish gaberdines and gentile coral necklaces, and coats and furs. Mostly furs. An infinity of furs.

This was a pawnshop that had been managed for years by Grandmother Gitl. Although crippled and bedridden, she ran the business with a firm hand, kept the money under the pillows next to her, and never let anyone near the cashbox. But Grandfather's domain was the pledged items. His task was to take the pawned object and return it. One needed the brains of a prime minister to remember who owned each pledge. Maybe Grandfather Moshe Yossi had the brains of a prime minister, but he didn't rely on his ministerial brain alone. Who could tell what might happen? So he came up with an original idea. He himself sewed a piece of paper onto every item and labeled it in Hebrew: "This gaberdine belongs to Berel." Or: "This fur belongs to the goy Ivan." Or: "This necklace belongs to the peasant woman Yavdoche."

Ah, but what if one Berel came to redeem his gaberdine and was given another Berel's garment? Well, there was a solution to that too. Both Berels' gaberdines were taken out, and the man was told to choose his garment. No Jew would claim another man's gaberdine as his. If this happened with a goy, then it was bad. But there was a way out of that too. (A scholarly man also has good ideas.) Grandfather would ask Ivan to kindly identify his fur. Every Ivan knows his fur so well he could easily give an identifying sign. Every item had to have one. Nevertheless, despite all these ideas, Grandmother and Grandfather often quarreled over the labeling. Grandmother Gitl pleaded with him:

"Listen, you old fool. Since you're already writing 'This is Berel's gaberdine,' is it so hard for you to write just one more word—'Berel Stutterer'? Or if you're already writing 'This fur belongs to the goy Ivan'—why don't you write his family name, Ganev? Or: 'This necklace belongs to the peasant woman, pug-nosed Yavdoche.' "

But Grandfather Moshe Yossi—may it not shame him in the other world!—was terribly stubborn. Just *because* she wanted it this way, he refused. And he wasn't entirely wrong. A crippled, bedridden woman took the liberty of bossing her husband around and calling him an old fool in the presence of the grandchildren! Now this Reb Moshe Yossi Hamarnik wasn't just anybody. He was a man who studied Torah and prayed day and night. He either studied or prayed. He observed all the fast days and didn't eat on Mondays and Thursdays as well; and he ate no meat at all during the week, except on Sabbaths and holidays. He was the first to arrive in shul and the last to leave. He began the Friday night Kiddush when people in other houses were already asleep. This prompted Grandmother Gitl to grumble and scold:

"As far as I'm concerned, it doesn't bother me. I've gotten used to being hungry. But you have to have some consideration for the children. It's too late for the little orphans."

Of all the grandchildren, Grandfather Moshe Yossi grew fond of only one—Sholom. Yes, he was a scamp, he was high-spirited, but he had a good head on his shoulders. He might turn out to be somebody if only he'd agree to spend more time with his grandfather in the room with the sheepskins, and not always run to the river with the Bohuslav children to watch them fish, or to the woods to pick pears or do other foolish things.

"If your father were a decent man," said Grandfather, "and if he hadn't become tainted by Bible study and Hebrew grammar and by Moshe Dessauer and other heretical ways, he would by rights leave you here with me for several terms at least. Then, with God's help, I'd make a pious Jew of you. You'd become a true Hasid, a true Kabbalist, with fire and zeal. But as is, what will become of you? You'll end up as a nobody, a nothing, an empty-headed boor, a scamp, a rascal, an idler, a prospective convert, a desecrator of the Sabbath, a pork gobbler, a sinner against the God of Israel."

"Moshe Yossi! Will you stop pestering the child?"

God bless Grandmother Gitl, thought Sholom, redeemed from his grandfather's hands. For a gang of Bohuslav rascals was waiting for him outside.

Nevertheless, there were times when Sholom loved his grandfather. Once, he met him sitting with his tallis bag under his arm at Grandmother's bedside. He was flattering her, speaking softly, bargaining and asking for money. However, she refused. He wasn't asking for himself, he countered, but for charity, for his poor Hasidim in the little shul. But Grandmother was adamant.

"It's not necessary. I have my own orphans—they're in greater need of pity."

Another time, Sholom found his grandfather sitting in his private room, in tallis and tefillin, head back, eyes closed, as if transported from this world. God's Divine Presence seemed to rest on him. When he woke his eyes shone and sparkled, and his face was less fleshy. Smiling through his fearfully large, thick mustache, he said softly:

"The forces of Edom will not rule much longer. Salvation is near, very near. Come here, my child, sit with me a while, and we'll talk about the end of days, the Messiah, and what will happen when the Messiah comes."

Grandfather Moshe Yossi began to tell his grandson of Messianic times. He described it with such fiery colors, enthusiasm and passion that Sholom didn't want to leave the old man. Sholom thought of his first and best friend, Shmulik. But the difference between Shmulik and Grandfather was that Shmulik spoke of treasures, wizards, princes and princesses—things that were part of the world of here and now; while Grandfather Moshe Yossi disdained this world and brought himself and his grandson, who listened with great suspense, to the other world—to the righteous, the angels, seraphim and cherubim near the Seat of Glory, and very close to *Him* Himself, the King of the King of Kings, the Holy One Blessed Be He. There one could find the Wild Ox and the Leviathan, the balsam perfume known as Afarsemon and the precious Preserved Wine. There the righteous sat and studied; there they took pleasure in the Divine Presence and basked in the glory of the Hidden Light. This was the light that God had set aside for the world to come during Creation, when He saw that mankind did not deserve to have it. And the Holy One Blessed Be He stood there in all His glory serving the righteous like a father. And from up above, from heaven, at the very place where the old Holy Temple had stood, a new Holy Temple descended, made of pure gold, diamonds and precious stones. The kohanim recited the priestly blessing, the Levites sang, and King David stepped forth playing a violin and singing: "Sing to God, O ye righteous."

At this point Grandfather Moshe Yossi began to sing out loud. He snapped his fingers, his eyes fluttered shut, his face glowed with ecstasy. He was no longer of this world, but far away, transported to the *other* world.

41. A Jewish Bird Man

An Old Tale—How Jews Lived among the Nobles—The Tragedy of a Poor Lessee

 Don't think, however, that Grandfather Moshe Yossi was always in the other world and had nothing to tell his grandchildren about this world. Oh no! He had plenty of stories to tell about Jews in olden times, Hasidim and Kabbalists of long ago, and the nobility and their treatment of the Jews.

One especially memorable tale concerned a Jew who died as a martyr for the Sanctification of God's Name. It's given here in summary, for Grandfather Moshe Yossi—may he forgive me for saying so—was terribly long-winded and would jump from one point to another till you found yourself lost in Boiberik.

The story happened long ago, even before the time of his grandfather, may he rest in peace, the founder of the Hamarnik clan. Why was he called Hamarnik? Because he lived, ran a mill, and leased a farm in a village called Hamarni. Another Jew named Noah, who ran an inn, lived in this village. Noah was a simple, God-fearing man; he prayed day and night and recited psalms. He seemed to be a penitent. People said he was a lamed vovnik, one of the thirty-six hidden saints. His wife did all the work. His sole task was to pay the rental installments at the nobleman's estate and renew the inn lease every year. Despite the minimal livelihood it provided (he barely made ends meet—he had many children, you see), he always feared the lease would be given to someone else, for many others were interested in having the inn.

One day, when he went to the nobleman to renew the lease, he found a crowd assembled for a banquet. After eating they prepared for the hunt. Horses and carriages, droshkies and drays, and dogs of all kinds were lined up waiting for the hunters, who had huge feathers in their hats and horns in their hands. Everything on a grand scale. Everyone was ready to move.

I haven't come at the right time, thought Noah. The nobleman won't want to talk about the lease now. But Noah was mistaken. When the nobleman rose from the table with his guests and was about to mount his horse, he saw the Jew humbly standing there, dressed in rags.

He turned to him with a pleasant mien and asked, "How's the Jewish lessee?"

"Sir nobleman," Noah replied, "I've come about the yearly renewal of the lease."

At this the nobleman, drunk as a lord, laughed and said: "For how many years do want the inn?"

"Well, I'd like to have it for a few years," Noah said, "but it's been the custom of his illustrious lordship—"

But the nobleman cut him short and said, "Fine. This time you can have it at the old rent for ten years. But on one condition: I want you to become a bird."

The Jew looked at him. "What do you mean, you want me to become a bird?"

"Simple," the nobleman said. "You have to go up on the roof of that barn. See it? You pretend you're a bird and I'll take aim and try to shoot you in the head. Understand?"

The other noblemen burst out laughing and Noah pretended to laugh too. He thought the nobleman was joking, that he'd taken a drop too much.

"Well?" the nobleman asked. "Agreed?"

What should I say? Noah thought, then out of curiosity asked, "How much time will you give me to think it over?"

"One minute," the nobleman said, deadly serious. "The choice is yours. Either you climb up to the roof and pretend you're a bird, or tomorrow you'll be out of the inn."

Noah almost died. What should he do? One couldn't dally with a nobleman. Especially since he had already given the order to bring a ladder. Apparently, it was no joke. So Noah spoke up once more.

"And what will happen if you hit me, God forbid?"

The assembled noblemen now laughed even more. Noah was confused. He didn't know if the nobleman was joking or serious. It seemed he wasn't joking, because he told Noah to climb up to the roof or go home and clear out of the inn. He was about to go home, but then remembered he had a family to support. So he began pleading with the nobleman to give him at least a few minutes to say his final prayers of confession.

"Fine," said the nobleman, "I'll give you a minute for confession."

One minute? What could he say in one minute besides Shema Yisroel? Especially since they were already pushing him up the ladder. So Noah said "Hear O Israel" and "Blessed be the name of his glorious majesty forever and ever." Weeping, he began to climb the ladder. What should he do? It was a heavenly decree. A family man burdened with many children. No doubt it was fated that he die a martyr. But perhaps God would take pity and perform a miracle? If the Almighty wishes it, He can do it. Noah was a man of great faith. Jews of the old school!

He climbed to the edge of the roof, continually weeping and softly saying Shema Yisroel. Tears poured out of him, but he was hopeful that God might still have mercy. If the Almighty wishes it, He can do it. Meanwhile, the nobleman had no time to lose. He told Noah to stand straight—Noah stood straight. Then he told him to bend over—Noah bent over. Then he told him to spread his hands—Noah spread his hands. Look like a bird—Noah looked like a bird.

Then the nobleman—perhaps he really meant to or was only joking and the Almighty made it real—fired and hit Noah right in the forehead. Noah fell like a shot bird and tumbled down from the roof. That same day he was buried in the Jewish cemetery. But the nobleman kept his promise. For ten years he let the widow stay at the inn, despite the many better offers for higher rent. Noblemen of the old school!

Grandfather had many such stories about Jews of the "old school" and noblemen of the "old school." The children would have loved to listen to them again and again, if not for his habit of extracting a moral from every tale ("You must be a pious Jew and have faith") and jumping from the moral to preaching and rebuking the children for following their evil inclinations. "You don't pray, you don't study, you don't serve God, but day and night all you want to do is go fishing or pick pears or just fool around with all the Bohuslav boys, the devil take them one and all!"

42. Days of Awe

The Bohuslav River and Forest—The Old Shul—Grandmother Gitl's Kapores Ceremony—Grandfather Blesses the Children

 It's hard to say which was livelier and more delightful—the Ross River, the Bohuslav woods, or the Old Shul. It's hard to say which was most tempting. The river was great fun. There the coachmen watered their horses. The water carriers filled their barrels. Barefoot women and girls with thick calves washed laundry, beating it with a wooden paddle so lustily that sparks flew. Scores of boys bathed and splashed, fished and learned to swim there, undressing behind the rocks, then jumping into the river with shouts and shrieks.

"Look at me swimming!"

"Watch me float on my back!"

"Look at me making bubbles!"

Everyone chattered and performed stunts. Everyone knew a trick. The Pereyaslav orphans were terribly envious. Then one of the boys approached, naked as the day he was born. His name was Avreml and he was black as a Tartar with dreamy eyes, a face flat as a noodle board, and a nose like a bean.

"What's your name?" he asked.

"Sholom."

"Do you know how to swim?"

"No."

"Then don't just stand there. Come here and I'll give you lessons."

Not just teach, mind you, but give lessons, which is altogether different.

The Bohuslav woods were no less delightful. They were full of pears, hard as stone and sour as vinegar. Still, they were pears. And free! You could pick as many as you wished. Just reach out and grab them. Wild pears grew high. So you had to climb a tree and shake the branch with all your might, otherwise the pears wouldn't fall off. In the woods you could find nuts too. Hazelnuts. They ripened late and were covered with a shell bitter as gall. And they had no kernels either. Those would come later. But no matter. They were still nuts. You could fill your pockets with them. For what you picked with your own hands was sweeter. Picking pears and nuts takes know-how. And Avreml knew. He was skillful at everything. He was good-natured and always in good spirits. There wasn't a mean bone in him. Only problem was—he was poor. His mother was an impoverished widow who cooked for the Yampolskys. When Uncle Itzi found out, he immediately reported it to Grandmother Gitl, who in turn summoned Sholom to her bed, gave him a pear from under her pillow, and told him repeatedly: "Don't you dare see boys like Avreml again, for if Grandfather Moshe Yossi finds out that his grandsons are playing with such riffraff there'll be no end of trouble."

She was quick to say, "Don't see . . ." But Sholom couldn't help seeing Avreml at least twice a day, morning and night, when he said Kaddish in shul. Avreml too was an orphan who said Kaddish for his father in the Old Shul. Ah, how many Kaddish sayers there were! And all of them said Kaddish by the eastern wall. When Moshe Yossi's grandsons came with their grandfather to the Old Shul for the first time, he took them straight to the shamesh and told him in no uncertain terms that he wanted the boys to say Kaddish right next to the Holy Ark, for they were children of a good family.

The shamesh, an old man with a bent back and red, rheumy eyes, politely heard Grandfather out. He didn't respond, but put a big dose of snuff into his nose, cleaned his fingers quickly, held the snuffbox out to Grandfather, tapped his fingernail on the top, and silently offered him some snuff. This meant: "I'm glad you told me these children are from a good family, for now you can be sure I'll consider them the apple of my eye."

The Old Shul of Bohuslav had such a magnetic quality that the Pereyaslav orphans, as they were called, became attached to it as if they were born and bred there. To them everything in it had an awesome grandeur, sanctity and grace. The stamp of antique beauty, former greatness and ancient holiness encompassed the entire shul, a miniature Holy Temple.

But if the Old Shul looked like a smaller version of the Holy Temple all year long, during the Days of Awe—from Rosh Hashana through Yom Kippur—the little orphans considered it the Temple itself. They had never before seen so many Jews or heard such praying. It was a mishmash of all kinds of Hasidim, including Lubavitch, who prayed ecstatically, clapped their hands, snapped their fingers, and sang strange melodies, humming and bim-bamming.

Occasionally, they went into ecstatic trances for a few minutes, then once more they sang and hummed and bim-bammed and snapped their fingers.

This was a new kind of praying for the Pereyaslav orphans. A spectacle of the first order. But nicest of all was that Grandfather Moshe Yossi outdid all the other worshipers in the Old Shul. He wasn't a Lubavitch Hasid, just a strange Hasid with his own ways, customs and crazy habits. He took the liberty of remaining in shul on Sabbaths and holidays long after everyone else had gone home. Uncle Itzi, who lived in the other half of the house, was already eating supper; the smell of the holiday dishes and gefilte fish wafted from their stove. The children were dizzy with hunger. The delicious aromas went right to the pits of their stomachs. Grandfather, meanwhile, was still praying, singing and bim-bamming. Grandmother Gitl quietly slipped the children pieces of honey cake several times so they wouldn't faint with hunger.

"You'll remember the time when you landed among madmen," she said with a laugh.

Uncle Itzi meanwhile had finished eating, said grace, and poked his head in through the door:

"Father isn't home yet? Ha, ha."

Not enough that he had already finished eating, but he had to snicker too.

At long last God had compassion and Grandfather arrived. He flew into the house dragging his coat behind him, the sleeves on the floor, and after a hearty "Gut yontev!" made Kiddush at once, singing it out so loudly the entire street heard him.

"For the sake of the poor orphans, one would think you'd give up those crazy antics of yours and cut it short," Grandmother reprimanded him.

But he didn't hear her. He was still in an ecstatic fervor, off somewhere in distant worlds. He ate with one hand and turned the pages of an old tome with the other; and while briskly swaying, he cast one eye at the book and another at his grandchildren and heaved a deep sigh. The sighs were directed at the little orphans, whose souls were infatuated with material things; they thought only of eating and of submitting to the evil inclination and all its desires.

After the meal he rebuked them for this and gave them a long morality discourse. He saw to it that the fresh challa, the gefilte fish, the sweet parsnip stew, and all the other holiday treats so skillfully prepared by the crippled, bedridden Grandmother Gitl should stick in their throats.

So much for Rosh Hashana. The Eve of Yom Kippur was even nicer. In Grandfather Moshe Yossi's house that day was distinguished by two ceremonies which especially impressed the orphans. The first, on the night before Yom Kippur, was Kapores. They had performed this ceremony back home too, but in Bohuslav it was different. Here Grandmother Gitl took responsibility for this mitzva. She and Chaya Esther's children performed the ritual together. Sitting in bed, she summoned the children and gave each one a live fowl, a rooster to the boys and a hen to the girls. She opened her big Siddur and pointed with her crooked finger to the prayer. The older children read it by themselves, while the smaller boys and the girls recited the prayer word by word, loudly and with a melody:

"Children of man who dwell in darkness and in the shadow of death, bound by misery and iron . . ."

While doing so she wept bitterly, like a mourner who weeps after dead kin. And when it came to the youngest orphan, the baby girl scarcely one year old, Grandmother nearly fainted from the sobbing. Now the children began to cry, and looking at them, the adults burst into tears. A terrible wailing broke out. During that awful Sabbath when their mother lay on the ground covered with a black cloth, the orphans hadn't wept one tenth as much as they did now during Grandmother's prayer.

The other ceremony took place the following morning, on Yom Kippur eve, after coming home from the Old Shul where the children got pocketsful of honey cake from the head trustee. Grandfather Moshe Yossi had told the children last night after Kapores to come for a blessing immediately after morning prayers.

Grandfather was in a festive mood, but strangely attired for the holiday. On top of his old tattered satin gaberdine he wore an outlandish robe made of an odd, stiff, rustling cloth which no money in the world could buy anywhere today. He wore a fur hat made of sewn tails and a white winged collar around his bare neck. A long fringed and tassled sash girded his gaberdine. Today his big mustache and bushy eyebrows seemed less fierce than usual; his face looked gentle, forgiving, even friendly.

"Come here, children, and I'll bless you," he said cheerfully, and invited all of them into his dark narrow alcove full of sheepskins. He placed his two hands on every child, closed his eyes and threw back his head. Then he murmured and murmured and murmured something softly; he sighed and groaned deeply as the long sleeves of his satin gaberdine touched the children's heads. When he finished, the orphans looked at his face. His eyes were glowing but red, and his lashes, mustache and beard were wet with tears.

43. Sukkos

*A Shared Sukka—Grandfather Prays and the Children Want to Eat—
Simchas Torah Joys*

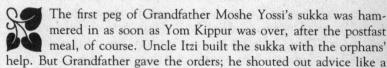 The first peg of Grandfather Moshe Yossi's sukka was hammered in as soon as Yom Kippur was over, after the postfast meal, of course. Uncle Itzi built the sukka with the orphans' help. But Grandfather gave the orders; he shouted out advice like a master architect.

"This goes here. That, there. That'll go in. That won't."

More amazing, Grandfather and Uncle Itzi weren't even on speaking terms. Feuding. This grieved Grandmother Gitl. She had only one son who would say Kaddish in one hundred and twenty years, and he didn't say a word to his father. Did you ever hear of such an outrage?

In the shared sukka two tables were prepared, one for Grandfather and the other for Uncle Itzi. Each table had its own bottle of wine for Kiddush and its own challas, candlesticks and candles. Aunt Sossi made the blessing over the candles on her table, and Grandmother Gitl was carried out to the sukka in her little bed to light the candles on her table. Then Uncle Itzi came from shul and had to wait until Grandfather would finally remember to come home and make Kiddush first. Rudeness was out of the question. After all, "Honor thy father." Still, Uncle Itzi left the house occasionally and looked into the sukka, each time with another comment.

"He's not back?"

"This year the Hasidim are praying later than usual."

"Hmm, soon the candles will burn out and we'll have to eat in the dark."

The children, however, finally had their revenge on Uncle Itzi, who was a harsh man without feelings—they were glad that he too had felt what it meant to go hungry.

Finally, Grandfather returned, wished everyone a happy holiday, took out his Rabbi Jacob Emden Siddur, a small but thick and complete prayer book. In the sukka he sat down and began to chant the passages welcoming the Patriarchs into the sukka. He chanted and prayed, and prayed and chanted.

And as if for spite, from the kitchen the aromas of peppered gefilte fish and freshly baked challas teased the children's palates.

"Dip us into the hot fish sauce and you'll feel the true taste of Paradise," the challas seemed to say.

Meanwhile, Grandfather Moshe Yossi continued what he was doing. Praying. The candles in the sukka were flickering—but he kept praying. The children were faint with hunger, exhausted and sleepy—but he kept praying. Suddenly Grandfather jumped up, rushed to the table and rapped out the holiday Kiddush so beautifully everyone brightened. Then Uncle Itzi chanted the Kiddush at his table. Next came Chaya Esther's orphans, one after the other, at which Grandmother Gitl let drop a tear. In short, it took a while before they finally could dip the challa into the honey and see a piece of fish and feel the pepper on the tips of their tongues.

So passed the first two days of Sukkos. The last days were even worse. It was so bad that on the night of Simchas Torah Uncle Itzi couldn't take it any longer. He called the orphans into his house and said:

"Children, do you want to see something nice? Go to the shul and you'll see a sight."

He didn't have to ask them twice. Holding hands, they went to the shul. It was pitch dark outside. Everyone was already at home eating. All the shuls were closed and dark. In the Old Shul, however, there was still light. The boys opened a door very softly, peeked in, and saw something incredible. There was only one person in shul—Grandfather Moshe Yossi in a tallis, holding his Rabbi Jacob Emden Siddur in one hand and a Torah in the other. Pressing the Torah to his heart, he circled the bimah slowly and like a cantor chanted the prayers for the Hakofes.

"Helper of the Poor, save us!"

A pall of fear mingled with laughter swept over the children. They took one another by the hand and ran back home.

"Well? Did you see a sight? Nice, huh?"

These were Uncle Itzi's first words. He laughed saying this, but his eyes teared. And the children took a dislike, not to Grandfather Moshe Yossi, but to Uncle Itzi.

But the following morning, on Simchas Torah, the scene changed radically. The children remembered the joys of the Simchas Torah celebrations in their old hometown, Voronko. The entire village got drunk as Lot. From the rabbi to the police chief, everyone drank whiskey. Everyone reveled and danced; you could have died laughing from their antics.

In half-goyish Pereyaslav, Simchas Torah was also festive. Even a man like Uncle Pinny became dead drunk and danced a Cossack dance. It was a sight to see a Hasid like him with long ritual fringes dancing a Cossack dance. And let's not forget Dodi Kahanov. When Dodi was in his cups, he insulted his good friends and raked them over the coals, ostensibly smiling all the while and kissing them. People barged into friends' houses with a hearty "Gut yontev," brought up jars of sour pickles from the cellar—and whiskey flowed like water.

But how could you compare all those previous Simchas Torahs with the one the Pereyaslav orphans celebrated in the Jewish town of Bohuslav? The houses, the streets, the very cobblestones—everything, *everything* sang and clapped, danced and made merry. Older Jews weren't the only ones to get drunk—youngsters too staggered on their feet. Even Uncle Itzi, usually quiet and terribly glum, became intoxicated. He tucked his earlocks behind his ears, folded the skirts of his long gaberdine, and pretended he was in modern garb. But best of all were Grandfather Moshe Yossi's capers that day. Although he drank but one tumbler of whiskey and half a glass of wine, he was drunker than fourscore sots. The way he kicked up his heels was the talk of the town.

"Well, what do you say to Moshe Yossi Hamarnik?"

"Go see what Moshe Yossi is doing!"

But Moshe Yossi wasn't doing anything. He was merely dancing in the street. And how he did dance! He danced and leaped, clapped and sang. And he wasn't dancing alone—he was dancing with the Divine Presence, with the Holy One Blessed Be He. He unraveled a scarf and held one end; the other was supposedly held by the Divine Presence. He twisted and turned as if dancing with a bride, taking different steps: forward and back, left and right, and then once again forward and back, left and right. He did this repeatedly, head back, eyes shut, a beatific smile on his face. He snapped his fingers, hopped and sang with increasing vigor:

> Moses was happy on Simchas Torah,
> Lam-tedri-dom, hey-da!
> Be happy and merry on Simchas Torah,
> Lam-tedri-dom, dom dom dom!
> Hey-da, dri da da!
> The Torah of Moses, hey-da!

The longer he danced the bigger the crowd became. All the youngsters in town came running to welcome Grandfather Moshe Yossi and watch him dance and sing and clap. Young scamps cheered him on and helped him sing his Simchas Torah melodies, while the faces of his Pereyaslav grandchildren burned with shame. But Grandfather Moshe Yossi was transported to a far-off realm; he saw no one. He continued dancing with his beloved Divine Presence, holding on to one end of the kerchief, while the other was held by the Almighty. He smiled and snapped his fingers, danced, jumped and sang with increasing vigor:

> Moses was happy on Simchas Torah,
> Lam-tedri-dom, hey-da!
> Be happy and merry on Simchas Torah!
> Lam-tedri-dom, dom dom dom!
> Hey-da, dri da da!
> The Torah of Moses, hey-da!

44. The Holiday Over—Back Home

Intrigues and Plots Among Family—The Children Outstay Their Welcome—They Long for Home

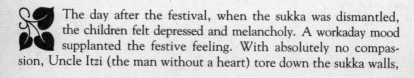 The day after the festival, when the sukka was dismantled, the children felt depressed and melancholy. A workaday mood supplanted the festive feeling. With absolutely no compassion, Uncle Itzi (the man without a heart) tore down the sukka walls,

ripped off the thatching, gathered up the planks, and with murderous fury removed the pegs (what did he have against them?). However, he left the four corner posts. But that was even worse, for these bare uprights bore witness to the ravage.

"Look, Jewish children," they seemed to complain and lament, "look what can become of a Jewish sukka."

Jews, only yesterday drunk as Lot, dancing and clapping and silly as children, suddenly became sober and well-behaved; they were almost ashamed to look one another in the eye. A strange sadness encompassed the town; Bohuslav sank into an extraordinary gloom. And most gloomy and sad were the Pereyaslav orphans. For as long as the children were guests, they didn't feel bad in Bohuslav. But as time passed they sensed they had outstayed their welcome. In his tallis and tefillin Grandfather Moshe Yossi sat by himself on his sheepskins in his little room, either praying or studying, humming and snapping his fingers, or sighing and talking softly to God. Sometimes he told the children his wonderful stories of long ago or preached to them: Why weren't they pious, why didn't they want to serve God? Because of them the End of Days was being delayed; because of them the Messiah was not coming; and because of them Jews were suffering the torments of hell, and myriads of souls could not be redeemed.

The children had heard all this before from their cheder teacher, from Grandma Mindy, and from just plain Jews who loved to preach and threaten them with Gehenna. They were sick and tired of all this. The politics at home between Grandfather Moshe Yossi and Grandmother Gitl was far more fascinating.

Day and night there were intrigues and secrets, whispering and gossip. Uncle Itzi and Aunt Sossi constantly complained about Grandmother Gitl: it was impossible to get a penny from under those pillows of hers. They also complained about Grandfather Moshe Yossi: he was too pious, so pious he was senile. "He's too old," they said quietly, with strange puckered smiles. Grandmother Gitl complained about her daughter-in-law and her one and only son. "They don't respect me as befits a mother. I know they're just waiting for me to shut my eyes. The inheritance is what they're looking forward to, the inheritance. But to spite them, I'm going to keep on living, even though death is a thousand times more preferable. For what good is my life, if you can call this living? I'm a cripple, I buried my lovely Chaya Esther, a mother of so many children, ah woe is me, calamity!"

With her twisted hands Grandmother wiped a tear from her eyes, called the children, put her crooked hands under the pillows, and gave each a few pennies. Seeing this, Aunt Sossi's little Chava Liba, with the red little cheeks and tiny lips, reported at once to her mother. Aunt Sossi immediately told Uncle Itzi and both whispered, "To her *own* children she's stingy, but *stranger's* kids are given a fortune." The children heard these remarks and were sickened by them.

The situation worsened daily. The children felt unwanted. They saw the family watching them as they ate; they heard comments behind their backs about their "healthy little appetites." The food stuck in their throats. Everything in that house revolted them. They longed for a letter from their father as if for the Messiah, and wondered when they would return home.

Soon the good Lord came to their aid; the glad tidings arrived. A Pereyaslav coachman named Noah brought a letter and added a postscript of his own to the children: "Get into the wagon and come back home." Like all other coachmen, Noah too had a covered wagon and horses. He called himself Reb Noah, but he had two flaws. He was hoarse and bald. Which wasn't so bad either. "I got hoarse," he explained, "during Simchas Torah. This past Simchas Torah I drank brandy. What I mean is, I always drink brandy. But in honor of Simchas Torah I really filled up my glass. In fact, I had to be revived. And as for my being bald, well, that's because as a child I didn't let them wash or comb my hair. I was a stubborn mule. So by force they had to pull out my hairs, one by one."

But all this had nothing to do with the trip. Something else prevented them from setting out. Even though Noah was specially sent from Pereyaslav to Bohuslav to bring back Nochem Rabinowitz's children, the coachman couldn't resist the temptation of looking for another two or three passengers for the return trip. That would be found money. So Noah rode around in the market, one day, a second, and a third; meanwhile his horses were devouring oats, and there wasn't hide nor hair of a prospective passenger. The children's resentment grew. Then finally came the wonderful news! They were going home. Witness the fact that Noah rolled out the wagon and was greasing the wheels!

"Now even if all the kings of the world come, it's too late," he said. "Even a wagonload of gold couldn't make me stay in Bohuslav another hour. No, sir! This town can burn or sink into the ground! You don't know Reb Noah!"

The children dashed into the house. They prepared for the trip, and said good-bye to their Bohuslav friends, to the Old Shul and the little yellow shul, to the Ross River, and to Grandfather and Grandmother. While they did this, Grandfather Moshe Yossi was, naturally, moralizing, and told them to be observant Jews, and Grandmother Gitl wiped her eyes with her twisted hands. But Uncle Itzi and Aunt Sossi muttered a chill "Good-bye." Their joy at seeing the "stranger's children" leaving was marred, however, because not everyone was going. Only the boys. The two girls were staying on in Bohuslav. Why? Simple. Grandmother Gitl said she wouldn't let them go. She didn't want her Chaya Esther's children to fall into the hands of a stepmother.

"Well, and what if the boys fall into a stepmother's hands, is that all right, ha, ha?" said Uncle Itzi with a little smile. He smoothed his earlocks and looked at the pillows behind which lay Grandmother Gitl's fortune.

"How can you compare boys and girls? Since when does a boy listen to his stepmother? A boy spends the whole day in cheder. And what does a girl do? A girl stays at home to tend the stepmother's children."

But this still didn't satisfy Uncle Itzi. He stroked his earlocks, looked at the pillows, smiled and said cannily:

"And what if all the children had been girls, ha, ha?"

"Then I would have kept all the girls with me," said Grandmother.

Uncle Itzi didn't smile now, but continued in his elliptic fashion:

"Where would you have gotten the money to support so many girls?" (Without a "ha, ha" this time.)

"God would have helped me," said Grandmother calmly, "just like He helped me raise a Kaddish like you who is so eager to get the inheritance and is afraid it won't be enough for him."

"Itzi!" called Aunt Sossi from her little room. "Itzi, come here. I have to tell you something."

The children were delighted with Grandmother Gitl for cutting Uncle Itzi down to size and were overjoyed at going home.

Still, the word "stepmother," which they had heard for the first time, distressed them. Did it mean that they would have a stepmother? What was a stepmother anyway? And why was it so bad that Grandmother Gitl already felt sorry for the children in advance?

They were certainly keen on seeing this stepmother. It made the journey back home worthwhile.

Home! Home! Home!

45. A Stepmother's Invective

A Stepmother—An ABC of Curses—First Creation—
A Lexicon of Abuse

 Why do people make such a big fuss over a stepmother? Judging by all the talk, the children would have thought a stepmother had horns. At every step they were threatened with stepmother.

"Just you wait, you little rapscallions, till your father goes abroad and brings you back a stepmother. Then you'll see what kind of God we have."

What more do you want? If the sun was dim, people said: "The sun is as warm as a stepmother."

There had to be something to it. The world wasn't crazy.

One day Father disappeared. Weeks went by. Where had he gone? No one was saying. The older people whispered to each other, out of earshot of the children; they winked more than they spoke, But in cheder one day the teacher blurted it out. He asked the children:

"Has your father already returned from Berditchev?"

To this diplomatic question, the rebbitsin added with even greater tact: "So soon? Do you think that bringing back a stepmother for the children is so simple for a widower?"

Now we finally knew that father was in Berditchev looking for a stepmother for his children. So what was there to hide? Was it really that big a secret? Because even before Father returned with the new goods he didn't hesitate to write that God had blessed him with a worthy match from all points of view: familial lineage and wealth. God willing, he'd soon arrive with his find. He asked, however, that no one tell her how many children he had—no need for her to know this right away. In time she'd learn it on her own. And anyway she wouldn't have to be responsible for all the children. The older ones were already grown up, and the two little girls were with their grandmother. He wasn't washing his hands of them, God forbid.

Children were children. But under such bitter circumstances it would be a good idea to keep secret for a while the existence of some of the children. "Otherwise," Father wrote, "there is nothing new. Everything is fine. With God's help we shall soon see each other in good health. Yours, . . ."

If not for the wrinkle with the children, this letter would have made a good impression. The children felt it most of all. True, they knew that Father loved them and considered each one precious. But the fact they were to become contraband merchandise for a while stung them and prompted strange thoughts. But not for long, for soon a message reached them at cheder:

"Your father has come home with a stepmother from Berditchev."

"Mazel tov," the rebbitsin called. "May you live to bring better tidings!"

That day the teacher dismissed the children early.

At home the whole family had gathered—Uncle Pinny and his sons, Aunt Hannah and her daughters. They all sat around the table drinking tea, pretending to eat honey cake and preserves. They smoked and chattered aimlessly. The remarks were disjointed; no one listened to anyone else, for everyone was immersed in his own thoughts, looking over the stepmother, and appraising the bargain that Father had acquired in Berditchev. Everyone was apparently pleased at first glance. A respectable-looking woman, no fool—and above all, amiable, obliging, good-hearted and kind. So what were they all babbling about? What was all that nonsense about a stepmother?

Only much later, in a week or two, did Stepmother show her true disposition and fiery temper. First, her language, her authentic Berditchev stepmotherly vocabulary—glib, juicy, blooming. Every word was accompanied by a curse, delivered good-naturedly.

For example:

If she said "eat," she'd add: May the worms eat you!

Drink: May leeches drink your blood!

Yell: May a toothache make you yell!

Sew: May they sew shrouds for you!

Go: Go to hell!

Stand: Stand on your feet till you drop!

Sit: Sit on scorpions!

Lie: Lie six feet under!

Talk: Talk in delirium!

Silence: Fall silent forever!

Have: Have troubles!

Not have: May you not have any peace!

Carry: May an ill wind carry you away!

Carry in: May you be carried in on a stretcher!

Carry out: May you be carried out feet first!

Carry around: May you be carried around in a basket!

Carry away: May you be carried away to the cemetery!

Now take an innocent word like "write."

Write: May they write prescriptions for you!

Written down: May you be written down for death!

Written up: May you be written up in shame!

Written off: May a madman be written off a madhouse roster and you be written in!

Sometimes when Stepmother was in a good mood and latched onto a word, she'd twist it and turn it and stretch it like dough—there was no stopping her. She'd let it out in one breath, like the Megilla reader rattling off the ten sons of Haman on Purim, and in rhyme no less:

"God Almighty, may you be bitten and smitten, eaten and beaten, swell and yell; may you get gout and shout, have aches and breaks and itches and twitches, dear merciful Father in heaven!"

The hero of this autobiography must admit that many of the curses and maledictions in his works came straight from his stepmother's invective. Very early on, before Sholom knew anything about writing, and never even dreamed he would be a writer, he wanted to jot down all of Stepmother's curses just for the fun of it and collect them into a little dictionary. He assiduously gathered them one by one until he had enough material to alphabetize. He sweated over this for a couple of nights and assembled quite a nice lexicon, which if memory serves him went something like this:

A—abusive, addlepate, aggravator, animal, ape, apostate, argumentative, ass

B—backscratcher, bandit, bathhouse flunky, beggar, boaster, broom, bum

C—cardsharp, carouser, clunk, creature, creep, crook

D—dogcatcher, dolt, dope, dummy, dunderhead, dupe

E—eager beaver, eccentric, edgy, eerie, empty-headed, equivocator

F—failure, faithless, fathead, flea, fool, fresh brat

G—gadabout, ganev, gawk, ghastly, golem, goose, goy

H—haggler, halfhearted, half-wit, Haman, harebrain, hoaxer, humbug

I—idiot, idolator, ill-made, imbecile, impulsive, informer, insolent, Ishmael

J—jackal, jack-in-the-box, jaundiced, jealous, jerk

K—kennel-keeper, kicker, kill-joy, knave, knothole, knucklehead

M—malingerer, measly, meddling, milksop, misfortune, monkey, mummer, murderer

N—naughty, ne'er-do-well, nervous, nincompoop, ninny, nitwit, nomad, noodlehead, nudnik

O—oaf, obnoxious, obstacle, obstinate, oddball, off-beat, opinionated, outlandish

P—pauper, peculiar, pepless, pest, pickpocket, pig, pimple, pipsqueak, plague

Q—quack, qualmy, queasy, queer, querulous, quick-tempered, quicksilver, quivery

R—radish, ragamuffin, raggedy, rambunctious, rascal, rattlebrain, reeking, reprobate, robber, rusty

S—sap, screwball, seedy, shlemiel, shrimp, snitcher, sniveler, snotnose, softhead, swine

T—tagtail, talebearer, terror, testy, thickwit, thief, tippler, turtle

U—ugly, ulcer, ululant, unclean, uncouth, unthinking, upstart, usurper

V—vassal, vengeful, vice-monger, vindictive, viper, visor head, vixen, voracious, vulpine

W—wacky, warped, wart, washpot, whelp, windbag, wise guy, worm

X—xanthic, xenophobic, xeric, Xerxes, xyster

Y—yackety-yak, yapper, yawner, yawp, yeller, yellow, yelper, yokel, yowler

Z—zany, zealot, zebra, zero, zigzag, zombie, zookeeper, zwieback

This was the future Sholom Aleichem's first work, and he called it *A Stepmother's Invective*. What happened with it could have led to a terrible catastrophe.

Because of its strict alphabetical format, the writer took pains to rewrite this lexicon several times. Father evidently noted that his rascal seemed to be unusually busy. One evening he came up behind Sholom, looked at his work and confiscated the manuscript, which he read from A to Z. Not enough that he read it himself, he also read it to Stepmother. But a miracle occurred. It was hard to determine if she was in fleeting good humor or was just ashamed to show anger. In any case, a strange frenzied laughter overtook her. She almost got apoplexy from the shrieking. Her favorite words were "pipsqueak" and "visor head." "Pipsqueak" was her monicker for Sholom, and "visor head" was a tag for one of the older boys who constantly sported his new cap.

Who could have foretold it would end with laughter? You can be sure that the young lexicographer recited the Prayer of Deliverance for the happy outcome.

46. On the Bench by the Gate

The Inn—Invited Guests—Dreams about the Treasure

Do you know what an inn is? It's not a rooming house and not a hotel, but something in between. Or both rolled into one. Nochem Rabinowitz's inn, from which he earned his livelihood, was a true inn. It had a large courtyard with big stalls for horses and wagons, and large rooms and beds for guests. Most rooms had several beds, but the average guest got only a bed, not the entire room. Unless of course he was someone special, rich and well dressed. Such guests, however, called "loaded guests," were few and far between. Most came only for a bed. They took neither samovars nor service. Instead, a huge samovar was brought into the lobby and each of the bed-guests filled his own teapot—take as much boiling water as you want! Here's to your health, fellow Jews!

Morning and evening the Rabinowitz inn was a pleasant sight. People crowded around the table, eating and drinking. Everyone talked at the same time, prattling on and smoking—the smoke was so thick you could cut it with a knife. They talked about everything under the sun. One spoke about the fair—he was a fair goer. Another, a grain dealer, about wheat. This one chatted about doctors—he was ailing and coughed. That one discussed cantors—he loved singing, go do him something. Off in a corner a man swayed in prayer, singing the morning blessing in a falsetto.

Meanwhile, Reb Nochem Rabinowitz, the landlord, a rather frail man with a thick cigarette in his mouth, wearing a round yarmulke and a cat-fur coat, sat at the head of the table like a king, listening to everyone at once. However, he did this with one ear, for with the other he was listening, albeit unwillingly, to Stepmother's invective, which flowed out of her, honey-smooth and slick as oil. She was settling accounts with her stepchildren and, before she was even fully awake, liberally dispensing ill wishes left and right. This one she jabbed in the ribs, another's neck was tweaked, a third she kicked in the stomach. She wanted one child to go dandle her baby, another to go to the market and help her carry the baskets, and the third to go to hell.

The children obeyed. They did everything Stepmother asked, for times were bad; there was no business. They studied only half a day in cheder, the other half they helped Father wherever they could. One helped serve the guests inside, and another sat on a bench by the gate to shout "Here! Turn here!" to the passing coachmen.

Being outside was of course preferable to enduring the din, the hell, and Stepmother inside. Sitting on the bench by the gate was no work. It was child's play, all fun. Especially in the summer when the wagons clattered by noisily, whips flying and hooves clomping. The coachmen had just collected passengers from the river steamer and wanted to pass each other. They raised so much dust you couldn't see the passengers' faces, even though you knew they were there. All the boys and all the servants from the inns ran toward the wagons with a merry tumult: "Here, uncle! Turn in here!" The coachman responded with a flick of his whip, flew by them, and vanished into the thick cloud of dust, leaving the boys and the servants empty-handed.

This happened during the summer, when the Dnieper River was navigable. In winter, when it stopped flowing, the inn got another kind of clientele. Huge wagons came laden with merchandise packed in mats and reeking of tar. These guests didn't eat Sabbath meals and didn't rent rooms. They thought nothing of sleeping on the floor or in the courtyard next to the wagons. They bought only hay and oats. Such customers provided little joy and less profit. Sitting on the bench by the gate in freezing weather was no fun either.

Sholom will never forget the times he sat on the bench by the gate. In the summer heat he roasted in the sun; in winter he froze like a dog, wrapped in a torn fur coat and in boots that begged for mending. He banged one foot against the other and hoped for the arrival of a coachman or a covered wagon with guests. If he saw one he'd stand, run toward it and shout, "Here! Turn in here!" But as if in spite, the drivers whizzed by and stopped at a nicer inn, at Reuben Yasnegradsky's, which was right across the street. There, people said, the rooms were large and furnished with easy chairs, mirrors and many other amenities that the Rabinowitzes did not have. That's why they were always packed with wealthy guests while the Rabinowitzes' place was so empty, it was for the dogs. Sholom was terribly peeved. At whom? God! Why didn't He make him Reuben Yasnegradsky's son rather than Nochem Rabinowitz's?

For Sholom, Reuben Yasnegradsky became a symbol of luck, wealth and all-around success. Getting rich guests became Sholom's obsession, a second treasure he now dreamed of, like the one he had dreamed of long ago when he knew Shmulik. He imagines that every passing wagon has prominent people, rich guests wearing bearskin coats. A coachman passes right by their entrance and before Sholom can say "Turn in here!" the driver of his own accord says "Whooaa!" and stops his wagon. One distinguished guest after another emerges, each in a bearskin coat. The servants bring in their yellow leather suitcases, packed with luxurious goods. Every bag weighs a ton. The guests march into the inn and each one orders a room, a samovar, and daily lunch and supper. Father, wearing his yarmulke, comes in smiling and greets them warmly.

"Do you plan to spend the Sabbath here?" he asks.

"Why one Sabbath? Why not three?" they reply.

It turns out they're merchants who have come to buy wheat; now Father can earn a nice commission on this as well. Why shouldn't he derive some benefit too? Then Stepmother comes in, wearing her silk Sabbath shawl. Face flushed with joy, she casts an eye on these rich guests and asks softly:

"Who brought them here?"

"It's me. I brought them," Sholom answers proudly, delighted with his on-the-spot fabrication, and pleased that the family will have at least one good day at their inn. And a good Sabbath as well. Oh, what a joyful Sabbath it will be. And why only one Sabbath? Why not three?

Too bad it was a fantasy. Yes, the wealthy guests in the bearskin coats and yellow suitcases came indeed; however, they stopped not at their inn but across the street at Reuben Yasnegradsky's. Oh, what mean, rotten people! It would be no skin off their backs if they came to our place, thought the constant dreamer, and returned to the house frozen through and through. He saw that Father in his cat-fur gaberdine was bent over a book, while Stepmother fumed as if in fever.

"No one came? Then what will I do with the bread I baked and the fish I cooked? Throw it to the dogs? Or do you think"—she turned to the stepchildren—"I'll save it for you? Stale bread isn't good enough for you, right? It'll stick in your throat. Or maybe your stomach won't digest it. A pampered bunch, bless you all! Spoiled brats! They couldn't leave you in Bohuslav with the girls, could they, to get measles over there, instead of taking you back here, may the devil take you, where you eat up a storm, may the worms eat you and gnaw you while you're alive, so that pieces fall from you like they fall from me when winter comes, may agues and plagues come over you!"

Here began the familiar invective, and Sholom the dreamer forgot he was freezing and ran out into the cold again, to the bench by the gate where it was more pleasant. At least there one could sit peacefully and dream that God might indeed send some rich guests in bearskin coats with yellow leather suitcases who might indeed stop at our inn and not at Reuben Yasnegradsky's. God could do it if He wanted to!

47. *The Lottery Agent*

Lottery Tickets—Great Hopes, Little Gains—Writing a Novel

Frail, quiet and pensive Nochem Rabinowitz must have been made of iron to bear Stepmother's yoke, listen to her invective and abuse, see her tormenting his children, and not even utter a word. No one will ever know how much inner anguish this caused him. But he never showed it and never complained to anyone. Maybe that's why Stepmother honored and respected him, was never gruff with him as she was with his children, and appreciated him after her own fashion. Her life wasn't easy either; she suffered and worked like an ox in a large house with a troop of children—her own and someone else's.

Perhaps she respected him because she saw how esteemed Nochem Rabinowitz was in town, even though everyone knew he wasn't rich; in fact, he could hardly make ends meet. Not a foolish woman, she was merely embittered and lost control of herself when angry. Forthright by nature, she didn't hesitate to speak her mind. Since Father paid no attention to her invective, she didn't pester him when he perused a book, played chess, or just chatted with a guest. Father's friends were maskilim, intellectuals, the cream of the town's intelligentsia, who deserve to be depicted in detail.

Foremost was the learned, heavyset lottery agent who, it was rumored, was somewhat of a heretic, despite his traditional long gaberdine and thick earlocks. Nochem Rabinowitz called him "a profound and erudite man." The two of them could spend all day together, talking incessantly. Where did they get so much to talk about? During his frequent visits, the lottery agent either brought or borrowed a book. Stepmother nicknamed him "Elflock" because of his dense, tangled beard. But in town he was called the lottery agent because he sold tickets issued by the Saxony and Braunschweig agency. He wore dark glasses (he had sensitive eyes) winter and summer, and always walked about in high galoshes. Not boots but galoshes—white socks and galoshes. Though absolutely impoverished, he was an optimist of the first order. He was sure his customers would win the grand prize someday and then his lot would improve too. He asserted that no one but Nochem Rabinowitz would win, for no one else needed the grand prize so badly. He may also have given similar assurances to his many other customers, for almost the entire town of Jews played the lottery. But Nochem Rabinowitz had faith in the agent as one has in a Hasidic rebbe, and both anticipated the grand prize like Jews awaiting the Messiah, sighing, yearning and waiting—any minute he'd bring the happy news: "Mazel tov, Reb Nochem, you've won the twenty-five thousand rubles . . ."

Sholom remembered that Father could never sit still during the final drawing. He would sigh more than usual, yawn mightily and, as if feverish, wouldn't be able to find his place. Sholom would get excited too; he looked forward to that great day perhaps even more keenly than Father. He was sure that Father was the sole candidate for the grand prize. Here again his friend Shmulik's treasure came into play. Sholom thought of this for days on end. He knew the numbers on Father's tickets by heart. He saw them in his dreams. God couldn't possibly be so mean. Why should He care if Father's number won? God could easily do it—what could be easier?

Sitting on the bench by the gate, Sholom saw the lottery agent from afar. As he strode along in his high galoshes, Sholom ran to his father with the news. "He's coming."

"Who?"

"The agent."

"So what?"

"What do you mean? Today's the big drawing."

Sholom saw his father's yellow, wrinkled face pale. His careworn eyes lit up for a moment, then darkened again.

The lottery agent came in huffing and puffing. (He had asthma and Stepmother would say, "Let it stay with him!") First he had to catch his breath and say good morning. Father didn't ask him a thing. If he had news, he would be the first to speak. The agent sat down, pushed his hat back, wiped his brow with the skirt of his gaberdine, and gave his report: "It's terribly hot outside. Literally burning." Then a period of silence. Neither of them said a word. Then the agent untied his greasy red- and green-spotted kerchief redolent of herring. (Here he kept all the lottery tickets.) His hairy hands trembling, he removed a big sheet of paper and scanned a long list of numbers. There! He found it. He gazed at Father through his dark lenses:

"If I'm not mistaken, Reb Nochem, I think your number is 16,384, right?"

"I don't understand your question," Father responded with a smile. "If *I'm* not mistaken, you have a good memory. You know everyone's number by heart."

"By heart, you say? Maybe. Well then, it's 16,384."

He looked through his dark glasses and tapped the list with his finger. Sholom felt his heart would burst any minute. Come on! Let's hear it already. But the lottery agent was in no hurry.

"Your number," he said slowly, "has won, Reb Nochem. Yes, it won."

A yellow cloud floated across Father's face and disappeared. Sholom himself felt like shrieking "Cock-a-doodle-doo!" But he controlled himself and swallowed every word the agent said.

"You've won, but it's a small prize. A very small one. Let's see, after deducting a tiny commission and all other expenses, it will come to . . . it comes to . . ."

Little Sholom almost fainted.

". . . to eight rubles and sixty kopecks. And if I'm not mistaken, you owe me twelve rubles fifty, and there's a previous debt, if you remember, of three eighty. So that adds up to sixteen thirty, right? So then it looks like you still owe me seven rubles seventy. Am I right or wrong? Now you probably want a new ticket. So I'll give you one. Here, Reb Nochem, choose a number. This time, God willing, you'll surely win. As sure as it's Tuesday all over the world. All right? Have you picked a number? Which one? 8613? May God grant good fortune! Best of luck! What are you staring at"—the lottery agent turned to Sholom—"you little rascal? How far have you read in *Songs of Glory*, you little scamp?"

The lottery agent had lent Sholom *Songs of Glory*, by Naftali Herz Wessely, and other books by Adam Ha-Cohen, Lebensohn, Kalman Schulman and Reb Isaac Ber Levinsohn. The scamp swallowed them as he sat on the bench by the gate. Father was proud that his son was already reading such books. "Do you at least understand what you're reading?" he asked. Sholom was ashamed to say yes, for he didn't want to boast to his father. But the agent answered for him. "Of course the scamp understands them, and quite well too. Why shouldn't he? You see, this little squirrel is a bit too young for Mapu and Smolenskin," the agent concluded.

Just because he said Sholom was too young, the little squirrel suddenly craved those books. He stole over to the bookshelf, helped himself to Mapu and Smolenskin, and secretly dipped into each.

The first book he snatched was *Love of Zion*, by Abraham Mapu, which he devoured one Sabbath while lying on the floor, tingling with excitement. He wept and shed bitter tears over the fate of the unfortunate Amnon. And like the hero of the novel, he fell madly in love with the beautiful, divine Tamar, perhaps even more than Amnon. He saw her in his dreams and talked to her in the language of the Song of Songs, hugging and embracing and kissing her.

The next day the infatuated Sholom walked around like a shadow. He had a splitting headache; his appetite was gone. This puzzled Stepmother. "The reason is—a bear croaked in the woods," she said sarcastically, then proceeded to snoop and investigate why the boy had stopped eating.

The *Love of Zion* incident ended this way: Occasionally, Sholom earned some pennies running errands for the guests at the inn. With this money he bought paper, sewed the sheets into a booklet, ruled them with lines on both sides, and set to work—writing a novel in the manner of Mapu's *Love of Zion*. It was an original novel, à la Mapu, using his style, diction and basic format. However, Sholom called his book *Daughter of Zion,* and his heroes Solomon and Shulamis. Since he lacked free time to write during the day—half he spent studying at cheder and half helping at the inn—he had to work at night by the light of a kerosene lamp, writing in his small script, writing and writing, until—Stepmother heard some scratching and saw a light. She rushed out of bed barefoot, sneaked up to the door, and saw what the rascal was doing. Then she raised such a rumpus that everyone in the house woke in a fright, assuming the house was on fire.

But the sole reason for all the commotion was the wasted kerosene.

"They're going to burn kerosene here, huh? May you all burn, dear God! A plague on you! Catch cholera! Burn in hell! Die an unnatural death!"

To be sure, Father confiscated the unfinished novel, *Daughter of Zion,* along with the stolen *Love of Zion.* The author of *Daughter of Zion* waited for the ax to fall. But the upshot was that Father showed the manuscript to the lottery agent before anyone else. The latter enthused over the calligraphy, the language and style, then pinched the rascal's cheek so lovingly it turned black and blue.

"You don't know what a treasure you have, Reb Nochem. Strike me dead, if you do! Something will come of him. You'll see what will become of him. Come over here, you scamp, let me at least give those red balloon cheeks of yours a healthy pinch, the devil take you, cheeks and all!"

48. Accomplished Sons-in-Law

A Goy Preaches to the Jews—Lazer Yossel and Magidov, the Accomplished Sons-in-Law—A Thousand Pages of Talmud by Heart

 Besides the lottery agent, the town's exquisite young intellectuals—the accomplished sons-in-law—also frequented Nochem Rabinowitz's house.

Every town has its own customs and ways. In Pereyaslav sons-in-law were in fashion. The householders in those days considered it a kind of sport, and they squandered money left and right for a suitable candidate. Goods of this sort were acquired mostly out of town. Rarely was a match arranged at home. Except of course if the father of the bride was broke. But whoever had the means for a dowry imported an accomplished son-in-law from Lithuania or Poland, as befitted his taste, style and fortune.

Uncle Pinny's son-in-law, for instance, wasn't imported but came from nearby Luben. He was a young Torah scholar, immersed in the world of spirituality; he didn't even know what a coin looked like. For her pretty daughter, Aunt Hannah got a son-in-law from Yagotin who was so good-looking he could have been on stage. Neither overly smart nor well versed in Talmud, but handsome. The Sabbath after the wedding, when the young couple was escorted to and from shul, a crowd formed to gape and assess who was better-looking. Some said she was more beautiful; others insisted he was. Both heard these loud remarks, blushed, and became even lovelier. For the parents this sufficed. They'd made a hit, their merchandise was admired, and the town talked about them. What else was needed but popularity?

Often, people even came to blows over sons-in-law. Of course, they didn't whack each other with sticks, God forbid. They merely argued and insulted each other over who had a nicer son-in-law. Women stuck out their tongues and thumbed their noses at one another. Sometimes they meted out slaps too. But then they were rebuked by Domanovsky, the clever justice of the peace, a goy who understood Yiddish. But he was still a goy. After all, how could a goy appreciate the pleasure of leading a son-in-law to shul on the Sabbath, all decked out in new clothes from top to toe, putting him on exhibit in a seat way up front by the eastern wall, giving him Maftir, and then hearing him sing out a Haftorah from the bimah the like of which hadn't been heard before, while the women push one another at the window of the women's gallery to get a better look at him? "Where is he? Where?" No, a goy would never understand this even if he were the wisest man in the world.

Most often, however, the merchandise quickly tarnished; it glittered briefly, then looked workaday, like scuffed or out-of-fashion fabric. In a year or two, the onetime brand-new son-in-law became like all other Jews; yesterday's prince, that exquisite piece of goods, grew a beard. The yoke of earning a living obviously lay heavily on him. It was a pity to see the former sparkling son-in-law, yesterday's prince—who had been on exhibit at the eastern wall seemingly just last Sabbath—relinquish that prestigious spot to a more recent acquisition, the new prince and darling of the crowd, and regard him with envy. His young wife, who had reigned here as queen not too long ago, now joined all the other women who elbowed their way to the window of the women's gallery: "Where is he? Where?" That's the way of the world. To quote the Bible: "A generation goes and a generation comes." In fact, a bit of philosophizing now wouldn't be out of place, but since we're talking about accomplished sons-in-law, let's proceed.

Two bright chaps in our town were the exception to the usual run-of-the-mill sons-in-law. That's why they continued to shine in Pereyaslav long after their weddings. Unlike others, their luster did not fade, nor did they go out of fashion. One was called Lazer Yossel; the other, Magidov. The former was brought from Korsun by a rich leather merchant who had a rather homely daughter but offered a substantial dowry. Magidov was extracted from somewhere in Lithuania by a contractor who supplied the government with horses. The contractor gave the Litvak a beautiful daughter, a strapping piece of girl, *and* a nice dowry, not including gifts and free board and whatever else your heart desires.

When they arrived, Pereyaslav went wild; it turned topsy-turvy. For a long, long time people in town and the surrounding region talked of their weddings, which even nowadays are still remembered. Don't ask what fortunes those two weddings cost! Whether the daughters were happy is another matter. As far as we know, one divorced her husband after his gift to her—several children—and left for America. The other's husband was either a teacher or a matchmaker, or perhaps both rolled in one. One thing, however, was certain—he was a pauper. But we're not talking about the present. We're citing what happened long ago, in times gone by. Then the parents were in seventh heaven. Mothers-in-law compared notes on the great treasures they had acquired. One bragged to the other women that her son-in-law was like a coverlet for the Torah. At which another went even further and boasted that *her* son-in-law was a Torah.

They had every right to boast. There was reason: Lazer Yossel was a genius. He was a young man who reportedly knew 1000 pages of Talmud by heart. Not 999, but 1000. Don't even mention the Bible! Moreover, he was a master of Hebrew, a first-rank stylist, and had an excellent hand. He was spunky, funny, a cunning blade. People whispered that he was somewhat of a freethinker too: he skipped prayers, disregarded fast days, carried a handkerchief on Sabbath, wasn't scared of a woman. Remarks like these were made in Uncle Pinny's house. But it was nothing compared to knowing 1000 pages of Talmud by heart.

The other son-in-law, Magidov, was also a genius. He too knew 1000—not 999—pages of Talmud by heart, was also an expert in Bible, Hebrew grammar and composition, and was an excellent public speaker. But he was neither funny nor a cunning blade. On the contrary, he delved too deeply into philosophy; his thinking was skewered. No matter what you said, he thought the opposite. An obstinate man, a Litvak!

Naturally, Nochem Rabinowitz didn't let pass the wonderful opportunity of having these accomplished sons-in-law examine his little Bible expert and see how that little devil wrote Hebrew. Both men agreed that Sholom was indeed a little devil and that his gifts should not be wasted. He should set a goal for himself and become someone special. The two sons-in-law praised him to the sky and said: "You can never tell what this little devil will be someday."

The lottery agent with the dark glasses, who spent his time in the company of young people, also chimed in and added: "I've always said that you can never tell what will become of this rascal."

The little devil, or rascal, stood nearby and heard everything. His soul trembled, his heart burst with pride, and his head spun like a man climbing a high ladder, with people down below shouting encouragement. It was no trifle to be praised by people who said, "You can never tell what he'll be someday."

Father was in seventh heaven. Still, each of his sighs tore out a piece of Sholom's heart. It meant: "I agree that you can never tell what this little devil will be someday. But advise me what to do with him? Go ahead, tell me."

One man gave him a suggestion, radical but to the point. And Father listened to him. It came from Arnold, one of Pereyaslav's leading intellectuals, a young philosopher who lived on the outskirts of town, in the suburb called Pidvorke. To him we'll devote a separate chapter.

49. Arnold of Pidvorke

A Suburb of Pereyaslav—Arnold the Heretic—Legend of the Exodus from Egypt—A School for Rabbis and a Gymnasium

Almost every town in the blessed Pale of Settlement had its suburb, whose population was mostly gentile. The Jews who lived there weren't like the ones in town. They looked more rustic; they weren't as sharp as the town Jews, and a little more ignorant. They wore high boots and smelled of sheepskins. They used different Yiddish expressions. Their laughter was boisterous— "Ho, ho, ho" and not "Ha, ha, ha." And they rolled their *r*'s: "Rrreb Morrrdecai rrrequests the honorrr of yourrr prrresence at a brrris."

Pereyaslav had such a suburb—Pidvorke—separated from the town by a wooden bridge and little river. It was different in mien and mood. Townspeople with time to spare strolled there to breathe the fresh air of the orchards and to smell the grass. Young boys and girls took Sabbath walks there. Of course, not together, God forbid. Separately. But in crossing the bridge they met anyway, stopped, exchanged glances and remarks. Sometimes they moved and touched each other with an elbow, whereupon both boy and girl blushed and hearts began to race. After several meetings in Pidvorke they began to write letters secretly and sometimes a romance ensued. We shall soon see the outcome of one such romance. Meanwhile, let's return to Arnold of Pidvorke.

Nochem Rabinowitz had a good friend in Pidvorke named Benjamin Kalman. Years ago, Benjamin Kalman had been Nochem's partner. They loaded ships with grain and sent them to Königsberg and Danzig. Lately, however, Benjamin Kalman's fortunes were in decline, his former luster dimmed, his business deals were limited in scope, and he proceeded cautiously. But the former partners' friendship was unaffected. Benjamin Kalman often came into the inn to sit and chat. But he did most of the talking. He loved to talk, especially to tell stories about his younger brother, Arnold.

"My Arnold! You won't find an intellectual like him anywhere. No one knows as much. No one is more honest than my Arnold. You haven't the faintest notion what sort of Arnold my Arnold is! He's some Arnold." And so on and so forth.

His brother Benjamin Kalman wasn't the only one who talked about him—*everyone* talked about Arnold. He was a hero in town. First of all, he was along in years. Either a bachelor, a widower or a divorcé. In any case, without a wife. A Jew without a wife was a rarity. And besides, he was a notary too. A Jewish notary was definitely a rarity. Have you ever heard of a Jewish notary before? Actually, he wasn't a full-fledged notary yet, but he was on his way. Studying to be one. As soon as he passed his exam he'd become a notary. Except of course if he didn't pass the exam. But why shouldn't he pass it?

"He'll certainly pass it," said Benjamin Kalman, "and he'll certainly become a notary, no doubt about it. Don't mess with my Arnold!"

Everyone knew what a notary was, including Sholom. In Pereyaslav there was one notary, a gentile named Novov. Novov the notary. But Sholom didn't know what "passing an exam" meant. Where does he have to pass it, when does he have to pass it, and how does he go about passing it? He heard these things being discussed but it went over his head. For example, it was said that Arnold wrote for newspapers and that the entire town, Jews and Christians alike, were afraid he might write about them in the *Kievlianin*. Sholom didn't understand what they were afraid of. And, anyway, who was the *Kievlianin*? Sholom also repeated what he had heard—that everyone trembled before Arnold. They feared his mouth and his pen like the Angel of Death. Hiding from him was impossible, and bribing him—no one had that much money. "They'll get it from him," Benjamin Kalman would say with a little smile. "If he wanted to dirty his hands, he'd write all of them up in the *Kievlianin* from head to toe. There won't be a soul he won't have written up. Don't mess with my Arnold!"

Most fascinating—and very characteristic—was that Arnold lived under one roof with his brother for years without exchanging a word with him. They were angry at each other. Nevertheless, one would have given his right hand for the other. "My Arnold!" "My Benjamin Kalman!" No one, whether in Pidvorke or in town, ever saw them together or heard them talking to each other. They didn't even eat at the same table.

In Benjamin Kalman's house, Arnold had his own little room in which sacred texts and secular books were stacked to the ceiling. He lived by himself, like a recluse. Strange brothers. Arnold was peculiar too. And he was among Nochem Rabinowitz's frequent visitors. But his visits weren't like those of other Pereyaslav maskilim. He didn't just come in to wag his tongue or speak drivel; he came with a new book, with an issue of the *Kievlianin*, or with a complaint about the town and its ringleaders.

Sholom respected him most of all. He didn't leave Arnold's side, didn't miss a word he said. Was this the Arnold who would pass an exam and become a notary? Was this the Arnold who wrote for the *Kievlianin* but didn't want to dirty his hands? Why did one have to dirty one's hands when writing for the *Kievlianin*? Sholom couldn't take his eyes off Arnold. He liked Arnold because he was a very pleasant, congenial man. He wasn't tall, but thin and wiry, as if made of steel. He had a well-trimmed yellow beard, and no hint of earlocks. He wore a short jacket and carried a slim cane. His tongue was razor sharp. Fire and brimstone. Spoke of God and the Messiah. Mocked the Hasidim. Demolished the fanatics. "I have no use for piety— honesty is what counts. Be honest, not pious," he said, and his tart, venomous laugh resounded in the room.

Sholom wondered how a Jew dared to say such things. But evidently he could. Arnold of Pidvorke was allowed everything, for his name was Arnold and he was a notary; that is, he would become a notary.

Sometimes Uncle Pinny was also present at Arnold's harangues. He shook with laughter and admonished, "Oh, Arnold, Arnold." By which he probably meant: "How can the earth abide a wicked man like you?" Nevertheless, even Uncle Pinny thought highly of Arnold because of his honesty. His integrity was famous in town. Honesty was an obsession with him. Arnold feared no one; he looked everyone straight in the eye and told the unadorned truth. And above all, he derided the rich and didn't give a damn about money. Now tell me, how can you not be fond of a man like that?

Arnold, however, didn't admire anyone. For example, he wasn't too enthusiastic about Uncle Pinny. Yes, he was a fine man with a nice beard, but Arnold didn't think highly of him. Arnold respected his brother Nochem much more. "Because Nochem Rabinowitz is neither two-faced nor a foolish Hasid." You could say whatever you pleased to Nochem. You could complain about a Hasidic rebbe and even about Moses. With his own ears Sholom heard Arnold say that he didn't believe in the Exodus from Egypt. "It's nothing but a legend. The whole story is just a legend." Sholom pondered over the word "legend," and concluded that it probably came from the word "lie." A legend, then, no doubt meant a little lie. Luckily it wasn't a big lie . . .

One day, Arnold of Pidvorke came running with a thick book. "Here, look what Draper says about Maimonides. Maimonides was court physician to the Turkish Sultan for thirteen years. And to get the job he converted. Imagine! He was a Moslem thirteen years. *Your* Maimonides, *your* author of *Guide to the Perplexed.* Now what do you say to that?"

Luckily, Uncle Pinny wasn't present. Had Uncle Pinny been there, I don't know what would have happened.

Sholom's father apparently boasted to Arnold about his son's writing, and asked him what course to follow with him and how to make him "someone special."

"Well, forget about his scribblings! Dump them in the garbage. They're not worth the paper they're written on. If you want to make something of this little fellow, enroll him in the district school. From there all paths are open to him. Then you can send him to the government rabbinical seminary or the gymnasium."

As soon as Sholom entered the room the conversation stopped. (Arnold told him about it later.) Even though Arnold's criticism of his "scribblings" and the rather dishonorable place he suggested for them displeased Sholom, Arnold still became Sholom's best friend if only for the word "gymnasium." That word was music to Sholom's ears. He was enchanted not so much by the word itself (whose meaning he still didn't know) but by the fact that he would be a gymnasium student. Now that was something! He knew what a gymnasium student was; he had seen one with his own eyes—the only Jewish gymnasium student in Pereyaslav. His uniform had white silver buttons, and on his cap was a silver badge. His name was also Sholom, but he was called Solomon. He was like all the other boys, yet he wasn't like them at all. After all, he was a gymnasium student, a different sort of creature, as we shall soon see.

Meanwhile, let's return to Arnold's suggestion, which let a cricket into the house. From then on words like "classes," "exams," "rabbinical seminary," "gymnasium" and "doctor" constantly chirped in the house. No matter what the subject, sooner or later one of those words came up. Everyone had an anecdote to tell: How a poor yeshiva student left his school barefoot and made his way to Zhitomir to the rabbinical seminary. How a Hebrew teacher's son, a Litvak, disappeared, and everyone thought he had gone to America; finally, it turned out that he had taken examinations for all eight classes and was now studying, so people said, to be a doctor. Only a Litvak could do a thing like that.!

"Shush! Listen to this. Take our Yenkel the Medic's sonny boy. How much more does he have to study to be a doctor?"

"He's still a long way off! It'll be a year of Wednesdays before Yenkel the Medic's son becomes a doctor."

Yenkel the Medic's son—that's Solomon the gymnasium student, the subject of our next chapter.

50. The Gymnasium Student Solomon

Yenkel the Medic's Son—Envy—The Wine Cellar—Kosher for Passover

Each doctor in Pereyaslav had a nickname: Fatso, Hunchback, Blackie. All of them were gentiles. There was just one Jewish doctor, and he wasn't even a full-fledged doctor, but half a doctor: Yenkel the Medic. But he played the role as if he had a license. He wore a cape, wrote prescriptions, and loudly pronounced the Latin name of the medicine.

"Take a tablespoon of Kali Bromali every two hours and a teaspoon of Natri Bromatri every three hours and you'll feel better in the morning. And if you don't feel better, you'll feel worse. Then call me and I'll come again."

The town preferred Yenkel the Medic to all the other doctors because you could talk to him. You learned what caused the pain in your stomach and why you had to take cod-liver oil for the rheumatic ache in your leg. (What connection was there between your leg and your stomach?) But Yenkel had one great attribute. He didn't haggle over fees. Whatever you gave him was fine. He didn't even look at the sum. However, his fingers poked in his pockets for a while and he soon guessed the size of the coin. If it was too small, he would return it and say that no money was needed. This made you feel uncomfortable and you gave him another coin.

He had another nice trait: he listened to you and loved to talk and tell stories, mostly about how talented his children were. One of them, Sholom—called Solomon—was already a gymnasium student. After the gymnasium, God willing, he would enroll in the university and would graduate as a doctor, a doctor with a diploma. A full-fledged doctor.

"I wish it were Passover already," Yenkel the Medic sighed. "God willing, my Solomon will come for the holiday and then you'll see a gymnasium student."

Sholom also looked forward to the holiday so he could have a look at him.

Finally, Passover came. Now Sholom would see what a gymnasium student looked like.

Yenkel the Medic wasn't sufficiently observant to run to the shul on the holiday. After all, he was a bit of a doctor. Half a doctor, true, but still a doctor. Nevertheless, for the sake of his son, the gymnasium student, he came to shul too. Washed, scrubbed, hair slicked down, happy. He sat in the first row, right opposite the eastern wall. Next to him stood his son, Sholom, or Solomon, wearing his uniform with silver buttons from top to bottom and a strange cap—a cap with a badge. He held a little Siddur and prayed, just like a normal person. Neither the adults nor the children took their eyes off this gymnasium student with the silver buttons. He seemed to be like everyone else—an average boy—yet he was different. He was a gymnasium student. As he thought of this, a deep sigh tore out of Sholom's heart.

After prayers, Yenkel the Medic did not rush home. To some he was the first to say "Gut yontev," while others greeted him first. But the important thing was the conversation about his son.

"Is that your gymnasium student, Reb Yenkel? Well then, welcome and hello."

Everyone greeted him from all sides. He was only a boy—yet grown men with beards were saluting him. Where was he studying? What was he studying? What would he do when he finished? What was his goal?

"What's his goal?" Yenkel laughed. "His goal is, ha, ha, ha, to be a doctor. A full-fledged doctor, ha, ha, ha."

Yenkel the Medic's son a doctor? A full-fledged doctor? In any case, he'd surely make a living. Even old Jews were amazed, although one wondered what prevented *their* children from becoming doctors—

and this puzzled them too. No one had stood in their way. But since *their* fathers hadn't let *them* become doctors, they didn't want *their* children to become doctors. Their consolation was that their children would remain Jews. But what was the rub? Livelihood. Eh! He who provided life will provide livelihood too. Take Yuzi Finkelstein. He didn't become a doctor and look how rich he was—they would have been happy with a fraction of his riches.

"How much longer does your little one have to study, Reb Yenkel?" people asked as they inspected Solomon from head to toe.

"My Solomon?" Yenkel the Medic stroked his beard and did a little jig with one foot. "Oh! He still has a long way to go." He counted off on his fingers the years of study in the gymnasium and at the university. Then there was interning at a hospital or perhaps a military hospital where you become an army doctor, almost an officer, with epaulettes. Ha, ha, ha!

Yenkel, a short man with a flat nose and curly, heavily pomaded hair, wearing his cape like a true doctor, seemed to be the happiest man in the world. And there was no happier boy in the world than the little gymnasium student with the red cheeks, the silver buttons and the strange cap with the badge. Both left the shul amid a crowd of townspeople. The grown-ups gathered around Yenkel. The children tried to get as close as possible to Solomon. He seemed to be an entirely different creature. He even smelled different.

Never before had Sholom envied anyone as much as the fortunate gymnasium student. Why couldn't he be in his shoes? Why wasn't he Yenkel the Medic's son? His name was Sholom too. Why should God care if Nochem Rabinowitz and Yenkel the Medic exchanged identities? At night, Sholom dreamed about the student. He also daydreamed about him. He thought of him constantly. The student became a mania, an idée fixe, another Chaim Fruchstein . . . Sholom envied the youth; he was terribly envious. But he lacked the courage to go and talk to him. How could he talk with a gymnasium student? How could he approach a boy whose name was Sholom but who was called Solomon? In his fantasy Sholom imagined himself a gymnasium student who was no longer called Sholom but Solomon. He wore a uniform with silver buttons, a cap with a badge, and all the boys envied him and marveled: "Is that Nochem Rabinowitz's boy, the gymnasium student? Is that the one who used to be called Sholom?"

Imagine Sholom's joy and elation the day Father told him that,

God willing, the next day he would begin school. He had already seen the principal and applied for the preparatory school.

"You'll finish the preparatory class in six weeks and then go to the district school. And from there, God willing, you'll go to the gymnasium, and from there, even higher . . . With God's help, everything is possible, as long as you apply yourself a little more."

If he hadn't been so shy before Father, he would have let out a whoop of joy. Apply himself? What a question! But he was in a fog about the district school, the identity of the director, and the meaning of "preparatory classes." He remembered Arnold's remarks and suddenly thought of Yenkel's son with the silver buttons and the strange cap. His heart became full, his head spun. Tears of joy brimmed in his eyes. But he stood there like a stone, a clod who couldn't count to two. But the clod was waiting for the moment when he'd be alone and then he'd let himself go. He'd slap his cheeks and thighs, roll on the floor, hop for a mile on one leg, and sing:

> Solomon, Solomon,
> Gymnasium student, Solomon.

"But in the meantime, begging your pardon, go rock the baby and then sit down and help me chop raisins."

Stepmother speaking, naturally. For the reader's information, the family had to chop raisins because the inn alone did not provide a living. So Nochem Rabinowitz opened a wine cellar and hung out a sign:

WE SELL WINES FROM THE SOUTHERN SHORES

Father himself made the wine from chopped raisins but called it various names, among which Sherry and Madeira come to mind. There was also a red wine called Monastery Wine Kosher for Passover. This was the children's favorite because it was both sweet and tart. An added syrup made it sweet, while the raisin pits gave it a tart flavor. Its red color, however, was Father's secret. Whenever the children were sent to the cellar for a quart of wine, they ran to the Monastery Wine Kosher for Passover and took several gulps. Despite this, the wine provided them with a fine livelihood—more than Father's other business ventures.

51. The Scholarship

Father Adamantly Supports the Scholar—A Stipend—Tumult in Town—The Dreams of the Treasure Begin to Come True

Things are easier said than done. Entering the district school was neither easy nor smooth. The first hurdle to overcome was Uncle Pinny, who moved heaven and earth to prevent it. "What? Take a child and make a goy out of him with your own hands?" he argued, visibly upset. Pinny didn't calm down until he had exacted a promise from his brother that he wouldn't let his children write on the Sabbath. Indeed, Father stipulated this condition to the principal: his children would not be at school on the Sabbath. Another condition was (at that time Jews were still able to list conditions) that the Rabinowitz children would leave the classroom when the priest taught his lesson. Both of Father's wishes were respected.

The children's second hurdle was the language. When they began school they understood so little Russian everyone made fun of them—teacher and classmates. It seemed the very benches were laughing. This hurt Sholom. He was used to laughing at everyone, and now everyone was laughing at him. And his friends, the little gentile lads, weren't silent either. As soon as classes were over and the Jewish children—the little Yids—came into the yard, the gentile boys threw them to the ground and, laughing good-naturedly, pinned their arms and legs and smeared their Jewish mouths with goyish lard. Crestfallen, the Rabinowitz boys returned home, afraid to tell what happened lest they be taken out of school. As it was, Stepmother was seething and fuming against the "scholars" (that's what she called them after they enrolled in the new school). Since Sholom was more diligent in his studies than the others, she persecuted him most of all. But then something happened that took the wind out of her sails and kept her quiet.

One fine morning Sholom was pacing up and down the house, committing his lesson to memory. Father was praying in tallis and tefillin. Stepmother was doing her work: nagging Father. She threw up to him the old offense of denying the existence of the older and younger boys and the little girls. She reminded him of his children's healthy appetites and, may no evil eye befall them, what incredible stomachs they had. She also didn't forget the rest of his family. None of this bothered Father. He prayed facing the wall, as if she weren't talking to him. But then she let loose with a stream of invective against Sholom for walking around and studying:

"This fine and dandy scholar thinks he's a big shot. He thinks he's free of all responsibilities except eating. As if we had a troop of servants here, or a house filled with maids! It's all right, it's not beneath your dignity, you fine and dandy scholar with your crooked boot, to bring a guest a samovar. Not a hair of yours will fall off, and it won't hurt your appetite or your chances for marriage."

The "scholar" was about to stop memorizing and go to the kitchen for the samovar. Suddenly Father tore himself from the wall, seized Sholom's hand and, in a raging passion, said in Hebrew (he didn't want to interrupt his prayers with a less holy language):

"No! Absolutely not! I forbid it! I refuse!" Then he continued in Yiddish. He attacked Stepmother vehemently, perhaps for the first time since his marriage. "From now on, don't you dare order him around! Not even for a second. You can boss all the other children, but not him. Sholom isn't like the rest. Sholom has to study. Once and for all. That's the way I want it, that's the way it is, and that's the way it's going to be!"

Whether it was because every despot and tyrant who hears a loud, emphatic word becomes frightened and falls silent, or because it was the first time Father had ever opposed her during their cordial relationship—in any case, a miracle happened. Stepmother bit her tongue and became quiet as a pussycat. Henceforth, her attitude toward Sholom changed completely. That is, she didn't spare barbs or curses, she still gibed him at every opportunity about his "classes," and she complained that he used up a ton of paper a week and three bottles of ink a day. She also purposely forgot to fill his lamp with kerosene at night, to prepare his lunch, and so on. However, she no longer bossed him around. Except, of course, for sweetly asking him to run an errand, watch the samovar, or rock the baby. But only if he was willing.

"Sholom?" Stepmother called gently in her Berditchev accent. "How come as soon you look at the samovar it starts boiling?"

Or:

"Sholom? Look here. How come the baby falls asleep the minute you rock it?"

Or:

"Sholom? How long would it take you to run over to the market? Half a minute. Not even that."

Sholom's success also stood him in good stead. When things go well, they don't stop. One day in class the principal, a rather nice gentile, whispered to Sholom that he wanted to speak to his father. Hearing the principal's request, Nochem Rabinowitz quickly donned his Sabbath gaberdine, pressed his earlocks even tighter behind his ears, and went to the principal's office. He was told that since his son Sholom was an excellent student, according to the law he should have a tuition-free scholarship. But since he was a Jew, he could only get a stipend (if memory serves, either 120 rubles a year or 120 rubles for half a year).

This caused a great hullabaloo in town. One after another, people came to ask if it was true.

"What then? Do you think it's a lie?"

"A stipend?"

".A stipend."

"From the government treasury?"

"No, from the Ministry of Education."

A link with the ministry was no trifle either. At night the entire family gathered to look at the scholarship boy. Whoever didn't see Father glowing and shining with pride that night has never seen a happy man. Even Stepmother seemed nice that day. In rare good humor, she celebrated with everyone and served the family tea and preserves. Sholom forgot the past and forgave her everything. Let bygones be bygones. Now he was a hero. Everyone looked admiringly at him. Everyone talked about him. Everyone laughed and was in good spirits. Aunt Hannah's children, who loved to joke with him, asked:

"What do you plan to do with so much money?"

As if they didn't know he wouldn't see a penny of it. As if they didn't know the money was needed for Father's business, the wine cellar.

Hold it! Look who had come—the thickset lottery agent with the dark glasses and high galoshes. He just wanted to set his blind eyes on the rascal and give that scamp a pinch on the cheek, tear out a piece of his flesh. And the accomplished sons-in-law, Lazer Yossel and Magidov, also came to congratulate Father and to sit down and chat about Haskala and enlightenment, about progress and civilization. But they were followed by Arnold of Pidvorke, who put a damper on Sholom's celebration.

First of all, he demonstrated to all present that they were asses. They didn't know what they were talking about. The scholarship wasn't a scholarship but a stipend. A scholarship was one thing, a stipend another. Secondly, Sholom wasn't the only prizewinner. Another student at the district school had also won a stipend of 120 rubles: Sholom's new school friend, Eli, whom we'll talk about later.

Meanwhile, the hero of our autobiography was in seventh heaven. It was clear that his old dreams about the treasure were slowly coming true. And his fantasy took wing and bore him far away to the world of imagination. He saw himself surrounded by his friends, who looked at him with shining-eyed envy. Sholom saw Father as a young man. What had become of his bent back? The deep furrows on his brow? The pale, careworn face? Father had become a new man. He no longer sighed. The whole family surrounded him, honored him and his son Sholom, the chosen boy, the happy lad who was so famous today everyone knew of him, even the government and the Ministry of Education. Everyone! Perhaps even the Czar!

52. His Friend Eli

Eli Dodi's Son—First Meeting at a Fire—Discussing Cosmography with Uncle Pinny—Desecrating the Sabbath—Being Called Author

Round white face, slightly pockmarked. A mane of hair that stood out, stiff, black, thick and prickly. Laughing eyes, strong, white teeth. Short fingers. A booming, resounding laugh. Fiery temperament. That was Eli, Sholom's friend through all their school years.

They first met on the night of the fire.

A fire is a spectacle, a free show, a fascinating mélange of all types of people, a mirror of all kinds of gay and tragic scenes. No need for a theater. The night is quiet, the sky deep with sparkling stars. A dog's bark is heard from afar. Meanwhile, the house is burning like a candle, slowly and quietly. It's in no rush. People flock in from all the streets. Sleepy at first, then bursting more intensely into life.

One by one, then in groups, then with troops of children. Men wearing ritual fringes rush into the fire to save what they can. Women scream, little children wail, young men crack jokes and girls laugh. The Rabinowitz children are there too. Suddenly Sholom hears someone's voice. It's a boy, whispering into his ear.

"They're coming."

"Who?"

"The firemen. Come, let's help them."

Holding hands, the boys run through the market to meet the firemen. While running, Sholom learns that his friend's name is Eli, Dodi the Scribe's son. And Eli learns that his friend is called Sholom, Nochem Rabinowitz's son.

Some time passed before they met again. This time it was during the day. In the street once more, at another free show. A black man with white teeth and a monkey had all the children in town trailing him. Such a marvel was a rarity in Pereyaslav. The usual entertainment was a blind bear who danced on a stick, a clown in red trousers doing his antics, or a gypsy putting a monkey through its paces. The gypsy and the monkey looked like twins. Both had wrinkled, hairy faces, bald heads and pathetic eyes, and both stretched out their dirty hands for a coin. The gypsy had a strange voice and spoke in a peculiar language. You couldn't help but laugh the way he shook his head and grimaced. "Give, sir. Good monkey. Amerikanski."

These two meetings sufficed for the two rascals to become friends. But God also arranged to have them in the same class in the district school; they even sat next to each other and met on the first day, when the teacher gave his opening lecture. Sholom saw Eli stretch out his hand, shake his head and pull a gypsy face. "Give, sir. Good monkey. Amerikanski." Well, try and be a hero and suppress your laughter. Naturally, both friends got their due, stayed after school, went without supper, and sealed their friendship forever.

From then on they became one soul. They went everywhere together. They studied side by side and got good marks. They promised each other to outdo all the gentile lads and to be the best in class. And they brought it off. They surpassed all the little goyim by far, and led every class. Sholom and Eli were the smartest in school— and the biggest rascals in town. No boy dared to do what they had the nerve to do; after all, they were scholarship boys, prizewinners, tops in school! And their mastery of Russian grammar! Mention a noun and they'd decline it in all the cases: nominative, accusative, dative, possessive, and so on. Say a verb and it would get conjugated. They were also supreme in geography. They knew why the earth was round, and whether the earth revolved around the sun or vice versa. Where does wind come from? What comes first, thunder or lightning? And how does rain originate?

However, the only subject that appealed to Sholom's father was geography. *That* could educate and enlighten you. Arithmetic was also good, for it sharpened one's mind. But it did no more than that. Take Yossi Fruchstein, for example. He was a simple Jew, had never studied anywhere. But he'd figure out the knottiest problem in his head. Or take the lottery agent. Where had he studied? In a yeshiva somewhere. But don't you think he knew algebra? So did Lazer Yossel. As for Arnold of Pidvorke—that goes without saying. For Arnold would soon take his examination. No, Father felt, say what you will, but geography was not mathematics. Geography had to be *studied.* It was a subject you had to know. Nochem Rabinowitz liked to discuss nothing but geography with his son. And he was delighted if a third person was present.

It was hilarious when Uncle Pinny was present. He stroked his beard, smiled, and poked fun at the little philosopher holding forth on geography. A young rascal like Sholom had the nerve to tell an older Jew, his own uncle, that the earth moved and not the sun. And what about the Biblical verse: "Sun, stand still in Gibeon!"? That's a problem, right? "And if, as you say, thunder comes before lightning, how come we see the lightning first and then hear the thunder?" Uncle Pinny asked for the fun of it, and held his sides laughing.

"And now you tell me that the earth is shaped like a ball, it's round like an apple. Go ahead, prove it."

"If you take the trouble," Sholom replied, "to get up early tomorrow morning and look at the top of the monastery at sunrise, you'll see the rooftop getting the first light."

"Sure! I have nothing better to do but get up at dawn for you and look at the top of the monastery for your geography, ha, ha, ha."

No, Uncle Pinny was not pleased. Neither with the classes nor with Sholom's friendship with Dodi the Scribe's boy. Who knows what bad paths he might lead him to? Uncle Pinny had already heard some nasty things about the two boys: They strolled in Pidvorke on Sabbath, they carried handkerchiefs in their pockets on the holy day, and they spoke Russian, not Yiddish.

Ah woe, it was all true. Every word of it. Indeed, they went to Pidvorke every Sabbath but not for walks, as we shall see later. And they not only carried handkerchiefs but also small change to buy pears. And the things they discussed! If Uncle Pinny had known what they talked about and what words they used! And if he had known that the two boys took a rowboat to the other side of the river! There, on the green grass, they read books (Russian ones) and sang songs (gentile ones) and daydreamed. Together they built castles in the air and wondered what they would do when they finished school. Where would they go? What should they study? What would they become? Truth to say, a gentile atmosphere reigned there. There was no Jewish content to these sweet dreams, for Eli had grown up in a home estranged from Yiddishkeit, even though— and the two were not connected—he got as many smacks from his father for not wanting to pray as did all the other children from their fathers. I suspect all fathers are like that. Even today you see fathers who do forbidden things but still want their children to be nice and pious and not follow in their footsteps.

Not wanting to pray was an old malaise among the children that dated back to cheder days. Skipping sections of prayers was a daily routine. But from the day they entered the district school they forgot about prayers altogether. Father knew this but feigned ignorance. Still, there were those who saw everything and opened Father's eyes to see how his children were gradually moving away from the straight and narrow path. This prompted the youngsters to absolutely refuse to pray, and even to feel a spiritual pleasure in this refusal. Not for nothing did their old cheder teacher once explain the meaning of a sin to the little sinners. "The sin itself isn't as bad as the joy of committing it." Sholom remembers to this day the taste of his first sin—desecrating the Sabbath. Here's how it happened.

Sabbath afternoon. The Jews had finished their lunch and were taking sweet naps. Not even a mad dog roamed the streets. So peaceful and still you could lie down on the street. The blazing sun was desert hot. The walls of the painted houses and the wooden fences of the courtyards begged to be written on. Sholom put his hands into his pockets and discovered a piece of chalk. He looked around. Not a soul. The shutters were closed. He heard the evil impulse telling him: "Draw!" What should he draw? He quickly illustrated the famous Russian song that all children drew as they sang:

> One dot, another, and a comma,
> A funny face with a straight line;
> One hand, another, and a circle,
> Two legs, a belly button, you're doing fine!

This made a round-faced little man with hands and feet and a smiling mouth. The artist was pleased with his picture. Just the signature was missing. Sholom looked around. Not a soul. The evil impulse egged him on. "Write!" But what should he write? Under the picture he added a Russian rhyme in neatly rounded little letters:

> No one knows the boy who penned this rhyme
> But you're a fool for reading this and wasting time.

Before he had a chance to reread his couplet, he felt two viselike fingers pinching his ears.

No reader will ever guess who had caught the hero of this auto-biography publicly desecrating the Sabbath. Naturally, none other than Uncle Pinny. Of all people, it was *he* who had to be the first to rise from his afternoon nap and go out to visit neighbors and say "Gut Shabbes." What happened subsequently is irrelevant. It's not hard to imagine that nothing helped—not pleading, not tears; Uncle Pinny took the boy, dusty with chalk, and led him home straight into his father's hands.

But that was nothing compared to what happened later when the entire town learned the news. Report of it even reached the admin-istration of the district school, and Sholom was almost expelled.* Father wept and had to go to the principal to plead for mercy. Since Sholom was a prizewinner and a top student, the principal obliged Father, commiserated with him, and did not expel Sholom. But later the teachers crowned him with a new name. When he was summoned to the blackboard, he was no longer called Rabinowitz. Now they called him either "artist" or "author," which they stretched into two mile-long syllables: "Au-thor!"

---

*He had previously been excused from attending school on the Sabbath, mainly because of the prohibition against writing on that day. [C.L.]

That name remained with him for a long time; in fact, for the rest of his life.

53. Among Cantors and Musicians

A Yiddish Book That Prompted Laughter—Cantors and Choristers—Joshua Heshel the Klezmer and His Band—Longing for a Fiddle

 Sholom had always had a penchant for writing. His goal was to write, not with chalk on walls, but to be a real writer, the author of a book. His old friend the lottery agent had predicted that Sholom would become a writer and write Hebrew like Zederbaum, Gottlober, Yehalel and other great figures in Hebrew literature. Then Arnold of Pidvorke said just the opposite.

"If this rascal ever writes, he'll be better off as a Russian, not a Hebrew writer. There are enough dilettantes, intrigants, teachers and do-nothings besides me writing for *Ha-Melitz*. Don't take Zederbaum, Gottlober and Yehalel as models, but Turgenev, Gogol, Pushkin and Lermontov."

In a word, choose either Hebrew or Russian. But no one even dreamed that someday the rascal would write in Yiddish. For was Yiddish also a language? Of course, they spoke no other language but Yiddish. But who knew that one could *write* in Yiddish? The Yiddish jargon, why that was something for the women! A man was ashamed to be seen holding a Yiddish book lest people consider him a boor.

Nevertheless, Sholom remembered an incident from his childhood. In Voronko, that tiny village off the beaten track, one little Yiddish book had a great success. Sholom recalled only that it was a slim booklet without a title page, with yellow, greasy, torn and tattered pages. On Saturday night, all the householders gathered at Reb Nochem Vevik's house for the post-Sabbath festivity. While Mother was busy in the kitchen preparing the beet borscht, the guests were amusing themselves. Father read aloud from a book of stories, and the guests sat around the table, smoking and laughing hysterically. They kept interjecting remarks to express their approval, and good-humoredly directed verbal abuse at the author. "What a devil! A cardsharp! Clever bastard! May an ill wind take his father's father!"

Even the reader himself couldn't contain himself and nearly choked with laughter. The children didn't want to go to sleep, and certainly not Sholom. He didn't understand a word, but liked seeing bearded Jews shaking with laughter, holding their sides, exploding with mirth. He sat on the sofa, saw everyone's beaming face, and envied the man who wrote that little book. His profoundest wish was that, God willing, when he grew up and became an adult, he too would write a book that would make Jews laugh and good-naturedly curse the author: "May an ill wind take his father's father . . ."

But writer or not, Hebrew or Russian, one thing was clear—he would definitely be educated. No two ways about it. He wanted to be an expert. He wanted to know everything. Even to play the violin. What connection, you may ask, was there between fiddling and knowledge? Well, there was a connection. In those days the violin played an honorable role in the program of knowledge. Along with other subjects it was part of one's education, like German or French for a child of a good family. No one expected any practical benefit from it, but if you came from a good home and wanted to be proficient, you had to know everything. Almost all the finest boys in town studied violin. Chaim Fruchstein, Tsali Merpert, Motl Sribne and many others played the violin. Was Sholom Rabinowitz any worse than they? But Father refused. He didn't like the idea. "It's not necessary," he said. "It's a waste of time. It smacks of being a klezmer at a wedding. Mathematics, geography, languages are something substantial. But scraping away at a fiddle—what kind of job is that?"

So thought Nochem Rabinowitz; from his point of view he was justified. But listen to the view of Joshua Heshel the Klezmer, a gentle man with two thick earlocks.

"What's one thing got to do with another? I also have children, no worse than any other Jewish children, and they're also wild rascals, and the devil hasn't taken them. But so what? Don't you think these rascals know how to play all the instruments?"

And what did Ben-Zion the Klezmer say? Ben-Zion, who taught all the boys in town violin, was a man with a flat nose, which accounted for his nasal twang. He tested Nochem Rabinowitz's boy, taught him the first two lessons of Bériot's *Music Guide,* and immediately asserted in his nasal way that Sholom was "falented."

Sholom couldn't tell if he really had talent. He only knew that since childhood he'd been dying to play the violin. Ironically, he always found himself in the world of music, in the company of cantors and musicians.

Cantors and choristers were almost always in their house, for Nochem Rabinowitz himself led services and had a good voice. Moreover, cantors hardly stayed anywhere else. On a Sabbath when the New Moon prayers were recited, a wagon would usually arrive on Friday afternoon packed with a strange bunch of blithe, high-spirited characters, all of them hungry. More often than not they would be tattered and raggedy, almost naked and barefoot, yet their necks were wrapped with warm woolen scarves. They attacked the inn like a swarm of locusts and ate everything in sight. It was axiomatic—if hungry people were present, they were no doubt choristers and a world-famous cantor. For days on end the cantor trilled and warbled, tested his coloratura, drank raw eggs. But the choirboys' shrieks made you climb the walls. They mostly had weak voices—but great appetites. Their singing didn't meet with much public approval, but they ate and drank their fill and left without paying.

Naturally, this rubbed Stepmother the wrong way, and gradually she got rid of the world-famous cantors. "Why don't you check in to Reuben Yasnegradsky's place? We have enough freeloaders of our own here, and plenty of screechers too."

The upshot was that Nochem Rabinowitz's children heard so much music that they knew which cantor specialized in which prayer, whether Pitzi the Cantor or Mitzi the Cantor, the cantor from Shedlitz, the one from Kavalarye, or Cantor Nissi Belzer. There were times when tunes just flew in the air of their own accord, when thoughts spun in Sholom's head and a haunting melody didn't let him sleep.

So much for singing. As for music, Sholom had even more opportunities of hearing klezmers, for both Joshua Heshel with the thick earlocks and flat-nosed Ben-Zion lived near the cheder. On their way to school the children had to pass Joshua Heshel's and Ben-Zion's houses. Well, actually, they didn't *have* to. They could easily have avoided them, and thereby shortened the walk. But Sholom loved passing by their places and standing under the windows and listening to Ben-Zion the Klezmer giving the children violin lessons, or hearing Joshua Heshel rehearse with his sons, who played various instruments. Wild horses couldn't have dragged him away.

Joshua Heshel's sons noticed Sholom. Once, Hemeleh, the elder boy, hit him with a baton. Another time they drenched Sholom with a pitcher of water. But to no avail. Then Sholom gave Hemeleh a cigarette—and a friendship was formed. Sholom became a frequent visitor at Joshua Heshel's house, where band rehearsals were held every Monday and Thursday. Sholom didn't miss one of them. Through Joshua Heshel's family he got to know all the musicians, their families, their wives and children, their customs and habits, their artistic-gypsy way of life, even their special klezmer lingo. Later, as Sholom Aleichem, he used this jargon in stories like "On the Fiddle" and in *Stempenyu, Wandering Star* and other novels.

So, as you see, no one stood in the way of Sholom's learning the violin. He had heard lots of music, and Ben-Zion asserted that he had talent. So what was missing? An instrument—a violin. But a violin cost money, which Sholom didn't have. The next step, then, was to find some money. But in the course of this search something happened. Comic, yet sad. A kind of tragicomedy.

54. *Thou Shalt Not Steal*

The Guest's Purse—The Deed and Regrets—
How to Get Rid of It

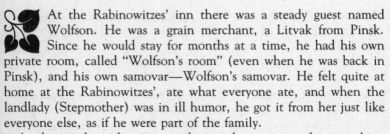 At the Rabinowitzes' inn there was a steady guest named Wolfson. He was a grain merchant, a Litvak from Pinsk. Since he would stay for months at a time, he had his own private room, called "Wolfson's room" (even when he was back in Pinsk), and his own samovar—Wolfson's samovar. He felt quite at home at the Rabinowitzes', ate what everyone ate, and when the landlady (Stepmother) was in ill humor, he got it from her just like everyone else, as if he were part of the family.

At the inn he either wore a short jacket or went about in shirt-sleeves, and smoked exceedingly thick cigars. He loved to talk with a cigar in his mouth and his hands in his pockets, chatting away without stop. His room was always open. The samovar stood on the table; the drawer was locked, but the keys hung there. One turn of the key and the drawer would be open. Everyone knew the contents of that drawer. Books, letters, invoices and money. A large, thick wallet stuffed with God knows how many banknotes and an old tattered leather purse full of silver and copper coins. A rather hefty sum. If only a boy like Sholom had half of it, he could have bought the best violin in the world.

Wolfson had often opened that desk drawer in the presence of family members. Unwittingly, Sholom saw that wallet bulging with banknotes and the leather purse filled with coins. Sholom's fondest wish was that Wolfson would someday lose the purse and that he, Sholom, would find it. That would be ideal. Returning a lost object is indeed one of the greatest mitzvas—but owning such a leather purse full of coins was an even greater mitzva. But that Litvak just didn't want to lose his purse. Sholom thought it over and swore that if Wolfson gave him his trousers to clean and forgot his purse there, he'd thumb his nose at him. It wouldn't be Sholom's fault if the purse slipped out during the cleaning. But Wolfson was no fool either. Whenever he gave the children his clothes to clean he would empty all his pockets. Once a Litvak, always a Litvak. This irked Sholom. He decided that if Wolfson neither lost nor forgot the change purse, he'd have a peek to see how much he had.

With this in mind—not to commit theft, God forbid, but just out of curiosity—Sholom sneaked into Wolfson's room one morning, stood around for a while, and pretended to clean the table, while the Litvak stood in the parlor with his thick cigar in his mouth, babbling away. But nothing came of Sholom's lolling about in Wolfson's room. As soon as he touched the cold keys an inner turmoil possessed him. His hands and legs trembled. He turned and left Wolfson's room empty-handed.

After this first unsuccessful attempt Sholom waited for a second opportunity. Meanwhile, he accused himself of being a thief. "You're a thief, Sholom. Even if you had only one bad thought, you're already a thief . . . a thief . . . a thief."

The second opportunity was not long in coming. Wolfson hated to be all by himself in the room. He preferred spending time in the large parlor with the other guests, smoking and talking as usual. Once again Sholom sneaked into Wolfson's room—this time not merely to look but to derive some gain. He was already a thief anyway. Once in the room, he bent over the table as if to take something from the other end. With his left hand Sholom held the cold key and turned it to the right—the lock sprung open with a soft *zzzing* and fell silent. He looked into the drawer and trembled.

First he saw the thick open wallet, overflowing with bills: red ten-ruble notes and yellow one-ruble notes. Who knows how much it added up to? If he slipped just one red bill from the pile, he'd be saved. Who would know? Then take it, dummy! But no. He couldn't. His hands shook, his teeth chattered, he couldn't breathe. He'd be better off looking at the leather purse—it was stuffed with coins. He wanted to take it, but his right hand refused to obey. Opening up the purse and removing some silver coins wouldn't be so bad either—but that was too much work. And if he put the purse in his pocket, the owner would miss it. Meanwhile, time wasn't standing still. The minutes dragged on. Each minute was a year.

Sholom heard shuffling. Aha, the Litvak was coming, dragging his floppy slippers. Sholom turned the key and left the room empty-handed again. He thought he would meet somebody—but no, there was no one. It was too late to go back. He should have done it sooner. What an opportunity missed! "You're an idiot, Sholom. You're a thief *and* an idiot!"

His third chance came later and went off smoothly. He avoided all preludes, didn't loll around, went straight to the table, opened the lock, put his hand into the drawer, took the purse, slipped it into his pocket, closed the drawer, and went to school with his books. He didn't rush, but went slowly, nonchalantly, almost indolently. But as he left the house the purse in his pocket scalded his flesh and he felt that under no circumstances should he keep it with him. Certainly not the first day. So instead of going to school, he slipped into the woodshed and hid the purse in the darkest corner, between the firewood and the wall. To remember the spot he made a sign for himself and then marched off to school.

If you've ever met someone with a flaming face and burning eyes, in a peculiarly heightened mood, someone who is prepared to go through fire and water for you, but is distracted and lost in thought, be aware that this fellow knows something that only he and God know. That's how Sholom looked that morning. He gazed at everyone with a guilty mien. It seemed to him that everyone knew his terrible secret.

His friend Eli, who knew him better than anyone else, asked:

"Sholomontchik! What's with you? Did you make another picture on the fence?"

"Shut your mouth, Elik, because in another minute I'm going to make such a picture on your face you'll forget who you are."

"Oh, really? Just you try. We'll see who will do what to whom."

Eli rolled up his sleeves, ready to demonstrate. But Sholom had no intention of fighting. He thought only of the spot behind the firewood where the purse lay hidden. In his rush he had even forgotten to examine its contents. He could hardly wait for classes to end so he could return home, slip into the shed for a minute, and plainly see how much he was worth.

At home he found the place in an uproar. Everything was upside down. The beds were undone, the kitchen topsy-turvy. The gentile maid was weeping; she swore by all that was holy that she knew nothing about it. Father was beside himself, ashen as clay. Completely bent over. Stepmother seethed, cursed, vituperated. But it was hard to fathom whom she was maledicting, for her curses were in the plural. "Taking something right from under someone's nose, may the devil take you." "A purse has sunk into the earth—may you sink into the earth!" "No one has seen the purse—may no one see you anymore." "Which guest would want to stop at this inn—may your mouths be stopped up!" And Wolfson himself stood there in his short jacket, the fat cigar in his mouth, hands in his pockets, looking at the children and smiling. "I just had it in my hands this morning," he said to himself, "and I didn't leave the house."

"Did you see the purse?" Father asked the children, and Sholom was the first to respond:

"What purse?"

Father, who was rarely angry, could no longer control himself and assailed his darling.

"What purse?" Father mimicked Sholom. "Look at that innocent! All morning long he hears 'purse, purse, purse' and he asks 'What purse?'"

"How much money was in the purse?" Father asked Wolfson.

"It's not the money I'm concerned about," Wolfson replied, "it's the purse itself. I just had it in my hands this morning and I didn't leave the house."

No, now was not the time to find out how much money the purse contained. Sholom was no idiot. Now was the worst possible time to inspect the purse in the woodshed. He wouldn't mind postponing the task a day or two. Meanwhile, he had to study geography and history till he knew them by heart, and complete a few theorems in geometry. Poor, perfectly innocent Sholom. The maid had already been fired. Stepmother was fuming. The entire house was in a dither.

Everyone was looking for the purse and Sholom joined them in the search. As he looked at his father's face, his heart grieved him. He couldn't bear to see him so hunched over and hear his sighs and groans. Now the thief first realized what a despicable deed he had done; he regretted his act and rebuked the evil impulse in him that had persuaded him to commit such a sin and brought him to such a pass.

Every hour felt like a year; the day stretched on forever. He managed to survive till nighttime, when the tumult subsided somewhat and household problems and concerns about livelihood temporarily diverted attention from the theft. Then the little thief slipped into the yard, went to the woodshed, slowly lowered himself to the ground, and removed the purse from behind the firewood. He opened it, looked inside—and found an old, worn-smooth coin which had been worth ten kopecks ages ago but was worthless now because no one accepted it as legal tender. And the purse itself had no value either. It was ugly and had a faulty latch; the leather was frayed and greasy, wrinkled at the edges, and yellow like an old grandmother's skin. Even holding such a purse was disgusting. For such a foul thing was it worth breaking one of the Ten Commandments, "Thou shalt not steal"?

When he returned, Stepmother asked him to bring the samovar to Wolfson's rooms. Each time Sholom brought it to him Wolfson would rub his hands and say in rhyme: "Oh, a samovar for me, now let's have a glass of tea!" This time, however, he added: "Well, what's new? Purse hasn't been found yet?" While saying this he looked right at Sholom, who sensed the subtle irony of Wolfson's words and glance.

But perhaps Sholom only imagined it. There's a proverb that says: "The cat knows whose cream she licked." And another: "A guilty heart is never at ease."

In any case, the thief hated Wolfson from that moment on: he couldn't stand looking at his Litvak face and listening to his Litvak lingo. In his heart Sholom cursed both the Litvak and his purse. But what to do with the accursed purse? Leaving it in its hiding place wasn't a good idea—someone might find it in the woodpile. If they hadn't fired the maid so quickly he could have quietly returned the purse. But with the maid driven away, the suspicion could fall on the children. Bad business!

At night it took Sholom a long time to fall asleep. It was all a bad dream. Was it really true? Was he really a thief? A common thief? He began to perspire. How low he had sunk! What would he do now? But soon he fell asleep and dreamed of purses. They weren't purses but living creatures, ugly, frayed, yellow and wrinkled, cold and damp, like insects, like frogs. They crawled all over his body, crept under his collar and into his armpits . . . Brrr!

He woke, looked under the blanket, touched his body—thank God it was only a dream. Still, how to get rid of the purse? The only solution was to chuck it where it would never be found. But where? Into the garden of the gentile neighbor? Deep in the cemetery? In the women's gallery of the shul? No, best to drop it into the river from the bridge. And the best time was Sabbath. That's what he decided to do.

Sabbath afternoon. End of summer. It was still warm outside. Jewish children walked around lightly dressed. Young girls still sported parasols. Among the strollers was Sholom, carrying the purse. It was hidden deep in his pocket and filled with pebbles so it would sink quickly. The only trouble was that the bridge was crowded—and he didn't want anyone to see. How then should he accomplish this? He paced back and forth and looked everyone in the eye. He could have sworn that everyone was staring knowingly at him. But perhaps he only imagined it. The same old story. A guilty heart is never at ease.

With God's help, the coast became clear. Sholom hid in a corner, behind a post of the bridge. He bent all the way over the guardrail and pretended to be fascinated by something in the water. He put his hand in the pocket where the damned purse lay, and felt something disgusting—a living thing, a snake. Slowly he took it out of his pocket, spread his fingers and let it go. Splash—no more purse. A circle formed where the purse fell. The round ripples grew wider. More concentric circles formed. Sholom could not tear his eyes away from the spot where his sin was drowned and his secret buried forever. But a pleasant voice broke his reverie; a sweet laughter echoed in his ears.

"Watching the fish? Ha, ha! What are you standing here and staring at?"

Sholom turned and saw the cantor's daughter and her girlfriend.

"Have you been here a long time?" Sholom asked the two girls.

"All the time, ha, ha!" They laughed. They considered it funny, but he was crushed, for they may have witnessed his deed.

Silly boy. His fears were in vain. A different kind of anguish awaited him, one totally unanticipated. He was fated to experience, as we shall soon see, a new drama, entitled "The Cantor's Daughter."

55. *The Cantor's Daughter*

Tsali the Cantor's Daughter—Passionate Love—An Exchange of Letters—Where His Letter Landed

The role played by gymnasium and university students in a big city was played by district school pupils in a small town. The only thing they lacked was a uniform. Otherwise they were considered celebrities, heroes in the full sense of the word. Everything forbidden to a plain cheder boy was allowed to them. For instance, it was all right to pull a prank on the shamesh in shul, bathe in the river beyond the bounds of the bathhouse, have fun with anyone their hearts desired, and even chat with a girl—as long as she came from a good family.

Girls went wild over the students. Nevertheless, I must add a caveat and say I'm not talking about flirting or romances. These contacts were on the purest and highest level, possible only between young children of both sexes. It's no exaggeration to say that the relations between angels couldn't have been more chaste and innocent than the relationship between the cantor's daughter and the young hero of this autobiography.

Sholom can't quite recall where, when and how they first met—and it's not that important. There was only one time and one place to meet: Sabbath afternoon at the Pidvorke bridge. Who spoke first and what they discussed is another conundrum. No doubt it began with a penetrating glance. Then came a smile. Then an accidentally-on-purpose touch of the elbows. Then a raised cap and "Good morning." Then a greeting sans the cap ploy. At subsequent encounters they would stop to chat for a few minutes about things in general, which led to plans for the next meeting.

He: Well, see you.
She: When? Next Sabbath?
He: When then, if not on Sabbath?

She: Where? On the bridge again?

He: Where else?

She: How about someplace else?

He: For instance?

She: Where will you be Simchas Torah for the Hakofes?

He: What do you mean where? At the Big Shul.

She: Why not the Cold Shul?

He: You mean where your father prays?

She: What's the difference?

He: My father will realize where I am.

She: Well, if you're a little kid who's afraid of his papa . . .

But he didn't let her finish, for her remark stung him to the quick. What? Someone was telling him that he was a little kid who's afraid of his papa? And who was saying this to him? But like a demon he found a way of twisting out of the situation. He said he had to tell her something important, but since she wasn't alone, but with a girlfriend, he couldn't tell her. The cantor's daughter blushed and winked to her girlfriend to move away for a while. Her friend obeyed and the two remained alone. The cantor's daughter was ready to hear the secret, and he began at once:

"I've wanted to tell you for a long time that," he stammered, "that I'd like to see you alone for once, without escorts and without girlfriends around."

"And don't you think I'd like to talk to you alone, without escorts and girlfriends? But I can't. They don't let me go by myself. My mother sees to it that I'm never alone. But don't be afraid of my girlfriend. She's a quiet, sincere girl and she also likes to talk to a boy. And if you want to know, she's also in love."

"Also in love? That means that you're in love too. Who's the lucky fellow?"

"People who know everything get old quickly."

Well, was any further commentary needed? Wasn't it obvious that this lucky fellow was none other than Sholom? And if there was the slightest doubt, just look at her beaming face and happy, radiant eyes. A familiar face. Familiar eyes. Where had he seen this pale face and blond, curly hair? Even her hand was familiar. A white hand with long, slim fingers. A smooth, warm, white hand. The first time in his life that he held a girl's hand.

Like a pious Jew who awaits the Messiah, Sholom looked forward to the happy holiday of Simchas Torah. But time dragged on too slowly. The days stretched like tar. He almost went mad. Without knowing why, he decided to pour out his heart in a letter. He spent one day and one night writing it. The words flowed like unimpeded water, like a fountain with all the taps open. Had he not run out of paper he never would have stopped. As poor as the author is, he would pay a fortune today for that letter.

Now only one thing remained. How to get it to her. How would she get the letter? There was only one solution: to send it to her via her girlfriend. Which meant making a third person a party to the secret, trusting a complete stranger. Perhaps this wouldn't be so bad either, but there was still a hitch: how to get to that third party. Easy. A fourth person would have to be dragged into the affair. The boy with whom the cantor's daughter's girlfriend was in love. Two young men—why this was another matter entirely! Two young men could talk without being disturbed and could settle the most secret matters between themselves. One small detail remained—to find that fellow and seal a fraternal bond. That seemed simple enough. But things are never as easy as they seem.

The young man, a clerk in a hardware store, was quite good-looking, but he had a pair of hands that could better be termed "paws." Approaching him almost caused a scandal. The store owner, a woman wrapped in furs despite the warm weather, had black hands and a sooty nose (she weighed out buckshot and nails and blew her nose with her dirty hands). That her clerk knew Rabinowitz's boy troubled her. What kind of business could a mere shop assistant have with Red Nochem Rabinowitz's son? That was number one. Secondly, when Sholom told the clerk he wanted to ask a favor of his fiancée, he got on his high horse. He looked like a rooster about to spring at a cat in a chicken coop.

"Who told you I have a fiancée?"

"I know her girlfriend."

"The cantor's daughter? Uh-oh! A bonebreaker!"

Sholom didn't understand the term. But judging by the fellow's smirk, he guessed that it wasn't a bundle of joy.

"Who's the bonebreaker?" Sholom asked.

"That's my business. But let's hear the favor."

Sholom took out the long letter from his pocket and gave it to the clerk.

"Please tell your fiancée to give this to the cantor's daughter and to send me an answer through you."

The clerk took it and inspected the envelope from all sides.

"Is that all? Come tomorrow and you'll probably have an answer."

A stone fell from Sholom's heart. The next day the clerk told him there was no answer. The same thing the day after: no answer as yet. Perhaps Sholom only imagined it, but the clerk seemed to smile slyly. His suspicion grew when the clerk sighed:

"Oh, if I could only write like you!"

"How do you know how I write?"

"My fiancée told me."

"How does your fiancée know?"

"From the cantor's daughter."

The explanation wasn't that preposterous, and Sholom enjoyed the compliment from the girl he loved. Nevertheless, doubts crept in of their own accord. The thought that the clerk hadn't delivered the letter but read it himself kept Sholom awake all night. He waited impatiently for an answer. It finally came on the eve of the holiday. The clerk ran toward him and gave him a folded yellow note, without an envelope, but sealed with coin-impressed wax. The long-awaited letter from the cantor's daughter was written with long, thin characters, which reminded Sholom of her long, thin fingers.

"I read the letter a few times with tears in my eyes," she wrote. "And I'm sorry I can't write like you. If I had wings I'd fly to you. If I could swim, I'd swim all the seas to come to you. If you think I sleep well, you're mistaken. I can't wait for Simchas Torah, because one heart is sensitive to another." Her note ended with a warning not to send any more letters through intermediaries for she was certain that others have seen it. At that point the clerk's big paws swam before Sholom's eyes. Hot and cold flushes swept over him as he pictured the clerk opening his envelope and reading the letter in which he had poured out his heart to the cantor's daughter. But his distress was short-lived, for soon it would be Simchas Torah, and soon he'd see, stand next to, and talk to the cantor's daughter.

56. The Simchas Torah Hakofes

*The Night of Simchas Torah—Poetry—Jews Dance—Women and Girls
Kiss the Torah—The Heavens Open and the Angels Sing*

If I were Goethe, I swear I wouldn't have depicted the sorrows of young Werther; I'd have depicted the anguish of a poor youth who was madly in love with a cantor's daughter. If I were Heine, I swear I wouldn't have written odes about Florentine nights; I'd have sung the praises of Simchas Torah night when Jews dance with the Torah, and women and pretty girls gather in shul and mix with the men—on Simchas Torah it's allowed. They kiss the Torah, jump up and down, and shriek, "May you live to next year!" To which the response is: "The same to you! The same to you!"

An hour or two before Hakofes the little boys and girls assembled and climbed up on the benches. They held flags with apples and lit candles. The flags fluttered, the apples were red, the candles glowed. The children's cheeks were as red as the apples, and their eyes glowed no less than the candles. The older boys, the ones who studied Talmud or were enrolled in the district school, wandered around the synagogue courtyard. The air was still mild and clear. Stars filled the sky. The whole world was festive—even the silence. Nothing could possibly mar the holiness of this Simchas Torah night when the Chosen People all over the world rejoice in their divine gift. So who cared if a gentile wagon passed by and raised a thick, smelly cloud of dust; or if a post chaise with an official inside flew by with its bells tinkling? The dust would settle, the sound of the bell would fade—and the night would remain holy and festive, for it's Simchas Torah all over the world.

A black cat scampered by with its velvet-smooth gait. It cut through the entire length of the synagogue courtyard and disappeared. In some distant gentile street a dog howled in a minor key and fell silent—and the night remained holy and festive, for it's Simchas Torah all over the world. Sholom breathed deeply. He was in high spirits; he felt grand. Proud. It's no trifle, he thought. Here I am, and it's the night of Simchas Torah. There's the sky, and there is God. My God! My sky! My holiday!

"Children! The Hakofes are starting."

They dashed into the Cold Shul, but nothing doing! False alarm. They were still saying the Evening Service. Tsali the Cantor was at the prayer stand, assisted by his two choirboys. One was a thick-lipped, swarthy fellow, a bass. The other was a pale-faced, emaciated youngster, a soprano. Reb Tsali, the cantor with the golden voice, was a tall, yellow-haired man with a nose like a shofar, thin curly earlocks, and a yellow curly beard that looked pasted on. It was incredible that such a freak could have spawned such a dear, tender gentle, lovely daughter.

The cantor's daughter was *his* daughter. Tsali the cantor was *her* father. He bragged to everyone that there was only one girl in the world like his daughter. Her only fault was—she didn't want to get married.

"No matter who you suggest as a possible match, she says no. But it'll do her as much good as cupping a dead man. When the right match comes along, she'll have to say yes. If not, we'll pull her by her braids. And if need be, there's also the cane," said Tsali in jest, lifting his bamboo cane with its yellowed ivory knob.

The Evening Service was over in the Cold Shul and Hakofes were still a long way off. First they chanted Ato Horeyso. The verses of the poem were assigned, one by one, to the prominent men who sat at the eastern wall. When each man's turn came, he stood and sang his lines. Although the melody is universally known, since everyone's voice and timbre were different, and everyone was apprehensive of his own voice, the tune didn't come out quite right and the little melodic curlicue at the end of the verse was entirely lost.

The Cold Shul was large, wide and spacious. It had no ceiling, only a roof. That's why it was called the Cold Shul. The roof was painted the color of the sky, a blue that was almost green. The painter had overshot his mark. The sparkling stars were too big. Each star was smaller than an apple, and looked like a gilded potato. The potatoes—that is, the stars—were not placed helter-skelter like stars in the sky, but were set in neat dense rows. Ancient brass chandeliers with the yellow-green patina of age hung on long brass chains from the center of the roof. The lamps on the walls were made of the same old green brass—all filled with burning candles. The shul, Sholom felt, was as bright as could be.

Where did so many men and women, youths and girls and little children come from? This was Sholom's first visit to the Cold Shul. He thought of the Biblical verse: "How goodly are your tents, O

Jacob." It wasn't easy to find a seat. Luckily, the shamesh recognized him. Since he was Reb Nochem Rabinowitz's son, a place had to be found for him, in the first row to be sure, among the prominent townsmen.

Which prayer were they up to? The noise and tumult were so great that neither the cantor nor the choirboys could be heard. In vain were the shouts of "Sha!" The shamesh's banging on the lectern did not help. Young women chattered, girls giggled, children whined. Sholom noticed a little boy with tears in his eyes. "Why are you crying, sonny?" Someone had accidentally knocked the apple off his flag and crunched it underfoot. What would he do now without an apple? he cried. Next to him sat a fellow with teeth bared, laughing at the youngster's misfortune.

"What are you laughing at?" Sholom asked, irritated.

"He's a dope!" The fellow continued grinning.

This vexed Sholom even more. "Were you any smarter when you were his age?"

Now the fellow stopped laughing and answered like a fresh brat.

"I don't remember how smart I was when I was his age, but I know for sure that I've got more wits in my left heel that you have in your entire head, even though you're at the district school and are Nochem Rabinowitz's son."

If this scene hadn't taken place in the Cold Shul among people he didn't know, Nochem Rabinowitz's son would have settled accounts with that fellow in a different manner. But he had to keep silent, for in a minute he could have been beaten up by that impudent lout. Anyway, amid the din Sholom heard the dear words summoning the worshipers to the Hakofes: "The scholar Reb Samson Zev, son of Reb Chaim Zvi the Kohen, give honor to the Torah." "The scholar Reb Moshe Yaakov, son of Reb Nachman Dov the Levite, give honor to the Torah." The Hakofes had evidently begun. Where was the cantor's daughter?

"O Lord, save us!" The first Hakofeh had ended with the merry tune of "Heyda!" and a dance. Again, the shamesh called out in his hoarse voice and summoned other men to carry the Torah around the shul for the second Hakofeh. And so the second, the third, the fourth Hakofeh were completed. The same melody and the same dance followed each Hakofeh. And the cantor's daughter was nowhere to be seen.

Sholom anxiously looked around. Perhaps she would still show up. But she wasn't there. Neither she nor her girlfriend. Could she have fooled him? Or perhaps she couldn't come. Maybe something had happened to her. Perhaps someone had found out about their tryst and locked her in the house. With Tsali the Cantor, a man who pulls braids and beats with a cane, anything was possible. Sholom's dark and gloomy thoughts knew no bounds.

Evidently the shamesh thought that since Nochem Rabinowitz's son was pacing back and forth, looking around, unable to sit still, he was dying for a Hakofeh. And perhaps one of the trustees had winked to the shamesh to honor Nochem Rabinowitz's boy with a Hakofeh. In any case, he suddenly heard his name: "Sholom, son of Reb Nochem, give honor to the Torah."

He blushed furiously. He couldn't abide the householders' looks. He felt like every boy who is called to read Maftir. And before he had a chance to collect himself, the shamesh gave him a large Torah, which he held in his arms as he stood in a line of men. The procession was moving, led by the cantor who sang, "Helper of the Poor, save us!" Women and girls pushed forward to kiss the Torah and wish Sholom long life. He felt bewildered by the unexpected honor, and proud that he was the only youth among so many adults—chosen because he wasn't just anybody, but was Reb Nochem Rabinowitz's son, a child of a good family. Then in the tumult he felt a kiss on his hand. "May you live till next year!" He raised his eyes and saw— it was she, the cantor's daughter, with her girlfriend at her side. Naturally.

The heavens opened and angels descended, singing songs of praise. They praised the world that God rules—such a good, sweet, beautiful, precious world. They celebrated the people God had created— such good, sweet, beautiful, precious people. Everything was so good, Sholom wanted to cry. And within him his heart sang to the angels: "Welcome to you, ministering angels."

Indeed, at first he felt embarrassed and ecstatic. Instead of kissing the Torah she had kissed his hand. Was it an accident? No, he saw by her smiling eyes that she hadn't done it accidentally. He was so surprised he almost dropped the Torah. He wanted to stop again and look into her beautiful eyes just to say a couple of words. But he couldn't. The men following him didn't let him stop. The Torahs had to be given to others. The Hakofes weren't over yet. When he handed the Torah back to the shamesh by the Holy Ark, Sholom turned, hoping to see the cantor's daughter again, if only from afar.

But he couldn't find her. He followed the next Hakofeh procession looking for her. But she had disappeared. He searched in the synagogue courtyard—she was nowhere around. Could it have been a dream? Perhaps he had imagined it. He still felt the kiss of her lips on his hands. He continued walking, oblivious to the ground beneath his feet. He had wings, it seemed, and was flying, soaring. The angels soared with him, carried him aloft, and escorted him to the Big Shul.

There the Hakofes were still under way. Father was in a rare good mood, in festive spirits. He looked splendid, handsomer than ever in his split silk gaberdine, whose yellow underlining showed through like spots. The two accomplished sons-in-law, Lazer Yossel and Magidov, stood next to him. Both were joking, and Father, as usual, listened and laughed.

"Why so late?" Father asked Sholom, not to rebuke him, God forbid, but out of curiosity.

"I was in the Cold Shul," Sholom replied. "They honored me with a Hakofeh there," he added proudly.

"Very nice of them," Father said, pleased.

The sons-in-law teased Rabinowitz's son.

"Did you meet the Helper of the Poor in the Cold Shul?" Lazer Yossel asked.

"What do you mean?" said Magidov. "Helper of the Poor in *that* place? More likely his grandson."

All three laughed and Sholom joined in the mirth. What a night it was! Such a night can only come on Simchas Torah at Hakofes.

57. *The Crisis*

Typhus—Reborn—Good-bye, Childhood

Whenever the author of this autobiography descends to the deep catacombs of his distant childhood, brings forth memories of bygone periods, delves into his later experiences, and considers all this soberly and judiciously, he marvels at his ability to survive so many merciless beatings, cruel deceptions and bitter disappointments—and still remain hale and hearty for fresh beatings, further deceptions and even greater disappointments. The blows themselves weren't as terrible as the disappointments and deceptions.

You can recover from a beating, but a disappointment leaves a scar in the soul forever.

Sholom had experienced spiritual disappointments and financial deceptions. As will be shown in future chapters, he knew how it felt to lose a fortune quickly per the advice of all kinds of Menachem Mendels. He can say with a clear conscience that he was less shaken by the monetary loss than by other people's deceit and by his loss of trust in others. The disappointment is what always embittered him and drove him to the grave.

Even in that period, when he was still a little pipsqueak and had made a fool of himself falling in love with the cantor's daughter, he already got his first taste of terrible disappointment. It was a blow that neither he nor anyone else had expected. One might have assumed, for instance, that the girl's parents would learn about the clumsy romance and break up the silly match. One might have expected Tsali the Cantor to take his daughter by the pigtails or give her a good caning. But who would have guessed that while the cantor's daughter was flirting with Sholom, she was in love with a goy, a clerk in Kotyelnikov's big hardware store, and that one Saturday night, not long after that Simchas Torah night, she would run away, enter the women's wing of the monastery, live with the nuns, and then convert and marry that clerk?

No writer's fantasy can imagine what life itself dreams up. Of course, Tsali the Cantor ran around, knocked on doors, spoke to influential people, was admitted into the monastery offices to see the abbess, and even spoke to the provincial governor himself—but nothing helped. The town was seething like a cauldron. The entire community was in an uproar. Had it just been a plain Jewish girl— well, what can you do? It's a tragedy! But it had to happen to a cantor, a religious functionary. Who would now let him officiate at prayers? But then the question arose—how would he earn his bread? Let's not even mention the humiliation of the Jews of the Cold Shul! Why did it have to happen to the cantor of *their* synagogue?

But all this trouble, humiliation and anguish could not be compared to the hell that was racking the soul of the lad who was madly in love with the cantor's daughter. She had so miserably deceived him, and exchanged him, a boy from a fine family, for a goy, a hardware store clerk. Why had she fooled an innocent boy, written him such letters, kissed his hand on the night of Simchas Torah at Hakofes, and sworn eternal love and other such things? She hadn't run off with the clerk because of a sudden, head-over-heels love affair. It had been planned well before. Sholom remembered that her girlfriend's fiancé, the one with the big paws, had once told him that the cantor's daughter was a "bonebreaker." Now he understood. And that drove him into such a fury that he began to revile himself. He cursed the day he first met her. He cursed the clerk with the big paws, and Kotyelnikov's clerk, and all the clerks the world over. Oh, how wonderful it would be if all the hardware stores in town burned down. Or if a hurricane swept away all the shops and houses. Or if the earth split open and swallowed all of Pereyaslav, the bridge and Pidvorke, like Korah. He didn't have an ounce of compassion for his own family, for strangers, for old people, for children or infants—every single one of them could go to the blazes! He cursed the world that God had created—it was a false, disgusting, loathsome world. And he cursed the people that God had created—they were false, disgusting, loathsome people.

Immersed in such misanthropic thoughts, Sholom returned home from school one day and felt that his head was heavy as lead. He saw spinning circles and odd shapes. The circles grew, the shapes melted like snow in the sun, and other shapes took their place. He refused to eat supper.

"Big deal! A bear croaked in the woods!" said Stepmother with her usual venom.

But Sholom couldn't stand on his legs. He lay down on the sofa. Father approached and felt his forehead. He asked him something and Sholom replied. But he didn't hear the question or recall his response. He just didn't remember. He thought he heard them say "stomach," "doctor," "pharmacy." Then he was given a teaspoon of something bitter as almonds. And his head—oh, his head! Round lumps appeared before his eyes and came out of his ears with a long, whistling sound. Like little ants, they burrowed beneath his skin into his veins. They tickled and hissed and bubbled inside his body. Purses, innumerable purses rolled down a hill. People wanted to catch these purses but could not . . .

But most amazing was that he saw everything though his eyes were closed. He couldn't hear because of the whistling in his ears, but he could see everyone. Everyone was here. A mishmash of long-gone chums and current friends. Others too. His old chum Shmulik, Pinneleh Shimmeleh's, Eli Dodi's, Uncle Pinny's son Itzl, the guest Wolfson . . . Most extraordinary was Kotyelnikov's clerk leading prayers and singing Ato Horeyso while the cantor's daughter was beating her breast and reciting, "For the sins we have committed." And then the hollow sounds of voices came out of the Cold Shul. Strange, whining sounds, accompanied by sobs—the dead praying. They prayed every Saturday night in the Cold Shul. They prayed with a minyan. Who didn't know that? Nothing amazed him, not even the gentile clerk singing Ato Horeyso in the traditional melody. But one thing puzzled Sholom. How was it possible that his chum Shmulik the Orphan had just been here and didn't ask about the treasure? How could he have forgotten such an important thing? Sholom opened his eyes to look for Shmulik but couldn't find him. Neither Shmulik nor anyone else who had just been there. Where had they all gone? Sholom closed his eyes again and listened to his heart beating and his temples pounding. He felt he was soaked in perspiration, swimming in a river of sweat. His fingertips were swollen, like after a steambath. His hair was wet and stuck to his forehead. He felt a cold hand on his. Heard a familiar sigh. He opened his eyes—it was Father. Next to him stood Wolfson, the lottery agent with the dark glasses, and many others. Everyone looked at him with compassion. He heard and realized that people were talking about him. "The crisis," he heard them saying, but didn't know what "crisis." And he was delighted that he had become so important, that everyone was so concerned about him. Most of all Father. He bent over Sholom and asked, "What would you like to have?" But Sholom didn't reply at once. First he wanted to orient himself and know what was happening with him. A few minutes later he got his bearings and knew where he was. He had been ill, evidently very ill, and now he felt better. Better? Excellent! When he understood almost everything, he licked his dry lips and said one word, and one word only:

"Gooseberries!"

Father exchanged glances with the others who surrounded the sick boy and asked him:

"Gooseberries? What gooseberries?"

"Preserves!" the sick lad said with a strangely gruff voice, which began thin as a soprano but ended with a bass. The sound of his own voice scared him. During his illness he had changed so much that when he got out of bed a couple of weeks later and dragged his feet to the parlor to look at the mirror he hardly recognized himself. Another person stood there. Previously he had been a little boy with big red cheeks, sprightly, lively, with smiling eyes, his hair trimmed, and with a curly shock of blond hair hanging over his forehead. Now his face had paled, his cheeks were sunken, his eyes larger and pensive. He also had grown taller. His blond curly hair had been cut to the scalp, like a Tartar's. He had changed completely.

But not only had his outward appearance changed. He had become entirely different. He had experienced a crisis deep within his soul. And he regretted his foolish, naive past, which would never return and which he would never, ever relive. And even now, recalling those happy years and moving on to other periods, he looked back with gentle longing and bade farewell forever to the beautiful years of his boyhood.

"Farewell, childhood!"

BOOK THREE

58. Sholom Gives Private Lessons

*The Meaning of "Giving Private Lessons"—Young and Old Teachers—
The Power of "Grammar"—People Use Pull—In the Pereyaslav
Municipal Park—At Stepmother's House—The Lottery Agent's
Compromise—Sholom Gets a Job and Packs His Books*

I don't know who first suggested that a youth not quite
seventeen, with no trace of a mustache, who hadn't even
completed his studies at the district school, should take cane
in hand, drape his jacket capelike over his shoulders, and march from
house to house giving private lessons. That meant instructing young
boys and girls in all the subjects offered at school, and preparing
them within a prescribed time for external exams or for admission
to school.

Taking examinations had recently become fashionable. *Everyone*
was preparing for them. Boys and girls, engaged youths, young householders, and mature, bearded men suddenly glued themselves to
Govorov's *Grammar*, Yevtushevsky's *Arithmetic*, Smirnov's *Geography* and Disterveg's *Geometry*; they began to learn Krylov's *Fables*
by heart and to study the dictionary. Exams became a kind of epidemic! Naturally, there were not enough teachers in town to handle
this epidemic. In fact, all told there were two professional Jewish
teachers: old Monisov, who had no teeth, spat when he spoke and,
what's more, was as deaf as a stone; and young Noah Bussel, who
taught French, wore a blue uniform and shiny boots, and charged
exorbitant rates.

There were also Itzi the scribe and his brother Abraham the
scribe—both well-dressed little men with red apple cheeks. Their
fees were low enough, but they waged undeclared war on Russian
grammar. Proper Russian spelling was a mystery to them. For instance, when it came to writing either "susha" (drought) or "Sasha"

(a nickname for Alexander), they mixed up the *s* and *sh* and created half a dozen combinations. A story made the rounds in town that someone had asked the two brothers to write the following sentence in Russian: "Sasha dried himself in a drought"—and they came up with two different Russian sentences.

True, this was only an anecdote, but how it mortified the poor souls when they heard it. It was exasperating. The brothers couldn't believe it. They had taught an entire town to write, children and children's children, and now young whippersnappers whose milk wasn't dry on their lips were spreading funny stories. But jokes aside, grammar was a current item. Without grammar, one could not budge. Things came to the point where even Uncle Pinny, who hated secular studies like a kosher Jew hates pork, conceded that grammar was useful. He was a man who did business at fairs, traded with Moscow, was esteemed by the gentiles, and spoke an excellent Russian. "But my grammar is poor," he said, pressing his five fingers together as he said the word.

Nevertheless, to bring his nephew Sholom down from his high horse, Uncle Pinny felt it necessary to add:

"But I still can't see why one has to go bareheaded, eat without washing, and write on the Sabbath. I would think it would be perfectly possible to know grammar *and* wear a hat and wash and make a blessing before eating and not write on the Sabbath!"

Like a true scholar, Uncle Pinny was apparently a vengeful man. He could not forget Sholom's youthful sin of writing on a wooden fence on a Sabbath long ago. But Sholom paid no attention to him. He was on a scholarship; he gave private lessons and earned money. People were tearing him to pieces; they were coming to blows over him. They wanted Sholom, and only Sholom, to prepare their children for the gymnasium. No one else would do! So how could he *not* be on his high horse?

People approached the lottery agent, since they knew he was a good friend of Reb Nochem Rabinowitz. They pleaded with him to please ask the father to persuade his son to spare at least half an hour a day for them.

"Folks say his son Sholom has a neat hand and that chances for passing the test are much better with him than with any other tutor . . ."

Father's heart swelled with pride. His soul gushed with joy—it was no small matter to see such admiration, even though the satisfaction was minuscule. What kind of a pleasure was it, pray tell, if you don't even have a chance to see your own child? The first part of the day he was at school, and then he was busy with private lessons till well into evening.

Then, at night, Sholom strolled with his friends in the municipal park. During the summer the Pereyaslav park was a Garden of Eden. There were concerts by a military band, led by the regimental bandmaster—a Jew with thick lips, black beard, and eyes as black as cherries. All the girls were in love with his baton, and he too liked them one and all. From afar he smiled to them with his thick lips and cherry-black eyes, and waved his baton ever more vigorously.

The trumpets blared, the kettledrums boomed, and the dust raised by strolling couples competed with the sweet fragrance of the blossoming elder tree, which filled the air with heady perfume. Only someone from Little Russia would remember and appreciate that sweet fragrance of a summer evening stroll in the municipal park. The park was scantily illuminated. There were no more than three or four gas lamps, and the glasses surrounding their dark, sooty lanterns were broken. A strong wind could easily blow the flames out. But who cared? In fact, it was nicer when it was darker. Then the youths and girls could stop, chat, laugh, and arrange to meet tomorrow at the same time, here on this path beneath the aromatic, blossoming elder tree.

Sholom returned home tired, excited and hungry. He ate whatever he found—a piece of herring, a slice of bream, a cucumber and some onion bread. Thank goodness, he had a good appetite. But what of washing one's hands and saying the Grace After Meals? Father didn't even ask if he had recited the Evening Service . . . It grieved him, but he preferred not to notice. Sholom didn't have time to say a word to the other children. Done with eating, he sat down to study and prepare his lessons for tomorrow. His reading by the light of a kerosene lamp vexed Stepmother. Her grumbling annoyed Father, which prompted Sholom to say:

"I'm going to buy kerosene and a lamp with my own money."

"Don't you dare do anything like that, or you'll drive me to the grave," said Father.

Hearing this, the lottery agent remarked, "I can't stand quarrels." Then he offered a compromise. "Since Sholom is already independent and earning money, thank God, and since he has to study and prepare for his last exam, it would only be right to leave the rascal alone. I suggest," the agent concluded, "that Sholom rent a room with meals until the exam period is over so he can continue to study in good health. And if he can't find a place, I'll take him."

Of course, Father refused to hear of such a crazy plan. But the lottery agent was so magnetic he could convince a stone wall. Moreover, he hated words. He liked action. So he left and returned with great news. Success: he'd found someone who would provide room and board and all the other necessities absolutely free, on condition that the rascal tutor the older children just for an hour in the morning, half an hour in the afternoon, and occasionally spend forty minutes or so in the evening with the smaller children.

"Well then, how many children does that come to?" Father asked.

"What do you care how many? Does Sholom have to feed them? He only has to teach them. And what difference does it make if there are three, five, or seven? Look, you know I'm a good friend and I won't lead you astray. So my advice is that the rascal pack up and move in, but soon, quickly, because lots of people are interested in a position like that. So get a move on! Giddyap!"

The rascal began packing. It didn't take too long, for his entire wardrobe consisted of a couple of shirts, a pair of socks, a tefillin bag, a little Siddur, and books, books, and more books. While packing, Sholom looked at his father—his face was yellow as wax. He twisted and chewed at his sparse little beard. Father couldn't find a word to say, but each of his sighs tore a piece of Sholom's heart. Stepmother, on the other hand, became effusive.

"I'm sorry, but I don't like the whole idea. First of all, what will people say? People will say—may plagues strike them dumb—that it's the stepmother's fault. That's number one. And furthermore, when a child lives in his father's house he can't go to ruin. One more mouth to feed, or one less. Big deal! The soup won't be any fatter if he goes."

When it came to good-byes, she even let fall a tear.

Seeing the rascal to the door, Father made him promise that he would come home for the Sabbath.

"During the week, well, be that as it may. But Sabbath—for goodness' sake, Sabbath! Can't you give me that bit of joy? Especially since it'll be a delight for you too. For where else is Sabbath celebrated like at your father's house? Who sings Sholom Aleichem like I do? Who else chants Woman of Valor so beautifully? Can anyone sing the Sabbath zemiros like me? And what about the Kiddush? True, all Jews make Kiddush. But God's Presence does not rest on all of them. Of course, the Sabbath is celebrated in all Jewish homes. But not into all Jewish homes come the angels of peace, fluttering, floating in the air, and filling the house with a quiet holiness, the sacred silence of the great, holy and beloved Sabbath day."

59. An Idyll

Guests for the Sabbath—A Hebrew Poet—Dante's Inferno *and Binyominson's Epic—How a Poet Broils Herring—At the Sabbath Table*

Having a guest for Sabbath was not only a mitzva, it was part of the natural cycle, a habit, a way of life for the average Jew of that time. A man like Nochem Rabinowitz, for example, couldn't understand how anyone could sit down to the Sabbath table without a guest. For him that would have been a ruined Sabbath.

The Almighty kept sending new guests his way. This time the guest was his son. That was good too. But he wasn't alone. In addition, there were two more: the lottery agent with the dark glasses— an old friend who sold tickets for the Saxony and Braunschweig lottery—and another guest called Binyominson, whom I'll describe now.

He was a Hebrew writer, a poet. He wrote a book entitled *The Valley of Jehoshaphat; or, Cholera*. In a beautiful, flowery Hebrew, the poet described how God, angry at a corrupt humanity, had sent cholera down to earth. The cholera came in the guise of a woman, naturally, an ugly, horrible harridan, wielding a huge knife with which she cut down people left and right. Obviously, Dante's *Inferno* was more terrifying and made a more lasting impression upon readers than Binyominson's *Cholera*. But that wasn't as important as language. His was a multihued, magnificent, sugar-sweet, flowery diction which cholera surely did not deserve. So much for his composition. Now let's turn to the poet himself.

Binyominson was gaunt but broad-boned; he had a shiny, square face and a beard so sparse that you could see the food going down his throat when he swallowed—it reminded one of a hungry goose. When he swallowed, his head moved up and down, also like a hungry goose. To compensate for his thin hair, he let it grow long. It hung down in curly clumps and was always smeared with something greasy to make it shine. He dressed in the German fashion and wore a high, hard hat. Everything was horribly old, but clean to a fault—neat, brushed and pressed. He did everything himself: laundered, ironed, mended, sewed buttons. At night he probably washed the shirt he wore during the day; his tie too was very likely his own handiwork. When he spoke, all his limbs went into motion, and his voice was impassioned. His face—eyes half-closed, directed up at the ceiling— elicited compassion. As Sholom watched the poet, he often wondered how Binyominson had looked thirty or forty years ago, as a youngster.

No one knew how he got there. Stepmother said that the lottery agent had dragged Binyominson in with him. "One shlimazl shleps another." Luckily for him, Stepmother was out on that fine day when the lottery agent arrived with Binyominson and his little gray suitcase. When she returned and saw the man with the little gray suitcase reading to Father from a booklet, she said at once:

"A shlimazl! The sort that should be thickly sown and sparsely grown." Then she asked, "How come he didn't find a room at Reuben Yasnegradsky's inn?"

But it was too late. One did not chase a guest from one's house, especially the kind of soul who needed nothing, wanted nothing, and demanded nothing. Binyominson slept on an old oilcloth-covered sofa in a dark little corridor between two rooms. When the samovar was brought, he filled his large kettle with boiling water. Then, from a yellow piece of paper he poured some senna leaves—"They're good for the heart," he said—pulled a piece of sugar from his pocket, and drank his tea.

He did the same with meals. In his little gray suitcase he had his own bread. The bread was dry and stale—the older the better (it was cheaper that way). Each day he bought a piece of herring for a kopeck. Holding it with the tips of his fingers, he walked slowly to the kitchen, excused himself a dozen times, and asked Stepmother to let him broil the herring on the hot coals in the corner of the oven. As the herring cooked, it protested noisily; it hummed and sizzled and gave off such an awful smell that you had to run from the house. Stepmother swore that next time she'd throw him out of the house along with the herring. But she never kept her promise. Because one would have to have a Tartar's heart to do this to a man who lived all week long on pieces of broiled herring.

Sabbath was an exception. When Sabbath came, Binyominson was a guest at the table along with everyone else. Head and shoulders above all the other guests. He was a gentle soul, a Talmud scholar, a maskil, a writer, a poet! It wasn't his fault, poor man, that he was a pauper. What could he do? If the choice were his, he'd have preferred being rich. But he had no luck—and he sighed. The master of the house also heaved a sigh and poured Binyominson a glass of wine. Then he filled his and the lottery agent's glasses and all three drank "L'chayim," not only for themselves, but for the entire House of Israel. The wine made them lively, their tongues loosened, everyone began to talk at once—but not nonsense, God forbid! They discussed Torah, sacred and secular literature, philosophy, Haskala and science . . .

Sholom, the youngest of the guests, also took part in the conversation; though he was considered almost a grown-up, he restrained himself in the presence of the adults. It was no trifle! He was a young man who already earned money and gave private lessons!

Since Sholom had ceased eating at his father's house and had become independent, the two other guests began to treat him as an adult and even spoke to him in the formal rather than the intimate mode of address. He became a customer of the agent, who sold him an eighth of a share in a lottery ticket. With the same tone and air of confidence he used with Sholom's father, the agent promised Sholom that, God willing, he would win the grand prize. And as for the poet Binyominson—he often visited Sholom and wrote at his desk when the latter was out giving private lessons. One day the poet brought his little gray suitcase containing his papers and stale bread. Instead of broiling his piece of herring every morning at the Rabinowitzes' inn and being humiliated by Stepmother, he preferred doing his chore in the house of Sholom's landlady, where he finally moved in, lock, stock and barrel, and settled permanently in his young friend's room.

This happened quite simply and naturally. Why shouldn't two people who liked and helped each other be together? Binyominson was a fine Hebraist, a poet. His younger friend had a private room, a bed so wide it was more like a field than a bed—would it harm anyone if two people slept there instead of one? Still, you might argue that Binyominson talked incessantly, never ceased praising his own verse, and read his long epics till late into the night with such enthusiasm and passion that tears actually stood in his eyes! No

matter, that was nothing to complain about. While the poet de-
claimed, his young friend Sholom had a delicious snooze; but Binyominson didn't mind. For when he read his stanzas, the whole world
could turn upside down!

One might ask what linked all these aforementioned characters?
How, for example, could Nochem Rabinowitz, a householder, half
Hasid and half maskil, be a kindred spirit with a Litvak and anti-
Hasid like the lottery agent with the dark glasses? And what bound
those two and the hungry, fervent poet Binyominson? And could a
wide-eyed youth with downy cheeks and blond, curly hair (after his
bout of typhus, his hair began to grow like grass after rain) feel that
he belonged in that company?

Sholom was a mature young man, drawn to the outdoors and to
the municipal park, where he longed to stroll with boys and girls he
knew. Then what was he doing here? Nevertheless, it must be said
that this was a rare idyll, an exceptional friendship; they were an
indescribably close-knit group. All four men looked forward to their
happy reunion on Sabbath, a meeting they eagerly awaited all week
long. If any of the four had some good news or something to show,
he saved it for the Sabbath. No matter how much the poet Binyominson tormented you all week with his poems, he saved the best
of them for Sabbath after lunch. "After lunch," only in a manner
of speaking. Actually, Binyominson showed everything he had accumulated for the week *before* lunch, *during* lunch and *after* lunch.
The lottery agent was much more practical than Binyominson.
When they returned from shul and Father chanted the Kiddush
and went to wash his hands, the lottery agent looked through his
dark glasses at the plate and said, "Now our poet will probably say
something."

And though the poet, poor soul, was starving—he didn't wait to
be asked again. Meanwhile the lottery agent was filling his belly,
stuffing himself, dunking the fresh challa in the peppery fish sauce,
washing it down with a little tumbler of strong whiskey, and rubbing
his hands.

"Excellent! Couldn't be better!" he exclaimed ecstatically.

His remark was puzzling. What was excellent, and what couldn't
be better? Binyominson's poems or the peppery fish sauce? Or was
it the little tumbler of whiskey? Or was it all of them rolled into
one? In any case, the high spirits that prevailed on this Sabbath lifted

even a prosaic soul like Stepmother up a notch. Done up in honor of the day in her Berditchev hairdo, she glanced amiably at the Sabbath guests and urged them to eat and leave all talk for the end of the meal.

In order to complete the picture and point up the idyll, I should mention another living creature who looked forward to the Sabbath guests: Feige Leah, the gabbai's wife. The author of these memoirs has already portrayed her in *Mottel the Cantor's Son*. This Feige Leah was really a cat, but since she was on the stout side, she was nick-named Feige Leah, the gabbai's wife. The children in the area had a weakness for pussycats and Feige Leah brought forth a litter of spotted cats every year. When they grew up, they were given away, but Feige Leah remained rooted in the house, firmly entrenched, a cat who knew her own worth and did not let herself be trampled underfoot. Stepmother, however, didn't consider her a privileged character. She was kicked, thumped in the ribs, and sometimes even beaten on the head with a broom. Why should she be any more immune than Stepmother's own children? And Stepmother's children didn't treat Feige Leah with kid gloves either. They tormented her, pulled away her kittens as they suckled, and tortured her nigh to death! But there was an excuse even for this (an excuse can be found for anything): why should children treat a cat any better than their own mother treated them?

Of course, when Sholom was at home he didn't let Feige Leah be unduly humiliated. Now that he was only a once-a-week Sabbath guest, Feige Leah welcomed Sholom as if he were still part of the family; she stood when Sholom entered, arched her back, rubbed her head against his legs, yawned mightily, and licked herself.

"What's new, Feige Leah?" Sholom bent down to pat her head.

"Meow!" Feige Leah responded, as if to say: "Oh well, thank God we're alive and can see each other!" Meanwhile, she kept rubbing against his leg and purring, looking a bit guilty, and waited for someone to throw her a morsel.

"A pity on living creatures!" the lottery agent sighed. Binyo-minson swallowed, looked at all three of his friends, and said, "I have a poem on that theme. It's called 'His Compassion for All His Creatures.'" Without waiting for anyone to ask, he looked up toward the ceiling and began reciting the poem.

60. Broken Hopes

The Coming Examinations—Building Castles in the Air—With His Friend Eli Dodi's—A Psalm—A Florid Letter to Chai Gurland—The Club in the Tobacco Shop—Gurland's Reply

 Time passed. Children grew. Summer came—the last summer of studies at the district school. Examinations were staring Sholom in the face. Within a week or two, he'd be finished. He was sick of school. He never really liked any of his classes, never considered them a source of learning and wisdom. The little bit of knowledge he had gleaned had come from the tree called Haskala. The fruits he hungrily devoured were Russian and Hebrew books, newspapers and journals. The club was of great help too; that is, the Pereyaslav intelligentsia, consisting of the lottery agent and Binyominson, and headed by the accomplished sons-in-law, Lazer Yossel and Magidov. But Sholom's ideal was Arnold of Pidvorke and his huge library.

The only good thing about the district school was his friend and classmate Eli Dodi's. He liked Eli for his sparkling personality and his comic actor's ability to imitate all the teachers. Together they played pranks, read books, had fun, and kept apart from all their other friends, most of whom were blockheads and clunks.

While other students studied for exams and feared failure, the two friends made fun of the whole world and didn't give a fig for the tests. It was summertime. A paradise outside. The best time to swim in the river and row toward the tall, green reeds by the distant shore. Beyond the meadow, sprinkled with scores of large red and white daisies, stretched a forest. They raced across the meadow to the edge of the forest in one burst of speed. Who would get there first? Both arrived breathless. They threw themselves face down on the green, fragrant grass and scraped the raw, sandy earth. There a fly crawled, a beetle strolled. Ants carried straw, bits of bark, or a pine needle with their front legs.

Silence. A strange, holy, lulling, soporific stillness. Once in a rare while, the silence was broken by the tweeting of a group of swallows passing overhead—a sign of coming rain. Or one could hear a lone frog croaking in the distant reeds: one *kwaa*, and he fell silent. Also a sign of rain—even though the sky was pure and clear, and not a speck of cloud was seen on the horizon. Sholom felt close to this forest, to the meadow, the daisies, the fresh earth and fragrant grass, all the creeping insects, the swallows, the croaking frogs. Indeed, with all of nature. Every thing and every person was part of one world, one family, one household. And they made all kinds of noises, just like at a fair—it was a world of its own, called Life.

The two young friends were happy in this world. Both were pleased with their lives; they were satisfied with their past, content with their present, and expected even more from the future. They had a long, quiet talk. A talk with no beginning or end. Most of it concerned what lay in store for them, what the future held. They made plans, built castles in the air; they imagined a sweet, variegated life that mirrors every young man's fantasy and is realized by no one on this earth . . .

But time was passing. It didn't stand still. After all, examinations were not child's play. Indeed, although Sholom and his friend were first in their class, no one could predict the outcome. The best student might fail. Only one person was supremely confident—the lottery agent.

"What exams! Who exams! Thumb your noses at them!" said the agent, who worried more about the rascal than Sholom's own father. Consequently, no one was as happy as he when Sholom brought home the good news one day that he and his friend Eli Dodi's were completely exempt from the examinations.

"Thank God, we're free! Exempt from exams! Going to live it up!" crowed the lottery agent. Overjoyed, that evening he brought to Sholom's room a herring and two biscuits, pulled a bottle of liquor out of his pocket, and, along with Sholom and the poet Binyominson, celebrated as God had ordained. And then as Binyominson himself put it, "a holy spirit descended" upon him, and on the spot he indited a poem entitled "To the Songmaster on a Three-Stringed Instrument, a Psalm."

Binyominson used the number three to represent the third class that Sholom had successfully completed. Now a new chapter had begun for him. What to do now? What would be his goal in life? All our old acquaintances offered suggestions. The accomplished sons-in-law, Arnold of Pidvorke, and other good friends each gave his own bit of advice. Attend gymnasium. Go to a rabbinical school.

Study at the university. Become a doctor. A lawyer. An engineer. Father was in a dither. With so many choices of professions and livelihoods his head began to spin!

The final choice, however, was the Zhitomir Teachers Institute, which had accepted the two excellent students, Sholom and his friend Eli, and awarded them government scholarships.

Applications had already been sent to Chai Gurland, the director of the Institute. To be on the safe side, Sholom added a letter he had written in flowery Hebrew to show Gurland that he wasn't dealing with some little tyke.

"Thank God we're rid of this!" the lottery agent exulted and wiped his dark glasses with the wet corner of his jacket (without his glasses the lottery agent's face seemed swollen and his eyes looked like little pillows). "The little rascal's position is already secure. I should have such worries about making a living! Whether he becomes a crown rabbi or a teacher, a decent man he'll be for sure! And we're also safe from the draft. Teachers and rabbis from that Institute are not drafted. All that's left now is to find a beautiful bride from a fine home with a dowry of about fifteen hundred rubles—then, as they say, we'll really be on the gravy train! Reb Nochem, why don't you have some of that Passover cherry liquor brought out?"

But, as it turned out, the lottery agent's festive joy was premature. This is what happened.

In the long run, none of Nochem Rabinowitz's occupations sufficed to make a living. Then, one day, along came a rich peasant, a gentile named Zachar Nestorovitz who thought the world of Father. Zachar gave him a storefront and a cellar of his large new brick house and opened a tobacco shop for him. Father's wine cellar was transferred here and business began to boom. As you remember, Nochem Rabinowitz's house had always been a meeting place, a club for maskilim and other people. Now the club became even livelier. Friends, acquaintances and just plain customers dropped in to visit. Whoever had some free time and wanted to meet somebody or know what was happening in the world came to the tobacco shop to smoke and chat.

Once the entire crème de la crème of the Pereyaslav intelligentsia gathered in the club. All our old acquaintances were there: Yossi Fruchtstein, the two accomplished sons-in-law, and Arnold of Pidvorke. Of course, the lottery agent with the dark glasses, the poet Binyominson and their young friend, the rascal, were present too.

A very lively discussion ensued and laughter resounded every minute, for Lazer Yossel, one of the sons-in-law, had asked everyone a simple question: "Do me a favor and explain the meaning of 'massive.' But without hands!"

Since it's impossible for a Jew to describe anything without using his hands, everyone demonstrated the word's meaning in his own way. That's what prompted the mood of hilarity.

Then, suddenly, right smack in the middle of the laughter, the door opened and the mailman came in with a registered letter. The return address was written in large Russian letters; Administrative Office of the Government Jewish Teachers Institute of Zhitomir.

"Aha, that's from him, from Chai Gurland!"

They opened the envelope and read the letter from the director.

"Since the Institute has a four-year course of study, and since from the papers and birth certificate it is evident that the applicant was born on the 18th of February, 1859, the candidate will have to present himself to the draft board in October of 1880—that is, three years from now. This means, one year *prior* to finishing his studies at the Institute."

This news struck us like a bomb, like thunder on a bright sunny day. At first, everyone began to argue and analyze the meaning of the letter. What was Gurland trying to say? And why didn't he conclude what should have been concluded? Perhaps something could be done; perhaps there was a ploy, a way out of this maze. But all the debating was for naught. Everyone realized, as sure as two times two is four, that it was all a devil's game—the chances of entering the Institute were nil. The birth certificate could no longer be changed. And Chai Gurland wasn't the sort to be party to chicanery. It was hopeless!

The hero of this tale regards that time as a transition period. He had to decide where he was going. He had to devise a plan of action and select a course for the rest of his life. He and his friend Eli Dodi's had long ago agreed that they would both go to Zhitomir, live and study in one room, stroll and row and go to the beach together. For vacations they would both return home. And boy, would they astonish their former friends with their Zhitomir uniform! They'd be a bit standoffish, and loudly speak of Pushkin and Lermontov, Byron and Shakespeare. Let everyone hear and realize what cognoscenti they were. Their friends would listen in astonishment and envy. Blushing girls would surround them pretending to fix their gloves; they'd cast glances at them and want to become better acquainted—in short, it would be Paradise!

Now all these dreams suddenly evaporated. No more Zhitomir, no more Teachers Institute; no swimming, rowing, vacations, friends; no more girls. Gone was Paradise. Good-bye, career. As for his father's face—a pity to look at it. As yellow as wax. New anxieties, new wrinkles, new sighs: "Help! What do we do now? Where do we turn?" Moreover, the poet Binyominson wasn't feeling well. He wanted to console everyone with a new poem, but ah, woe! The muse wasn't singing.

Also, the lottery agent had not come around lately. He had appeared several times for a few minutes, stating that he had an excellent plan for the rascal, which would set him up with a livelihood for the rest of his life and provide for his children and his children's children, but he had no time to elaborate. Then he left and wasn't heard from again.

61. The End of the Idyll

Three Rubles, Grammatically Correct—The Lottery Agent Leaves Us— The Poet Binyominson Vanishes

Nothing is permanent in this world. The aforementioned idyll was destined to end. One of the foursome departed prematurely, and directly after him, another—and the circle crumbled. First our old friend the lottery agent with the dark glasses and the high rubber galoshes, and soon thereafter the poet Binyominson.

Who actually was the lottery agent? Where did he come from? Who and what did he have in this world? For whom did he toil all his life, tramping through the mud, day in and day out, perspiring and longing for the grand prize? No clear, definitive answer can be given to these questions. Sholom remembers that the lottery agent often asked his young friend, the rascal, to do him a quick favor and write an address in Russian in his beautiful handwriting. The address was dictated as follows: Madame Freyda Itta, the town of Pagust, province of Pinsk, district of Minsk.

As the lottery agent dictated, he made several grammatical errors, which Sholom corrected, including the proper way to say "I'm herewith enclosing three rubles."

"Who needs grammar?" the lottery agent retorted. "They don't need grammar in Pagust for the holidays. They need money."

Not for naught do we have a proverb here in Volhynia: When a Litvak leaves home for seven Passovers, he even forgets to say good-bye. The lottery agent would always say he'd be right back —but would disappear for a long time. Later, no amount of nagging and questioning—"Where have you been?"—would help. You'd never get an answer from him. "I've been away. Don't worry about it!"

Now once again the lottery agent had disappeared, and no one knew where he was.

One morning while Sholom was teaching his students in his room, the door opened and his father entered.

"What happened?" Sholom cried out in alarm.

"Nothing. The agent isn't well. We have to go see him."

Along the way, Father provided Sholom with details. "Actually, the lottery agent hasn't been well for a long time. Lately, however, he's been seriously ill." The more details Father provided, the gloomier they became. "The lottery agent's condition is critical," Father concluded. "In fact, he probably won't survive. That is, what I want to say is—the lottery agent is no more."

Talking thus, they arrived at the synagogue courtyard. It was flooded with the rays of the blazing, end-of-summer sun. A crowd of half-naked and barefoot Jewish children played leapfrog and filled the courtyard with the shrill sounds of their healthy young voices. The Jewish street was full of life and joy. Although the air was suffocating, it was still wonderful. Here and there a lone tree could be seen, and bits of grass broke through the earth. The poured-out slops covered the dust that the children had raised in the course of their games. Still, it was summer, and they were outside; playing in God's world was a delight.

"This is where the lottery agent lives," Father said. And the two descended into a cellar that looked like a dark pit. Holding on to the damp walls, they opened the large, heavy, iron door latch and saw the following scene:

On the bare earth, covered with a black cloth, lay something round and pointy in the middle. By its head sputtered two candles, stuck into two bottles of different sizes and colors. In the middle of the room, on the other side of the flames, a shamesh sat on a bench, his gaberdine tattered and his beard tangled. By the right wall of this cellar room, side by side like a pair of twins, a pair of old, torn, high rubber galoshes stood forlorn, and on the sill of the only window, a large pair of cast-off dark glasses lay abandoned.

The funeral took place that same day. It's not hard to imagine the funeral when, first of all, the dead man was an unknown pauper and, secondly, he was reputed in town to be a quiet heretic. However, since Jews like Reb Nochem Rabinowitz, Yossi Fruchtstein, the two accomplished sons-in-law and Arnold of Pidvorke also participated in the funeral arrangements—this was the first, if not the only, funeral which Arnold attended—the rest of the town expressed interest. Everyone exchanged glances and soon a crowd gathered and grew. Gradually and unexpectedly, it became an imposing, magnificent funeral. The poor got wind of a "fat" funeral and cripples crawled out of the woodwork, pulling at sleeves, raising a fuss, demanding to know why charity money wasn't being distributed by the coffin. It was hard to convince them that the Jew who had died was as poor as they.

"Then why is he getting such a nice funeral?" they countered. "If he's not a rich man and evidently no rabbi either, how come he's so privileged?"

The sun was still blazing when the black-draped coffin was carried out of the dark cellar. The synagogue courtyard and the entire street was black with people. No one had summoned anyone else. People came of their own accord. No one wept, yet sighs were heard. No one delivered a eulogy, no one's jacket was rent in mourning, no one said Kaddish, no one sat for the prescribed seven days of mourning. But praises fluttered in the air.

"He was a good man."

"No saint, but a good man, a nice man."

"He cared for and supported a town full of poor people, secretly."

"Whatever he earned, he gave away."

"His last bit of bread . . ."

"He neglected himself for the sake of others."

"He tore money out of the hands of the living and the dead for the sake of sick old Jews."

"He hated to be thanked."

"He never spoke of his own needs, but always thought of the next person."

"He was a strange Jew."

"Not a strange Jew, but a strange man. Yes, he was a man, a mentch . . ."

It was a quiet but beautiful funeral. One could feel a sense of release. Thank God that people paid their debts, if not during one's lifetime, then at least after one's death. Even if it was only a bit of public esteem for so many years of suffering, anguish, torment and bitterness. But it was sad that he himself, the lottery agent with the dark glasses, could not rise for a minute and observe the honor he had been accorded. Perhaps . . . who knows? What do we know? One's head swam with thoughts about the immortality of the soul— in which the dead man believed, even though he was considered a heretic. Perhaps his soul was now following the coffin, and knew more than everyone there, much, much more. Who knows, who knows?

Gradually, as the funeral procession approached the cemetery, the crowd thinned out and only the lottery agent's closest friends re-mained—the members of the club. His gravesite was as modest as the agent himself. A mound of earth was shoveled over the grave; the mourners dispersed. No one wept, no one said a eulogy, no one recited Kaddish, no one sat shiva. At first, people in the club would occasionally speak of him. Then they stopped. Soon he was forgotten. Shortly thereafter, Binyominson the poet disappeared. For a while no one knew what had become of him. Then word had it that he was in Kiev. Later, Binyominson won fame as a participant in the great intellectual battle that had broken out among the sages of Kiev (we'll meet them in later chapters). His name became as well known as those of Moshe Aaron Shatzkes, Isaac Jacob Weissberg, Dubze-vitch, Darevsky. Much later, rumor had it that Binyominson had emigrated to America. There he had become a reverend and, nat-urally, was an "all-rightnik."

That's how our circle crumbled. The group disbanded. That ex-traordinary friendship came to an end. No more idyll.

62. Wandering for Half a Year

*Lonely and Forlorn—The Sheepskin Dealer—Seeking One's Fortune—
Competition and Small-Town Envy—Abraham the Klezmer—Sholom
Flees the World and Returns Home*

 After losing two dear friends, Sholom could not find his
place. He felt orphaned. He felt even more forlorn when his
sole remaining friend, Eli, also departed—for Zhitomir. Willy-
nilly, this prompted a feeling of envy. He knew quite well that it
was a nasty thought, not a genuine feeling. But what could he do?
He was angry. Why should his friend have such good fortune and
not he? Was it Sholom's fault that he was in a rush and came into
the world a couple of months too soon? Should he lose his career
over such a bit of foolishness and be deprived his whole life? Sholom
pressed his face into his pillow and cried long and bitterly. He felt
that heaven had tumbled down to earth; the entire world seemed to
darken for him. But for which plague wasn't there a medication?
The best doctor was time.

We would like to ask the reader to turn back the clock and recall
the steady guests at the Rabinowitzes' inn. One was known by the
strange name "The Sheepskin Jew." He would bring sheepskins to
his tannery, where they would be dried and treated. Then he would
make winter hats and fur coats for the peasants. When the Sheepskin
Jew came to the inn, people could smell him a mile away. That's
how pungent was the odor of the hides. At first, everyone in the
house would be sneezing constantly. Then everyone's nose became
so stuffed his sense of smell was deadened.

The sheepskin dealer himself was a fine man. Simple, good-
natured, openhearted. Crude and on the simple side, he loved to play
the role of cantor, and led prayers at the top of his voice. But he
had a lisp. When it came to making Kiddush on the Sabbath, he
raised the wine goblet, closed his eyes, and roared:

"The shixth day. The heavensh and the earth were finissed and
all their hoshtsh."

Choking with laughter, the youngsters slid under the table. The
Sheepskin Jew knew the children were laughing at him, but he
couldn't care less.

"You rashcals! You little peshtsh! Is it nice to laugh at an elderly

Jew? God will puniss you. You shcoundrelsh, you little shcampsh!"

This prompted another gale of mirth. Now both adults and children laughed—and he joined them.

The Sheepskin Jew helped Sholom leave his hometown and go out into the world to seek his fortune. He didn't leave for America, God forbid, or London or Paris, and not even for Odessa, Warsaw, or Kiev, but for a small town known as Rzhishtchev (in the Kiev province), not far from Pereyaslav.

In Rzhishtchev there were no Jewish teachers, said the Sheepskin Jew. They would plaster him with gold. He and his friends there had children who wanted to learn, and even if you stretched out and died, there wasn't a teacher to be found! The Sheepskin Jew swore that he'd treat Sholom as one of his own, like the apple of his eye!

In short, he built up such a desire in both the father and son to go to Rzhishtchev that it was difficult to resist the temptation. And so Nochem Rabinowitz took his son and sailed to Rzhishtchev on a steamer.

Upon arrival, they immediately set out for the Sheepskin Jew's house, where they were received royally. On the first day, the family served them hand and foot. They met the head of the household at work sorting skins. He was barefoot and in shirtsleeves. Seeing his honored guests, he at once put on his boots and gaberdine, and shouted into the next room:

"Seyne Seyndel, put up the shamovar, we have gueshtsh."

In a flash appeared a samovar, glasses, tea, coffee, chicory, milk, and the sort of butter cookies that an average Jew would allow himself only on Shevuos for a dairy meal, or for a woman's confinement. Supper was prepared—a king's banquet. Gefilte fish, fried fish, baked fish. Soup with rice, a broth with soup nuts—choose what you want. I won't even mention the meats—there were meats of all kinds. There were even two types of tsimmes. And then the samovar. Once again, tea, preserves, cakes. And when it came to supper, the sheepskin dealer asked his guests:

"Tell me, whatsh your preference in dairy goodiesh? Boiled kreplach, fried kreplach, or kreplach filled with kassa?"

"It makes no difference to us," the guests replied modestly.

To be sure, all three types were brought to the table. This was washed down with coffee and all kinds of jams. Father was bedded down in the living room on a velvet sofa, and for Sholom a bed was prepared on the other sofa. Both beds were made as though for princes. The next morning, Father bade them farewell and returned home, while the son remained with the Sheepskin Jew, taking room and board in exchange for tutoring the children.

The next day, lunch wasn't served with as much flair as the first day. Plain kasha and soup, a bit of meat, and that was it. The dairy supper consisted of some cheese, bread and butter. Mostly bread. The guest tutor was bedded down, no longer in the living room and not on a velvet sofa, but on an iron box from which he awoke with broken bones. On the third day, he got a piece of smoked fish and potatoes for lunch and a heartburn that almost made him faint. Instead of supper, only a glass of tea and bread were served. This time the tutor's bed was some thrown-together sheepskins on the floor. One had to be made of steel to withstand the stench of the hides. To top it off, a baby caterwauled in his cradle all night long, crying his guts out, not letting Sholom sleep. A small lamp smoked and sputtered; it gave Sholom a headache. The infant didn't stop yelling at the top of his lungs. It was pitiful!

Seeing that he wouldn't be able to fall asleep anyway, the tutor rose from the sheepskins to see why the baby was crying. It turned out that the cat had jumped into the cradle, made itself as comfortable as you please, and bedded down for the night. The tutor had to decide what to do now. Chase away the poor cat—it too was a living creature. Or let the cat be—but then the baby would bawl. So Sholom hit upon a plan (a wise youngster always comes up with something): he'd rock the cradle and then the cat would leave of its own accord. He knew this from experience. He had seen it all the time at home and school. Before a baby was placed into a new cradle for the first time, they would first rock a cat there for good luck. But a cat would by no means let itself be rocked. As soon as it was placed in the cradle and the rocking began—it would quickly jump out, ready to claw anyone's eyes out. That's what happened now. As soon as the tutor approached the cradle, the cat rose, jumped out, and disappeared. The little infant sensed it was being rocked. He stopped crying, calmed down, and fell asleep. The next morning, when Sholom told the story to the mother, she cursed the cat up and down, hugged her baby, and wished for herself any harm that might befall him. But the fact that Sholom didn't sleep all night bothered her no more than last year's snow.

There was no point in continuing this way, Sholom realized. He found room and board in another place and took his leave of the sheepskin dealer. And here began a pack of troubles, endless distress, and chagrin. One angry landlady after another, merciless cockroaches, biting bedbugs, scampering mice, rats and other disgusting creatures.

All this torment and pain was nothing compared to the intrigues he had to suffer from his competitors, his fellow teachers. Although they competed fiercely among each other, these tutors teamed up to wage war against the newcomer from Pereyaslav. They did their best to blacken Sholom's reputation, calling him a criminal, a thief, a robber—everything evil. They spread such gossip about him to the parents of his pupils that Sholom prayed to God that his summer stint of teaching would soon end and that he'd be able to flee with his life. The time he spent in Rzhishtchev was like a nightmare.

Only in one house, Abraham the Klezmer's, did he feel he was among human beings. Abraham was an authentic artist, a maestro who deserves to be depicted. Tall and broad-shouldered, he had a round, wide face, small eyes, thick brows, and long black curly hair. His hands were so large, coarse and hairy, the violin in his hands didn't look like a violin but like a tiny toy. He couldn't read music; still, he wrote his own compositions. He played so sweetly you could have melted listening to him. He was a kind of Stempenyu, and perhaps he was even head and shoulders above him.

In real life he was a Stempenyu as well. A strange sort. Poetic nature, a great lover of women and girls. But he also had a wife—not a witch like Stempenyu's; on the contrary, his wife was just like him. Tall, big, beautiful and wide. Perhaps a bit too wide. Wide enough for three. She and her husband were like two drops of water. Never angry, always happy, in good spirits, and constantly laughing. They loved to eat well, drink well, and live well. If they had the means, they bought the best and the most beautiful of everything. If they didn't have it, why then they put their teeth on the shelf and waited for God to send them some earnings, and then they'd kill a herring and enjoy life as God had ordained. God didn't deny them children either. They had an entire troop of them, all born with talent. They were all excellent musicians, and played various instruments. An extraordinary orchestra.

Into that house came the modern teacher from Pereyaslav. Here he felt like a fish in water. The maestro himself taught him how to play the violin. He didn't have to pay a penny. Abraham the Klezmer wasn't the sort to take money for such a sacred thing as divine music.

"But if you have a couple of pennies to spare," he said, "I'd like to ask you for a little loan."

The same held true for his wife. She needed a couple of kopecks to go to the market.

"Do you have any small change in your pocket?"

Naturally, there was always some loose change. So Sholom felt at home there. He became one of the family. And that sufficed for his competitors—the other tutors—to gossip about him, malign and bad-mouth him, and do likewise to Abraham, his wife and their entire household. They spread the news in town that the Pereyaslav tutor's entire earnings were handed over to the klezmer's wife and that they reveled and caroused there every night. The musicians played and Sholom and Abraham's wife danced!

In the klezmer's house, said the tutors in town, they didn't care that poor people were starving and little children were dying. The gossipmongers pulled pious faces and cast glances heavenward. And the ones who listened spat. What kind of connection was there to paupers, and what did it have to do with little children? And what did the spitting mean? Don't ask! When you're dealing with competition, logic drops dead. In short, Sholom barely made it through the summer term and fled from that accursed little town. Bound for home, he was afraid even to look back, and vowed to warn his children and children's children never to give private lessons in small towns. He decided to look for another career.

63. Back Home Again

The Joy of Returning Home—Another Meeting with Eli—Writing for Ha-Maggid—Darwin, Buckle and Spencer—Two Externs of the Old School

 No word rings as beautifully as "mother." None speaks to the heart like "home." To appreciate home, one should leave for a while, roam in strange places, and then return to familiar surroundings. Everything then takes on a new charm. Everything becomes twice as precious. One feels changed and reborn.

When Sholom returned for Rosh Hashana, the first thing he did was walk through town and breathe the air of all the streets. He wanted to make sure that all the houses, courtyards and gardens were in their usual places. The people he met had changed little. They greeted him amicably, and he was as cordial as possible to one and all. The youngsters he had left behind had stretched their legs and grown taller. He too, people assured him, had grown, become more mature; and he was in the height of fashion. His high-heeled shoes squeaked, and his trousers were modishly long and wide. He wore a short jacket and a soft beige cap. His hair was long like a poet's and brushed down like Gogol's.

His friend Eli, who had also just come for the holidays, looked entirely different. His uniform consisted of a short coat, buttoned to the neck, short, narrow trousers, a blue, broad-brimmed cap, and hair as short as a soldier's. Chest out, teeth gleaming, eyes merry, Eli didn't stop singing the praises of the Jewish Teachers Institute at Zhitomir. They were studying higher mathematics, reading Russian literature, and doing gymnastics, he said. Jewish subjects, however, were quite minimal: a chapter of the Pentateuch, a chapter of the Prophets, a bit of the *Code of Law,* and that was it.

"And that's the entire course of studies at the Teachers Institute?" Sholom asked. "And you're going to be a Jewish teacher, a rabbi among Jews?"

Sholom was also surprised that Eli had brought a pack of Russian poems from the Institute and not one in Yiddish—as if he had come from a Christian theological seminary. But this did not affect their friendship. They were always together. The two went everywhere. They had plenty to talk about—and even more opportunity to laugh at and mock the entire town. And just like long ago, in the good old days, they went to the river, rented a rowboat, and rowed far beyond the bounds of town.

The end of summer. The cold had not yet set in, but the meadow was no longer green. No trace was left of the red and white daisies. The reeds, now yellow and sparse, were still sunk in mud. The clump of woods was cloaked in red. It was too late in the season to stretch out on the damp and swampy ground. The friends sought out a fallen tree and sat down to rest. They exchanged experiences of their first half-year of separation. No detail was omitted; not the slightest event. Every impression was passed on, every meeting, every event. Amazingly, although both spoke at the same time, and both laughed and interrupted each other, they still heard and understood each other and had a wonderful time.

Then they fell silent; each became contemplative, introspective, alone with his thoughts. They were close and liked each other. They revealed almost all their innermost thoughts, but not all. No, not all. Each youth had his own thoughts, his own ideal, his own little world where no one else, not even a best friend, could enter . . .

A chill set in. The day began to fade. The sun was setting. The woods became overcast, as though wrapped in a light mist. The sound of a falling acorn echoed. The two youths awoke as if from an enchanted dream.

"Time to go home?"

"Time to go home!"

They rose and followed a narrow, crooked path through the meadow. As they skimmed over the little river in the rowboat and passed the yellow reeds, they sang a Russian (not a Jewish) song. It was dark when they returned home. Their cheeks flamed, their eyes sparkled. They had ravenous appetites and bought sweet watermelon and two fresh, soft, still-warm biscuits. They made a meal of it and were happy. They laughed for no rhyme or reason.

Any onlooker would have thought that these happy, healthy youths were satisfied and lacked nothing. Actually, only one of them (Eli) was truly happy. The other (Sholom) felt broken, dispirited. His only consolation was that everyone in town spoke about the Haftorah he had chanted in the synagogue, of his knowledge of Bible and Hebrew, and of his calligraphic skills. None of which his friend Eli could do. From where should Eli know how to write Yiddish or Hebrew? Only Nochem Rabinowitz's son excelled in this. He knew all the Haskala literature inside out. He read *Ha-Maggid*. People wondered why Sholom hadn't yet written for that paper. But how did they know that he didn't write for it? Perhaps he used a pseudonym.

So went the talk in Pereyaslav. A special halo was placed around Sholom; in his own eyes he grew taller and taller. He behaved circumspectly, no longer sought out his street urchin acquaintances. He joined the municipal library and carried home thick tomes. He read Darwin, Henry Thomas Buckle, Spencer. He palled around with the well-known enlightened young men in town. Self-taught and disciplined, they had plowed through Latin and Greek, studied geometry, algebra, trigonometry, psychology and philosophy. They were ready to enroll in the university that very day. They just lacked the means. Pereyaslav boasted two of these old-time external students. One was called Chaite Ruderman, the other Avreml Zolotushkin. Both are dead now and deserve to be recalled briefly in these memoirs.

Chaite Ruderman lived beyond the edge of town, separated from people and the world. He was a son of Moshe David Ruderman, a teacher portrayed earlier in this autobiography, and a brother of Shimon Ruderman. (Once, Shimon was about to convert, but the town saved him from the monastery and sent him to the Teachers Institute in Zhitomir.) Chaite didn't resemble his pale, asthmatic brother Shimon at all. Chaite was a strapping, broad-boned, good-looking young man with red, downy cheeks. After Moshe David the teacher died of asthma, his widow, Chaite's mother, became a waitress at weddings and baked honey cakes. This provided her with a livelihood and enabled her to support her son, who knew only one thing—books, books, and more books. But Chaite was estranged from everybody. Only rarely did anyone have the privilege of talking to him. Still, everyone knew of Chaite's profound erudition. This unknown philosopher astonished everyone who met him. He tore everything and everyone apart. He disparaged the entire world. His tongue was a file. His laughter gall. His humor venom. How did this recluse know the world? This was an eternal secret and conundrum. One summer day Chaite went to swim in the river, caught cold, and died of tuberculosis at the age of twenty-two.

The second philosopher and autodidact, Avreml Zolotushkin, was no recluse and no unsung scholar. He was a merry, dark-complexioned youth with fiery black eyes and black, kinky hair. Dark as an Arab, he had white, laughing teeth and a slightly hoarse voice. He loved to dress like an Englishman in checked trousers and an outlandish cap. In wintertime he wore a burly cape. He was as full of books as a drum is full of air. He knew Heine's poetry by heart. He loved Dickens and Thackeray, Swift, Cervantes and our own Gogol. He himself was a humorist. Without telling anyone, he wrote many funny sketches but didn't want to publish a line or show his work to anyone. By nature he was very obstinate, spiteful, mocking and introspective. He made a living by being a scribe in the town hall. His handwriting was as convoluted and curly as his hair. He died a bachelor at the age of forty plus.

These were the two stars with whom Sholom rubbed shoulders, and from whom he tried to learn as much as possible. But Chaite Ruderman and Avreml Zolotushkin got along like fire and water.

They did not know each other; they never even met. Nevertheless, they hated each other with such a passion that each one forbade the mere mention of the other's name. We shall probably meet them in the course of our further adventures.

64. Going to a Great Job

Loafing—Advice and a Letter of Recommendation—Out into the World Again—Left with One Coin—At the Gates of the Garden of Eden— A Chilly Welcome

Sholom's many professions came to naught. His lessons stopped; he had no money to continue studying. Freeloading in his father's house wasn't to his taste either, especially after he had already been on his own. Although Nochem Rabinowitz was proud of his learned son, it distressed him that he was idle and jobless. What would become of him? Moreover, his stepmother's dab of respect for her independent stepson suddenly vanished. By degrees she resumed her former attitude toward that "good-for-nothing." She looked askance at him and baited him with sly gibes, all of which tormented his father. Sholom either immersed himself in his books— or put on his hat, took his walking stick, and went to see the town philosophers, Chaite Ruderman or Avreml Zolotushkin, to discuss abstruse matters and world problems. As usual, Chaite Ruderman the pessimist berated everyone; he recognized no authority and looked down his nose at the whole world. On the other hand, the optimistic Zolotushkin quoted lengthy passages of Heine and Börne. He played with his curly hair and spoke in a singsong, wrought up like a Hasid quoting his rebbe.

But all of this was just a ruse to kill time. Sholom felt an emptiness in his soul; he regretted time and energy lost. He longed for work. He wanted to go out into the world. He was tired of his life. Sick of himself. Sick and disgusted.

But God, who abandons no one, also looked down at the forlorn hero of these memoirs. Israel Benditsky, his father's good friend, came to his aid. Although he was only a klezmer, Benditsky played the role of a respectable citizen in town. He regarded himself as a musical director and orchestra leader, and performed only at high-class, lavish weddings. His main source of income, however, was a well-kept, princely inn. He was also the only photographer in town. And besides, he was a very handsome man—tall, well-dressed, with an extraordinarily beautiful round black beard. He wore a black woolen cape, a high hat, and leather overshoes with brass-tipped heels. Glib-tongued, he was a sweet talker who interjected many Russian words into his conversation.

Benditsky frequently dropped into the club—that is, to the Rabinowitz tobacco shop—to chat. Once, while they were sitting and talking, Benditsky casually mentioned that a very rich Jew, a magnate named K., had recently visited him. This magnate lived in the Kiev region in the small town, or rather the village, of T. He had been searching high and low for the right teacher, a tutor in Yiddish and Russian, for his children. Said teacher had to be clever, knowledgeable, and come from a respectable family.

It turned out that Father had known this magnate for a long time. He was a regular fellow. Years back, when the magnate K. was just a little nobody in the employ of a nobleman, he had stayed in the old Rabinowitz inn. Hearing this, Benditsky called out:

"Then God himself has sent me to you. Listen to me. Sit down at once and write a nice letter in Hebrew as befits you and him and let your boy take it to T. and accept the job and congratulations all around, Amen!"

And that's exactly what happened. A letter was composed, a beautiful, festive Hebrew epistle, so felicitously phrased it could have moved a stone. The salutation alone took up three full lines. So many virtues and praises were sung that if this magnate deserved only a third of them, he would have been an angel.

Armed with such imposing protection, Sholom went out into the world once more, seeking his fortune. It must be admitted that the young teacher took neither extra money nor letters of credit. Most of the bit of money he had earned giving private lessons had been spent on his princely wardrobe. The rest was eaten up by trains. After all, a living soul must eat and drink. The trains stopped at every station. Passengers streamed out of the cars and dashed to the buffet. They bought drinks, freshly baked pastries, tea, or soda water. Sholom drank quickly and tipped generously, like a banker or a captain.

Ditto at every stop. The few coins vanished, melted like snow in the sun until a lone five-kopeck piece slid around in his purse. But

Sholom didn't give it a second thought. After all, he was heading for a sure thing. A great job! And armed with such a recommendation! He was riding high . . .

At dusk, when he arrived in T., he looked around and realized he was almost penniless, with only five kopecks to his name. But this didn't faze him. On the contrary, he never felt better in his life. The fact that he had freed himself from the intrigues of the teachers in Rzhishtchev—those leeches and pests—was worth everything. The sun was now on the other side of the forest. Sholom filled his lungs with salubrious fall air, redolent of oaks and pines.

The young teacher jumped off the railway car and went straight to the rich man's house to deliver the letter. The magnate chose to live removed from town in a white palace with a vast green garden enclosed with a brightly colored picket fence. Approaching it wasn't as easy as one might imagine. Worse than getting to see a nobleman. Still, when one was armed with such a mighty letter of recommendation, one could even go to the Czar. So thought our hero, but he was mistaken. For the Garden of Eden isn't as awesome as the path leading to it. To get to such a nabob you have to suffer all the torments of hell. Before being privileged to see this magnate's face, you must first undergo three trials. And even if you pass all three, you're still not finished. You might still leave empty-handed.

The first was a watchman, a tall, desiccated, bandy-legged gentile who waddled as he walked. His name was Pantalei, and his job was to sit at the gate as Mordecai did for King Ahasuerus. Next came Zhuk, a black hound with a cataract. This miserable one-eyed cur was chained to a tree—otherwise he would tear people apart. The third was a young retainer who wore a soiled shirtfront and a golden ring. His well-greased black hair was parted precisely in the middle, he smelled of eau de cologne and onions, and his ears were filthy and his fingernails black.

Passing these three barriers was no easy matter. First, you had to befriend Pantalei the watchman, for when he saw a stranger, he asked in Russian, "What do you want here?" Could Pantalei make head or tail of a letter of recommendation concerning a job? But Pantalei was not a bad chap. He considered a five-kopeck piece an excellent coin. So now Sholom's last kopeck slithered away! Pantalei was cooperative. Zhuk was far worse. True, the dog was chained. But a dog is still a dog. This miserable cur barked and leaped and pulled at the chain with all his strength. Fortunately, Pantalei was close by. He shouted at Zhuk, cursed him, taught him manners- –a full-fledged sermon.

But the most difficult stage of all was the retainer. He considered himself an overlord, asked you the most detailed questions, and put you to the test: "Who are you? Where do you come from? What do you want here?" Best to hold this clown at arm's length and talk down to him. If not—he'd walk all over you. Sholom knew this from experience. Then the retainer took him to task. Who was the letter from? What's written in it? What's your business? A job? What kind of job? In the factory or in the office? If it's the factory, all the jobs have been filled. And if it's the office, there are no jobs there either. Unless of course it's a teaching post, for which there are plenty of applicants. For instance, there's one who wears a cape. A very impressive teacher, but he has one flaw. He's an idiot. Shred him like cabbage and he wouldn't even know it. He does have one virtue, though. He has a beard, which means that the young masters and ladies will respect him.

"But they won't respect you, because you're still too young. You they'll eat up alive, is what our young masters and ladies will do, may a foul disease strike them all in one day!"

With these sweet words, the retainer concluded his remarks. He took the letter from Sholom, placed it on a little silver tray, and disappeared into the distant apartments. Several minutes later he returned empty-handed and without an answer. He reported that the magnate opened the letter, glanced at it, and put it aside without reading it.

We shall soon see what had happened.

65. Dream and Reality

At the Village Inn—Nosy Berel the Red—Sholom's Hunger and Flights of Fantasy—Another Dream of a Treasure—A Meeting with the Magnate's Daughter

 Despite this cold welcome at the hands of the magnate in T., Sholom nevertheless did not lose heart or hope. Those are the ways of a rich man, he thought. Perhaps he has other matters in mind. If not today, then tomorrow. Meanwhile, time moved on. Night fell. He had to find a place to sleep and finally located the only guest house in T., a rickety little inn. The owner was a young relative of the magnate—a redhead with a fiery red beard called Berel the Red. He had laughing eyes that closed when he spoke. He was a strange Jew, nosy to a fault. He wanted to know everything about you, and was always ready to help you in any way. That's what Berel himself said. He could give advice, run an errand, put in a good word for you with his rich relative, and even prepare a modest meal or a glass of tea. The big samovar was full anyway. Like it or not, drink tea you must.

After pumping the young guest as to who he was and who his father was, it turned out that Berel knew him quite well. He had often stayed at Sholom's father's inn. Now his guest became even dearer to him. "In that case," Berel said, "go wash your hands and eat with everyone else." But the youngster didn't like being considered a needy guest. He had enough self-respect to decline the favor, especially from a poor Jew who lived off the crumbs that fell from his rich relative's table. And so Sholom concocted a lie—he wasn't hungry; in fact, he had just eaten.

No matter how much Berel the Red pestered him to reveal what his business was with his rich relative—Berel claimed that he could perhaps help—Sholom would not disclose it. It was beneath his dignity to have a stranger, and especially a redhead, poke his nose into his private affairs.

Berel the Red, however, continued to quiz him. But the young man played dumb. As it turned out, Berel knew full well what Sholom wanted from his rich relative. He just wanted to hear it from his guest himself. And Berel told him that since his kinsman, the magnate, let it be known that he was looking for a tutor for his children, teachers young and old began streaming to him with documents and letters of recommendation from Bohuslav, Kaniev and Parashtche. "Jews are looking for a livelihood; they want a piece of bread" is how Berel expressed himself. The words "livelihood" and "piece of bread" rang like an insult in our young hero's ears. And to add oil to the fire, the redhead added, "It's really a pity on these candidates, for they're hungry, poor things." It seemed to Sholom that the redhead was aiming these remarks right at him. He apparently knew that our hero would go to sleep hungry.

Sholom didn't know if he dreamed this bizarre scene or fantasized it in a waking state: he had not brought the magnate a letter, but had just come to his house as a servant—on a par with all the other employees. The magnate took a liking to him and asked him who he was and where he came from. When he realized whom he was dealing with, he soon promoted him to foreman and head of the entire staff. And the watchman Pantalei, the hound Zhuk, and that clownish retainer were all scared to death of him. Sholom wrote a letter to his father, in flowery Hebrew, naturally; and the envelope wasn't empty either, but filled with several fresh and crackling hundred-ruble notes, a holiday gift for his father. In the letter he described his high position and financial success, told how he drove a carriage led by a team of six horses. Seeing him, people asked, "Who is that?" And others responded, "Don't you know who that is? That's the top man." "So young?"

It was well into the morning. Banging was heard from Berel the Red's kitchen. The smell of freshly baked bread and boiled milk wafted over to Sholom. Our hero dressed quickly, went to the magnate's courtyard, where the retainer informed him that the magnate had still not read the letter. With bitter heart Sholom returned to the inn, where Berel the Red closed his eyes and asked perfunctorily, "Well, what's new?"

"Nothing as yet," replied the young guest and slipped away from the redhead into his little room. He stretched out on his bed and covered his nose. He didn't want to smell the marinated herring and chopped onions that tickled his nose and teased his appetite to the breaking point. And in order to still his desire for food, Sholom closed his eyes and immersed himself in thoughts. On the wings of his kindled fantasy he flew to the world of imagination, to the magical world of sweet golden dreams, where he loved to seclude himself whenever he was alone. There no one had any mastery, not even his closest friends. That was the enchanted world which had remained from his childhood friend, Shmulik. A world of hidden treasures and two little magic stones, one called Yoshfe and the other Kadkod. He rubbed the first stone and made a wish. Breakfast materialized: hot, tasty doughnuts and butter cookies that melt in your mouth, and hot coffee and milk whose aroma seeped into every corner. Before he had a chance to pick up the coffee, he saw a rich broth with soup nuts, a quarter of a chicken, a roast duck garnished with carrots, and a matzo-meal kugel with goosefat. Also, rare vintage red and white wines that his father had saved for Passover and served only to select connoisseurs. Done with this magnificent breakfast, Sholom felt he needed rest. He rubbed the second stone and made another wish. At once he found himself in a crystal palace of twelve rooms. The walls were plastered with hundred-ruble banknotes. The ground was paved with silver coins and decorated with gold ducats. He saw ivory furniture and velvet bedding. Gold and silver, diamonds and rubies were everywhere. An orchard of the finest fruits surrounded him. Golden fish darted by in a brook. Divine music was heard—the greatest violinists in the world. And Sholom did nothing except dispense charity with a full hand. This one got gold, that one silver, this one precious stones, that one coins, this one foodstuffs, that one clothing—no one was left out, not even his worst enemy. On the contrary, he gave his enemies even more than his good friends so that they should feel . . .

Dreamy and hungry, our young fantasist awoke and, feeling queasy, once again went to the magnate's courtyard, where by now he was quite at home. Pantalei let him in. Zhuk did not pester him. The retainer was quite chummy. He slapped Sholom on the shoulders and informed him that he had spoken about him not with the boss but with his daughters. And while they were talking, one of the girls appeared. She was fat, had red cheeks and an upturned nose, and wore a short dress that came down to her pudgy calves. "That's him!" the retainer said, pointing to Sholom. The chubby girl looked him over from head to toe, hid her face in her hands, burst out laughing and ran away.

66. Tale of a Watch

Tricks to Still Hunger—History of a Watch—Sholom's Talk with the Watchmaker—The Tricks Don't Work

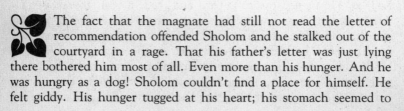 The fact that the magnate had still not read the letter of recommendation offended Sholom and he stalked out of the courtyard in a rage. That his father's letter was just lying there bothered him most of all. Even more than his hunger. And he was hungry as a dog! Sholom couldn't find a place for himself. He felt giddy. His hunger tugged at his heart; his stomach seemed to

have shrunk. He broke into a cold sweat. Which possessions could he sell and buy something to still his hunger? Were he in a big city, he could have pawned his overcoat and come up with a few kopecks.

Sholom searched all his pockets, then remembered his watch. But what could he do with his watch if there was no pawnshop in town? Sell it? In the marketplace that morning he had seen a large clock face inscribed with the words "Master Watchmaker." Here he might be able to sell his watch, however cheaply. Whatever he got would suffice—as long as he could buy something to eat.

Being hungry was awful. A gnawing feeling in his stomach; his hands and feet shaking. Worst, however, was the disgrace. He had no choice but to get rid of the watch. But Sholom's watch wasn't just a watch, it was a watch with a history. A story behind it. An historic watch. So first you must hear the history of the watch.

This happened at the time when the author of these memoirs was in the height of his glory as a private tutor. In his hometown, Pereyaslav, he had more students than a young teacher could wish for. But only one thing was lacking at these lessons—a watch. So Sholom saved his money to buy a watch. The best time to buy one was during a fair, when merchants and shopkeepers from all over gathered in Pereyaslav. Name it and you could buy it at that fair.

Sholom awoke one morning, took his walking stick, and went to the shops and booths in the fair where items made of gold and other expensive things were on display. The fair was held in August, when watermelons and canteloupes are in season. Apples and pears were piled up on wagons and on the ground. Jews ran around like poisoned mice, perspiring and exhausted. They did business. They took in money. Gyspsies swore, horses whinnied, sheep bleated, pigs squealed in their sacks. A blind beggar played a bandore. An old woman sold bagels. A young boy peddled kvass, Russian sour beer. Talking. Yelling. It was deafening.

Walking around the fair, rapt in thought, Sholom met a Jew with a red pimply face, strange darting eyes, and a dirty shirtfront. The man stopped him and spoke softly in a hoarse voice. Then he winked with his crafty eyes at a tall, thin nobleman with a long, upturned mustache and a Polish hat.

"This gentleman wants to sell something for next to nothing. Take a look. What do you care!"

At once the nobleman sidled over, pulled a piece of paper from his pocket, looked around, and unfolded the paper. A shiny, golden, brand-new watch sparkled before Sholom's eyes. After displaying the watch from afar, the man wrapped it in the paper and without a word hid it in his pocket once more.

The Jew was the one who spoke:

"It's a steal! He needs money badly. The gold on the watch itself is worth a hundred rubles."

"How much does he want for the watch?"

"I think he'll take half—fifty rubles. It's a great bargain! I'd buy it myself, but I don't have that much money with me," said the Jew.

"I don't either," said the youth, tapping his pockets.

"Well then, how much do you have?" asked the pimply Jew.

"All I have is twenty-five."

The man's crafty eyes sparkled and he stretched out his hand.

"Use it in good health!"

In a flash the money and the golden watch exchanged hands. Sholom felt a throb in his heart. What if the watch was stolen? Suddenly, he found no pleasure in his bargain; dark and gloomy thoughts plagued him: Perhaps they'll find the watch on me. Buying stolen goods is worse than theft itself. In short, Sholom already had regrets. But it was too late. He took the watch out of his pocket, inspected it from all sides—it was brand new and ticked with hammerstrokes. The heavy casing was of fine gold. Its face was as white as freshly fallen snow. Its dials like spears. The next step was to show the watch to a connoisseur for appraisal. His father too was a connoisseur of watches. But it was beneath Sholom's dignity to show it to his father. And he didn't want to admit that he had bought it on the street either. Best, then, to bring the watch to Henzl the Watchmaker.

Henzl was quite young, but extremely erudite. It was said in town that Henzl had invented a solar watch. You couldn't tell he was learned by looking at him. He was a plain-looking man with a broad nose. He had a thick, wide, flat finger with a long nail, with which he opened the watch cover. Then he put a magnifying lens in his eye, looked into the watchworks, and immediately assessed the attributes, flaws and worth of the watch.

After inspecting Sholom's bargain, Henzl shut the golden watch with a snap.

"It has a plain cylinder, not an anchor," he said. "It's worth five rubles at most."

"But what about the gold?"

"What gold? It's no more gold than I'm a cabinet minister."

"Then what is it?"

"Tombac!"

"What is tombac?"

"Tombac is tombac. It's neither brass nor copper, but tombac . . ."

Henzl removed his magnifying lens, returned to his work, and said nothing further.

It was this watch that our young wanderer wanted to sell to the watchmaker in the small town of T. Sholom strode into the shop confidently and saw an old, rather deaf Jew with cotton in his ears. The following dialogue took place between the old watchmaker and the young man:

"Good morning, Mr. Watchmaker. Do you have any good watches?"

"How many watches does the young man need?"

"Just one!"

"What kind of watch do you want, silver or gold?"

"I'll buy a gold one later. Meanwhile, a silver one will suffice, as long as it works properly."

"That goes without saying!"

The old watchmaker displayed a half-dozen new watches. Sholom selected one, then said: "Actually, I want to make a trade. That is, I'll take this new silver watch and will give you my old one . . . How much would you say it's worth?"

The old man inspected the watch from all sides, thought a while, and shook his head. Then he took the cotton from his ear, moving it from one to the other, as if this were somehow connected with the watches. Finally, he declared that he couldn't offer more than two rubles for the watch. And since his silver one cost nine rubles, the young man would have to pay the grand total of seven rubles to conclude the deal. Sholom approved, but made a counteroffer.

"Why don't you take my old watch in the meantime and pay me two rubles? In a day or so I'll come back and choose a new watch."

But the watchmaker did not like this new proposal.

"Why not?" asked Sholom.

"Just like that. I don't *buy* watches, I *sell* them."

Sholom had another idea. "I'll give you my old watch for one ruble—and done! Not for the money, but because I'm sick of this watch. I can't even look at it anymore."

"If you're sick of the watch," said the old man, "you can throw it away."

"I can't conclude the deal with you," Sholom explained, "because I'm short on cash. That is, right now I haven't got a penny to my name."

"Then why don't you come in some other time," the watchmaker suggested, "when you have some money?"

This exchange was repeated several times. Sholom spoke of money, the old man of moonbeams. Since God had created nudniks, Sholom hadn't seen such a stubborn nudnik as that old man!

Sholom put away his cheap watch and asked the watchmaker to hold the silver one for him. "Perhaps I'll come back today. I expect some money in the mail. And please don't be angry at me for taking up some time."

"It's all right," said the old man, but his pallor, sullen look and trembling fingers showed his irritation. Sholom barely made it to the door. Weak with hunger, he returned to his lodgings at Berel the Red's house and prayed to God that he wouldn't meet the landlord. For that red-haired Jew, Sholom thought, was the only one who had guessed that he was hungry.

67. An Angel in Human Guise

*Tearful Prayer at the Village Synagogue—God's Angel Appears—
An Invitation to Teach—Happiness Forever*

Next door to Berel the Red's inn stood the town bes medresh. Here Sholom secluded himself the next morning and, having nothing to do, stood and prayed. He prayed alone. For the few Jews in T. rose early, prayed in a minyan, and then went off to work. The only one who remained was the shamesh, a shoemaker. Since he had so little work, he also served as a shamesh. Seeing a strange young man with his tefillin bag, the shamesh-shoemaker approached and asked if he had a yorzeit that day. If so, he'd run and gather up a minyan for him.

"No, it's not a yorzeit, I just want to pray," Sholom reassured the shamesh.

"Enjoy it. Here's a Siddur." Then the shamesh left Sholom alone and went to the anteroom, where he began fixing an old pair of shoes.

Our young hero had never before prayed with such devotion and heartfelt sincerity. Even then he was already far from observant. That was the era of the Haskala, when piety was considered humiliating, when a fanatic was worse than a libertine, and even worse perhaps than an apostate today. But the desire to pray came from within him. A kind of religious ecstasy suddenly swept over Sholom and he burst out singing like a cantor. At the Silent Devotion he broke into tears. He cried for a long time from the depths of his heart. When he finished he felt much better, as if a heavy stone had been removed from his heart. He couldn't explain logically why he had wept. He just knew that the tears had come of their own accord and that his soul felt cleansed. Perhaps it was because of frayed nerves, perhaps his long fast. Come what may, today he would break the fast. Enough fasting! He rewound his tefillin, took his walking stick, and returned to his lodgings. At the threshold he met Berel the Red, who told Sholom that he had a visitor, a rich man from a nearby village.

"I think he's a close relative."

"Whose relative?"

"Yours. That is, not a relative, but somehow connected." And without further ado, Berel the Red took Sholom by the hand and brought him to a room reserved for the wealthy clients. There he introduced him to a young man sitting next to a samovar and drinking tea.

The young man, a sympathetic-looking chap with kindly blue eyes, a high, fair forehead, and a neat, rounded beard, rose politely, introduced himself as Joshua Loyev and asked his guest to join him at tea. Loyev winked to the landlord to bring an extra glass. He poured Sholom a glass of tea and offered him some bagels, cookies and pastries. Then young Loyev turned to our hero.

"The landlord told me that you're Nochem Rabinowitz's son from Pereyaslav. In that case, there's some kinship between us . . . Please eat and have some tea."

Never in his life, not before and not later, was a glass of tea so welcome as it was then. No food in the world tasted so delicious as those fresh bagels, cookies and pastries, which quickly disappeared from the table. Not a trace remained, even for politeness' sake. The guest downed everything like a hungry goose. By the time he looked around and realized it wasn't nice, it was too late. Meanwhile Loyev had figured out how they were related:

"Your father has an in-law named Abraham Joshua. This Abraham Joshua had a first wife who was related to me. She was my late mother's sister, that is, my aunt. Now do you understand? Distantly related, but still kin . . . Now tell me where you're coming from, where you're going to, and what you are up to."

When Joshua Loyev found out that Sholom had come here to teach, he asked:

"Do you want to stay here at K.'s place, or would you mind traveling a bit farther? If not, I suggest you come to our village and tutor my younger sister. My father too can afford to pay you as well as the local rich man, if not better . . ."

At these words, Berel the Red spoke up and wished he had a tenth of what that rich man possessed. And without asking Sholom's permission, Berel said that Sholom would gladly see Loyev's father and take the teaching position with pleasure.

What a strange Jew was Berel the Red! Who invited him to be a mediator? He didn't let anyone say a word and liked to talk himself.

Sholom, astonished at the turn of events around him, almost didn't believe his ears. This was either a dream or a hallucination, or perhaps young Loyev was an angel from heaven, descended to earth in the guise of a man. But it was beneath his dignity to show his pleasure. He listened to the conversation with apparent indifference, weighed his answer, and told Joshua Loyev rather vaguely:

"Your offer isn't bad. But, you see, I brought a letter of recommendation to the local magnate, a letter my father wrote . . . What will happen . . . ?"

"In what language is your father's letter?" Berel the Red interrupted.

"What do you mean what language? In Hebrew."

"The holy tongue," Berel repeated. He slapped his sides and began laughing as lustily as if eighteen demons were tickling his armpits! "Young man, you'll have some wait until my relative learns to read a Hebrew letter. I'm afraid you'll have to wait a long time!" At this point Sholom too had a good long laugh.

Within half an hour Joshua Loyev and his young protégé had formed a fast friendship, which grew from minute to minute. It turned out that Joshua was a young maskil, the sort of Haskala scholar produced by that generation. He knew Bible and Talmud, was versed in all the Hebrew books, knew passages of Mapu by heart, could discuss Maimonides' *Guide to the Perplexed* and Judah Halevi's *Kuzari*. He had a beautiful handwriting, but was a wee bit weak in grammar. In other things, he was Sholom's match. And besides, he was a likable fellow who loved people. In fact, his entire family loved people. Residing in a far-off village made them yearn for company. What was their business? They leased lands from Count Branitski and Count Molodetski. They lived the life of farmers, had their own horses and carriages, got along well with the neighboring noblemen, and were liked by the gentiles.

The stream of Loyev's remarks showed that they were dying for company in the village. He talked nonstop, as if he wanted to pour out everything that had been stored up inside him at home over a long period of time. He talked in Berel's house, he talked in the yard, he talked as they sat in the carriage harnessed to a pair of robust horses that would take the new teacher to the Loyev home.

"What do you think of these two horses?" Berel the Red asked Sholom when young Loyev left to talk to the coachman. Berel sang the praises of Joshua's father, his great wealth, and his unique personality.

"You have to thank God it turned out this way."

But it seemed that Berel wanted gratitude to be directed to *him*. Not on his life! Sholom wouldn't leave Berel with the impression that he had saved a man from hunger. Still, Sholom felt terrible that he couldn't pay for his lodgings. For now he was tight on cash.

"Tell me rather how much I owe you."

Berel the Red closed his eyes.

"For what?"

"For lodgings, for everything. I'll pay you as soon as I arrive at Loyev's house."

"Go on with you, go on! Don't make me laugh!" Berel laughed and pushed Sholom away. Just then a tall peasant with white eyebrows and smiling, submissive eyes entered. Andrei wanted the baggage of the young gentleman who was accompanying his young master. Sholom, ashamed that he had no luggage, said that his bags were in transit. They'd arrive later. Meanwhile he had only this little bundle which he'd carry to the carriage himself. But Andrei didn't want to leave empty-handed. Even a little package was good enough. And he picked it up with two fingers and carried it like a feather. A minute later Sholom sat with his young patron in a magnificent soft-cushioned phaeton. Andrei cracked his whip and two gray horses with arched tails carried our hero over fields and through forests to a new place, among new people. Sholom never even dreamed that there, in the village to which he was now traveling, he would find happiness for the rest of his life.

68. An Unexpected Examination

*In Bohuslav—Loyev—A Girl and Her Cavaliers—Rashi's Questions—
How to Write a Letter to a Factory Director—The Results
of the Examination*

It was near twilight when the young Maskil, Joshua Loyev, and his young protégé entered the town of Bohuslav. At their inn they met old man Loyev, who was waiting for his son. Old Loyev impressed Sholom. He had never expected a Jew to look like a general, a field marshal with a leonine voice. Joshua briefly described the young teacher, and where and how they had met. After listening to his son, the old man saddled his nose with a pair of white silver spectacles. Without undue ceremony, he earnestly contemplated Sholom and inspected him as if he were a fish in the market. Then Loyev stretched out a warm hand and greeted the teacher with a friendly look, as amicable a look as such a stern field marshal could muster.

"What's your name?" he asked Sholom.

Learning the young man's name, Loyev now spoke as softly as his leonine manner allowed him to:

"Now listen here, my dear Sholom, please be good enough to step into the other room. I have to discuss some matters with my son. Then I'll call you in and we'll continue our chat."

The other room was a guest parlor in the European fashion. Here sat Bereleh Etels, the innkeeper. A former dry goods merchant, in his old age he had become the owner of an inn. Bereleh, a man with a blue nose ribbed with tiny red veins, stood with hands folded, doing nothing. After speaking of his guests and their business, he said of himself: "God has punished me. In my old age, I have to sell noodle soup!"

His short, thin wife wore a bowtie-shaped headdress and a chain of little yellow pearls around her neck. She wandered around the house vituperating the innkeeper's children (she was a second wife), cursing the servants, abusing the cat, apparently dissatisfied with the entire world—a pessimist of the first order! At the window, reading a novel by Spielhagen, sat their youngest daughter, Shivke, a beautiful and extremely coquettish girl with a round, pale face. A few young men with trimmed beards—the cream of Bohuslav's intelligentsia—came to visit her and discuss literature. The blue-nosed innkeeper introduced the young teacher to this group. How the old man knew who the teacher was is a riddle. To prevent his being bored, the beautiful young girl turned to Sholom with a sweet smile.

"Did you read Spielhagen's *On the Sand Dune?*"

"Yes, I know all of Spielhagen."

"How about Auerbach?"

"Yes, Auerbach too?"

"And Bogrov's novel, *Memoirs of a Jew?*"

"That I know by heart!"

"How about the novel *What Is to Be Done?*"

"Who hasn't read Chernyshevsky?"

"What did you think of the heroine?"

"Vera Pavlovna? What sort of question is that?"

The beautiful young girl and her cavaliers were enchanted. One of them, a private attorney with the imposing name of Mendelssohn, tugged at his just recently sprouted mustache. It turned out that he was head over heels in love with the girl, and was fuming with envy at the young guest who had all of literature in his back pocket. The lawyer stared daggers at Sholom and deep in his heart probably wished that the newcomer break all his bones the next time he took a step.

But all this emboldened our young hero, and he began to speak trippingly on the tongue, citing entire passages by heart and throwing around names like Buckle's *History of Civilization in England* and John Stuart Mill's *On Liberty*. (An out-of-town young maskil has to reveal what he knows when he visits people he doesn't know.) And then right in the middle of Sholom's impassioned discourse, old man Loyev and his son Joshua entered and overheard the young Pereyaslav teacher's lecture to the assembled company. Loyev and Joshua exchanged glances, apparently pleased.

"Listen here, young fellow, let me ask you something," old Loyev sang out. "My son tells me that you're just as knowledgeable in our holy Jewish books as in their secular ones. Do you remember what Rashi says about the daughters of Zelophehad?"

Then commenced a long-winded discussion on Rashi. And Rashi led to the Talmud. At which followed a learned disquisition about scholarship and Haskala, as is usual among Jews who are at home in all the commentaries. This caused a sensation, a furor so great that old man Loyev placed his hand on Sholom's shoulders and said:

"Experience has taught us that despite all this learning and knowledge, when it comes to writing a letter, for example, one's tongue is tied. So, if you'll forgive me, please take this pen and write me a letter in Russian, addressed to the director of a sugar factory. Tell him that until he forwards a certain sum of money we will no longer provide him with sugar beets."

Obviously, this little letter was just a pretext to test Sholom. The letter was passed from hand to hand; the exquisite calligraphy amazed everyone. Here the merit of his teacher, Monish of Pereyaslav, stood Sholom in good stead. Reb Monish Volov had a natural gift for calligraphy. A golden hand. People displayed his handwriting all over town. He didn't write—he painted. Despite his total ignorance of the Russian language, this devout, God-fearing Jew competed with the writing teacher at the state school. It was incredible that such beautiful penmanship was done by a hand and not a machine. His students, including the Rabinowitz children, had suffered enough under Reb Monish's tutelage. But they drew sustenance from his handwriting and his beautiful Russian script, which in time became so useful to them.

But the examination did not end here either.

"If you don't mind," old Loyev added, "please translate this letter into Hebrew; you see, the director of the sugar factory is a Jew!"

That's how the old man explained his request, which of course was also connected with the exam. Without giving it too much thought, Sholom translated the letter into flowery Hebrew. He tried to make the script beautiful and artistic, and the lines thick, measured, gemlike and exquisite. And here too the merits of a former teacher, Reb Zorechl, came into play. What Reb Monish was for Russian calligraphy, Reb Zorechl was for Hebrew.

In short, Sholom passed the improvised exam with flying colors. His head spun from the effort. One of his ears burned. Fantasy took him on her wings and bore him to the world of sweet dreams and enchanted thoughts. He was beaming and happy. The old dream of a treasure had begun to be realized, and quite naturally: Sholom imagines that he arrives at his new home and becomes acquainted with Loyev's daughter. They fall in love, disclosing their secret to the old man. He places his hands on their heads and blesses them: "Be happy, dear children!" Sholom writes his father in Pereyaslav: "This is the story, dear father, please come." They send a carriage for him drawn by fiery steeds . . . Then smack in the middle of the dream his reverie was broken. Old man Loyev approached, called Sholom aside, and began to talk of mundane matters—that is, wages.

"Or would you rather we postpone it for later?"

"Yes, later."

Sholom felt like a man who had just fallen asleep and begun to dream—when suddenly someone came and woke him. The sweet dreams went up in smoke. His overheated imagination vanished like a shadow and the charm of the treasure and all the good, sweet thoughts disappeared.

Meanwhile, night had fallen and it was time to leave. Several miles still separated the town of Bohuslav from the village. A two-hour journey. The horses were already harnessed, and Andrei the coachman carried Sholom's valise into the carriage. The outside air was cool.

"Is that how you're going?" old Loyev asked Sholom. "Why you're as naked as Adam! You'll freeze, for goodness' sakes! Andrei! Give me a cloak!"

From under his seat Andrei drew out a warm woolen cloak. The old man himself helped Sholom put on the garment, which made him warm and comfortable. But he didn't care about that. Something else concerned him. Shivke, Bereleh's daughter, and her cavaliers were standing by the window, looking on, watching old Loyev help Sholom on with the cloak. It seemed to Sholom that they were laughing. Andrei too made him feel discomfited and ill at ease. He wondered what the peasant thought of him.

69. A Jewish Leaseholder

*A Wealthy Jewish House—Learning Etiquette—Old Man Loyev's
Library—An Extraordinary Jewish Landowner*

It was night when all three entered the village: the elder
Loyev, his maskil son Joshua, and Sholom, the young teacher
from Pereyaslav. After passing many squat, dark, peasant
huts, a large field, and a threshing area stacked with piles of straw,
hay and grain, the carriage slowed down in front of an imposing
courtyard. Before the coachman could stop the horses, the wooden
gate opened of its own accord. A hatless peasant bowed low to the
master and admitted the carriage. It glided briefly as if on a soft carpet
and came to a halt in front of an imposing white mansion. The roof
of this large, wide house was thatched with straw. Two big porches
(one on each side) graced the front, and a garden the back. The
house had many windows and was whitewashed inside and out. The
furniture was simple. There seemed to be dozens of rooms. Servants
scurried about like silent shadows. They wore soft shoes to lessen
the noise. No one dared say a word while the old man was at home.
The discipline was tight. The landlord alone was heard. His leonine
voice rang out like a bell. At a long, finely decked table in the first
spacious room sat a beautiful, tall young woman. She was the old
man's second wife. Next to her sat a girl of thirteen or fourteen,
their one and only daughter, a copy of the mother. Old Loyev introduced them to Sholom and they sat down to supper.

This was the first time that the young teacher found himself at
a patrician table where the meal was conducted with great formality
and served by a white-gloved lackey. This servant was only a simple
peasant named Vanka, but Loyev dressed and primped him like a
nobleman's retainer. For one unaccustomed to an assortment of plates,
and to spoons and glasses of varying sizes, it was rather difficult to
maintain aristocratic decorum and not violate the tenets of etiquette.
One had to be constantly on guard.

It must be admitted that Sholom had never known that while at
table one had to obey an entire corpus of etiquette. In an average
Jewish home this was not strictly observed. There everyone ate from
one plate, dunked his fresh challa in the gravy, or even ate with his

hands. In a middle-class Jewish home, one was oblivious to special rules pertaining to dining and negotiating knives, forks and spoons. In a middle-class Jewish home it sufficed to know that you have to leave a piece of fish or meat for the sake of good manners. Otherwise, one could sit the way one pleased, eat as much as one wanted, and, without fear of reprimand, pick one's teeth with the fork.

Who was it that introduced etiquette to the world? Who indited such a code a law, and where was it written? No, the young tutor had never read these rules of etiquette. His sole thought was to watch carefully what other people were doing. Naturally, he could not enjoy his food if he had to be constantly on guard, always careful not to take an extra mouthful, hold fork and knife improperly, sip the soup too loudly, or have someone hear him chewing.

The teacher also passed the etiquette exam with flying colors, but the first few times he left the table hungry. After all these fancy formalities, plentiful courses and excellent food, Sholom longed for a piece of fresh bread with herring and onion, hot baked potatoes in their jackets, still gritty with sand, and a dish of cabbage whose odor wafted in the air for a full day and night . . .

It took some time for Sholom to get used to the discipline of finicky formality. In the meantime, the youth had to keep up appearances and not display his democratic manners and proletarian habits, God forbid. In a word, he had to be like everyone else. Indeed, from the very first day he was not considered a stranger but an equal—one of the family. After all, he came from a good family. That was Loyev's decision. In fact, the old man expressed his opinion concerning the teacher directly to his face, telling him that he came from a good family, and that such a person must be treated with special consideration.

First, Sholom was given a private room, simply furnished but with all the comforts and the finest service. Tutoring his pupil took up two or three hours a day. The rest of the time was Sholom's own and he could do what he pleased—read books or write. He read everything that came his way. Old Loyev himself liked to read and constantly spent money buying new books. And since the old man read no other language but Hebrew, most of his library consisted of Hebrew titles. (Yiddish was not fashionable at that time.) Among the writers who adorned the library of this village magnate and landowner were Kalman Schulman, Mapu, Smolenskin, Mandelkern,

Gottlober, Yehalel (the pen name of Yehuda Leib Levin), Isaac Ber Levinsohn, Mordecai Aaron Guenzburg, Isaac Erter, Dr. Kaminer and Chaim Zelig Slonimsky.

Old Loyev knew all these books almost by heart. He loved to cite passages from them, and to speak about them again and again. Only rarely does one meet a man with such a memory, such a commanding manner of speaking. An orator! He also had an extraordinary sense of humor. He had a true talent for retelling a tale in his own fashion. A man of experience, he told stories that were interesting and full of suspense. Not only did he narrate, but he also poeticized, creating multicolored pictures. Wherever he was, no matter how many people were present, he alone was heard.

In brief, he was a rare sort, an original, a Jew like no other. It was amazing that a man who was raised in a pious Jewish home, in the Jewish town of Bohuslav, turned out the way he did. How did a Bohuslav Jew learn to conduct such an aristocratic household, to love the soil, and to devote himself to farming? It was fascinating to watch him in the morning as he stood next to the threshing machine by the river, in his high, shiny boots and velvet knee-length coat, giving orders to his workers, throwing the sheaves into the feeder, or operating the winnow and the sieve. He took part in every phase of the work himself: plowing, sowing, weeding, digging, reaping and processing the grain; he was with the horses, the oxen and all the domestic animals. He worked everywhere.

If we ever had to show other people an exemplar of a Jewish landowner, an authentic farmer, old Loyev could have been chosen. Christians said openly that people ought to learn from this Jew how to manage a farm, work the soil in the best possible fashion, and make poor workers content. All the village peasants, without exception, would have done anything in the world for him. Not only did they fear him and stand in awe of him—they loved him. They simply loved him because he treated them like human beings, like friends, like his children. These gentiles had never experienced such good treatment from previous landlords—the Polish noblemen. One should remember that the older generation of peasants had not yet forgotten the feel of serfdom on their bodies; they still bore the marks of beatings and blows. And now they were being treated like human beings, not like animals. That explained their trust in their landlord. Hardly a soul among them could multiply two by two. When it came to reckoning, they relied on the old man completely. They were confident that he wouldn't cheat them even out of a penny.

It's hard to imagine the different course Jewish history might have taken, and the role we could have played in the economic and political life of the land, had it not been for the Russian minister Ignatiev's edicts against the Jews, edicts forbidding them to settle in villages, or to buy or rent land for farming. I say this because leaseholders like old Loyev were no rarity either in this region or in others of the blessed Pale of Settlement. Jews from Bohuslav, Kaniev, Shpole, Rzhishtchev, Tarashtche, Zlatapolye, Uman and many, many other places left their little towns and headed for the villages. They leased large and small tracts of land from the noblemen and did wonders with them. They took poor soil and neglected ruins, and converted them into veritable Gardens of Eden. This is no exaggeration. The author of this autobiography heard these very words from the famous Russian landowner Vasily Fyodorovitch Simorenko, a Christian and a close business associate of old Loyev, whom we shall soon meet again. In a word, Loyev was a kind of nobleman, a Jewish landowner. Because of an evil decree, his kind has been uprooted and wiped from Jewish history, perhaps for many, many years.

70. *Life in the Village*

The Village Sofievke—Sholom Gets to Know the Outside World—Three Good Years—Tutor and Pupil—Like Brother and Sister—With Books, Fields and Neighbors

 The village, Sofievke, belonged to Count Branitski. Sholom came as an employee, a temporary tutor, but stayed on permanently and found his second home. Here, as we shall see later, the course of his life and future happiness were determined forever.

Meanwhile, the teacher spent almost three years at the village. He considered them the best, the most blissful years of his life. In every respect this was truly the springtime of his life. Here he was closer to nature, to God's world, and to God's earth—the earth from which we all came, and to which we shall all return.

In Sofievke Sholom realized that our place was here, in nature— and not there, in town. Here he became convinced that we are a part of the great outside world; that we always longed for and will always long for mother earth; that we always loved and will always love nature; and that we were always drawn and will always be drawn to the village. I hope that the kindhearted reader will forgive my short introduction. I can't think of Sofievke without expressing the feelings bound up with it. Having said this, we can now go to the village itself and depict in detail the happy village life.

Sholom slept in a large, bright room with closed shutters; when he woke in the morning, one thrust of his hands opened the window and the shutters. A shaft of light streamed in, bringing with it the warmth of the sun. The aroma of mignonette mingled with the scents of mint and wormwood, and with the fragrances of other unknown grasses once sown (so people claimed) by Count Branitski. But now nettles and thornbushes grew along with the tall grass of the steppes. It grew so high during the summer that both tutor and pupil often played hide-and-seek in six-foot-high grass and had to look for a long time until they found each other. The noise of the opening window prompted a cackling hen and her family to dash off to a side. But soon she returned, scratching and pecking at the dirt, teaching her little chicks to do the same.

It didn't take long to wake, dress and wash. Although it was still early when Sholom left his room, he found no one in the house. Old Loyev had long since departed for the threshing area and the noisy machine. Mrs. Loyev was with the turkeys, geese, ducks and other fowl—they had an entire kingdom of winged creatures. From the large fields came a slow procession of ox carts laden with grain. From afar, one could see the wheat field at a glance. Much of the wheat was already harvested and bundled into sheaves. The rest stood in ripe, yellow stalks, bending and waving in the breeze.

On the other side of the meadow, where the grain ended, were straight rows of beets with large green leaves. Spaced well apart between the rows stood the tall sunflowers, their fuzzy yellow heads like soldiers on guard. Birds loved to gather around the sunflowers and one by one pick out the already sweet white seeds. Beyond that lay the dense oak forest. When the noblemen still resided in Sofievke, they would hunt game there. Now that the land was leased by a Jew, the innocent rabbits and birds had no worries. Jews did not hunt. Jews found other uses for the forest. Old Loyev felled timber, and built barns, chicken coops, storehouses for the grain, sheds and stables for oxen and horses, wagons, sleighs, and numerous other farm implements.

After breakfast, when his first lesson was done, Sholom strolled in the garden, sometimes alone, sometimes accompanied by his pupil. It was hard to say when the garden was more beautiful—at Shevuos time, with the trees in full bloom, or in the summer, when the currants and gooseberries turned red. Or perhaps late in summer, when ripe apples fell from the trees and only the late-blooming, round black plums remained.

Each season had its own special charm and enchantment. The strolling tutor and his pupil always found something new in the garden, even if the gooseberries were still green as grass and sour as vinegar—it didn't matter. They pricked their hands and plucked the largest gooseberries, the ones that hung down and were translucent in the sunlight. Later, when the currants became red as wine and sparkled in the sun, they seemed to plead with you: Take some more, taste another bunch! And so it went, until one's teeth were set on edge. The same held true for the sour cherries and the sweet cherries and the other fruits, which ripened at different times. True, all these could be bought in town too. But they didn't have the same taste and smell as when you plucked them fresh from the tree. And especially if you were not alone but accompanied by a girl who was dear and precious to you, a girl who also considered you dear and precious, like a member of the family, a brother . . .

How could the pupil not have related to her teacher like a brother, when her parents treated him like a son? Sholom was not treated any differently than the Loyevs' own children. Like the Loyev children, the tutor too was surrounded with plenty, lacked nothing, had no worries and no concern with money. In that house, money did not exist at all. That is to say, there was money—and plenty of it. But with the exception of the old man, no one knew its worth nor felt any shortage of it. Everything was prepared lavishly and generously. Food, drink, clothing, shoes, even the rides in the gleaming horse-drawn carriage. There was a servant at every step, an unending supply of people and horses whenever you wanted them. When you appeared in the village, all the gentiles bowed and removed their caps. Born noblemen could not have felt better, freer and more honored.

The old man returned from work covered from head to toe with dust, straw and bits of stalks. He pulled off his long boots, washed,

changed his clothes, and took on a new look. He sat down at his
desk and looked through the mail. A young peasant lad had brought
it on horseback from the nearest post station (in Baranyepolye),
carrying the mail in a sack on his shoulders. After reading through
his letters, Loyev summoned Sholom to write replies to them. The
tutor did his work quickly because he understood old Loyev at a
glance and knew all the correspondence by heart. The old man hated
to repeat anything, and liked to be understood even before he had
finished. Himself a quick worker, he liked to see work swiftly done.

When the correspondence was finished, the family sat down to
eat. Invariably, there were several guests at the table. Most of the
time they were neighbors, leaseholders or merchants who had come
to buy wheat, oats, barley or other grains. As I said, a stern discipline
reigned at the table. No one dared say a loud word; only the old
man sounded forth like a bell. He never ran out of things to say.
For everything he had a story, a parable, a proverb which made you
think and laugh. He had no equal at telling an interesting story,
imitating and mimicking everyone down to the last detail. He had
true talent, even though other Jews considered him strange, an oddball, a crank, a madman.

Nevertheless, the merchants loved to deal with him because his
word was a sacred bond; even if the price increased after a deal was
made, you could be sure he would not renege on the sale. He acted
this way not out of principle or pretension—it was plain and simple
natural honesty, which knew of no chicanery and hated false, un-
derhanded behavior. In the business world, a man like that was called
a "crazy loon" (behind his back, of course), but merchants preferred
to deal with such a madman than with any other who was sane.

After the meal, when the old man and his guests talked and arranged business deals, the teacher and his pupil left to study, learn
and read. Most of all to read. They read everything that came their
way, indiscriminately, without system. Mostly, they read novels and
plays of the great classic writers, Shakespeare, Dickens, Tolstoy,
Goethe, Schiller, Gogol, along with potboilers by French writers,
such as Eugène Sue, Xavier de Montépin, Von Born, Achard and
other hack scribblers of the French boulevard.

After satiating themselves with books, they went to see the thresher
in action, or to the meadow where the men harvested grain and
bundled the stalks. It made Sholom want to roll up his sleeves and
take part in the work. But standing on the side and watching was

much easier than bending your back cutting grain and binding stalks. Looking didn't make you perspire or raise blisters on your hands.

But what an appetite it prompted later! They came home, had buttermilk and black bread, then went out for a stroll in the garden. Or they asked for a horse and carriage and rode with Andrei to the neighboring estates: to Guzipke, Kritohorbe, Zakutenitz. Everywhere they went they were warmly welcomed as beloved guests. The hosts didn't know what to give them first, so they were served tea from the samovar and fruit preserves. Sometimes they rode to Baranyepolye to see Postmaster Malinofsky. There they were treated to a bottle of liquor which the postmaster himself drank up, one little tumbler after another, for Malinofsky was a goy who loved to drink.

At other times, they would visit Dodi the Steward, who lived nearby—in fact, on the estate itself. Dodi's little house was much more fun than their big mansion. The treats one got there one couldn't manage to get at home. For example, only Dodi's wife would serve green garlics with sorrel schav. And where else could they indulge in fresh young pickles right out of the barrel, eaten with hot potatoes in their jackets? Or stuff themselves with sweet cabbage stems which Dodi's wife cut up, ready for sauerkraut? Or drink their fill of apple cider which had the taste of Paradise? A visit delighted Dodi's wife, and Dodi himself was in seventh heaven! But Dodi the Steward was a character in his own right and deserves a separate chapter.

71. Dodi the Estate Steward

*A Man of Nature—Old Loyev Reads the Story of Peter the Great—
Pessi Dodi's House—Sholom Writes Romances and Tragedies
and Gives No Thought to His Own Romance*

Dodi the Steward was a strong, well-built man—neither tall nor husky, but rather solid and muscular. He had yellow hair and somewhat squinty blue eyes. His shoulders—steel. His chest—iron. A hand like a hammer. Not every horse could take him. When he straddled a horse's back he seemed part of it; you couldn't tell where Dodi ended and horse began.

All the gentiles were in awe of Dodi. They were scared to death of his hand, although he rarely raised it to strike anyone. Except if necessary. Only when words no longer availed. The minute someone said, "Here comes Dodi," the peasants, their wives and their daughters (all of whom had been standing around gossiping) quickly set to work. When he was with the workers, he didn't just talk. He took the plow or sickle, the shovel or pitchfork, and with his own hands showed how the work should be done. It was hard to fool Dodi; stealing was impossible. For theft there was no punishment great enough. Drunkenness also incensed him. A glass of whiskey was all right, but becoming drunk, brawling and rioting—that was out. You took your life in your hands!

But you'd hardly recognize this manly Dodi, before whom an entire village of peasants trembled, when he stood in the presence of old Loyev. He was smaller than a child, meeker than a lamb. His hands at his sides. Holding his breath. No soldier stood in awe and respect before a field marshal as Dodi did before the old landlord.

Dodi had come to the village as a youngster and stayed on permanently. He grew in size and responsibility until old Loyev crowned him with the title "steward"—that is, he made him the foreman of the entire estate. Here Dodi married; here he earned his bread. He was given his own little house and garden, and provided with flour, straw, wood and two milk cows. He became a householder and a father of children. Still, he never dared to sit in the old man's presence. Not even for a minute. Only once in his entire life had he sat down in Loyev's presence, and an incident occurred that Dodi never forgot.

I think I mentioned that old Loyev loved to explain, to teach everyone, to share what he knew with others. One long winter night, Dodi presented a report of the estate finances, standing before the old man as usual. When he finished, Dodi waited to be dismissed. But old Loyev was in a good mood. He wanted to chat a while, not about estate affairs, but about peripheral matters and about his Polish neighbors.

Finally, the conversation turned to Poland and the Polish Rebellion. Then Loyev discussed the Russians and Russian history before Peter the Great. And since a book on Russian history in a Hebrew translation by Mandelkern lay on Loyev's desk, he began to read, translating the entire story of Peter the Great into Yiddish for Dodi. As he read, Loyev told Dodi to sit down. Dodi didn't dare. The old man repeated his command. This time Dodi had no choice. He sat on a chair next to the door, under the old grandfather clock. Dodi's head was not used to such lectures, and to top it off, he was seated. So gradually he began to nod. His eyes closed, stuck fast, and with the drone of the old man's voice, he slowly fell into a sweet sleep. Now we'll let Dodi sleep and say a few words about the grandfather clock.

The clock was an old invalid that had provided many years of service, and should long have been retired for a well-deserved rest in the attic among old, decrepit junk. But Loyev always had a strange affection for superannuated things—for an old, faded and cracked mirror that reflected a double image, for an old collapsed chest of drawers, from which pulling out a drawer was as hard as splitting the Red Sea! Among other such antiques was an old-fashioned ink-well that had been on his writing desk for years. Made of glass, it was shaped like a little boot and set into a black wooden container filled with sand. No money in the world could persuade the old man to chuck this old inkwell and buy a more civilized-looking one. But it had nothing to do with stinginess. Old Loyev was not stingy at all. On the contrary, he purchased only the best and most expensive. He just couldn't bear to part with an old object. The same held true for the clock, which on account of its advanced years needed a heavy weight. New weights were constantly being added. Before this clock tolled the hours, it wheezed and rattled like an asthmatic old man before he begins to cough. But when it rang out the hours, the clock really sounded off like a church bell. The "bong, bong, bong" was even heard outdoors.

Now let's return to Dodi. Dodi snoozed and Loyev read the history of Peter the Great and his wife, Anastasia. Suddenly the old clock decided to chime the hour of ten. Dodi no doubt thought it was a fire—the granary was ablaze. So he quickly jumped to his feet and shouted: "Water!"

Frightened, the old man put down the history of Peter the Great and looked at Dodi through his spectacles.

"I'm going to remember that look," said Dodi, "till my dying day . . ."

Sholom liked Dodi for his simplicity and calm. He was convinced that this man of nature had never uttered a lie in his life. Dodi's loyalty and devotion to his boss and his family was limitless. And because the teacher was treated by the Loyevs as a member of the household, Dodi too considered him family, and was prepared to go through fire and water for him.

In Dodi's view, everything connected with the Loyev family was on a higher plane. In any case, they weren't like other, average folk. Dodi simply deified the Loyevs—and this helped Sholom too. During the hot summer days or the long winter nights, Sholom and his pupil loved to drop in on Dodi and his wife for a quick visit. In that small house with its low ceiling that one could touch with a fingertip, they always felt better than at home. The schav with young garlics that they ate at Dodi's house during the summer, and the baked potatoes and fresh sour pickles or frozen sauerkraut that were served during the winter, were mouth-watering delicacies a thousand times better than the most exquisite dishes at home. Not to mention when Dodi's wife, Pessi, baked honey cake or rendered chicken fat—that was a holiday for the youngsters. Hot honey cake just out of the oven, or fresh, fatty cracklings that melted in your mouth like the manna the Israelites ate in the desert—these were no small matters.

Most of their visits were in the winter, when the trees were wrapped in white, like frozen corpses in shrouds. At such time Sofievke lost its summer charm and splendor. There was nothing better to do than to slip into Dodi's well-heated little house and refresh oneself with Pessi's delicious treats. Outside, awesome silence reigned. The snow was deep. No one came to visit the Loyevs. Sholom's heart was filled with gloom, his soul with melancholy. One solution was to ask Andrei to harness the horses to a wide sleigh. The youngsters buried themselves in fur coats and, covered with sheepskin blankets, rode to one of the neighboring estates, where they had a glass of tea from a hot samovar and then returned home.

But winter had its advantages too. There was plenty of time to read and write. During the nearly three years that Sholom spent in the village, he wrote much more than during a later ten-year period when he was already a writer named Sholom Aleichem. Writing never came so easily to him as then. Throughout the night he would write long, heart-rending novels, impassioned dramas, and complicated tragedies and comedies. Ideas poured from him as from a barrel. His fantasy spurted like a fountain. He never asked himself why he wrote all this. When he finished a work, he read it to his pupil and both were enchanted. Both were convinced that it was a masterpiece—but not for long. As soon as Sholom completed a new work, *it* became a masterpiece, and the earlier one was considered pale and wan by comparison. The best place for it was the stove. And so, up in flames went more than a dozen novels and scores of plays.

Neither of them doubted that the young man was born to be a writer. Both tutor and pupil spoke of this, fantasized, and they built the most beautiful dream castles. Discussing different plans and various works, they forgot their own plans. About this they never exchanged a word. It never dawned on them to articulate their feelings or to ponder the fate of their own romance.

The word "romance" was too clichéd, the word "love" too banal for what the young couple felt. Their relationship was so natural they could not have felt any other way. Would a brother ever dream of declaring his love for his sister? It wouldn't be an exaggeration to say that objective observers knew and constantly talked about the young couple's romance more than the two protagonists themselves. Both were too young, too naive, and too happy. Not a cloud specked their blue sky. They saw no opposition from anywhere. And most important—they never thought of it. During the nearly three years of their acquaintance, they never dreamed for a moment that they would ever separate. Nevertheless, the day came when they had to part. Not forever, but for a short time.

This happened when our hero had to report to the draft board.

72. *The Draft Board*

*Talk of the Draft—Saying Good-bye—A Letter of Recommendation—
Fantasies—Results of the Letter—Story of a Crippled Son—The Return*

One can confidently say that during these three years hardly a day passed in Sofievke without hearing the word "draft." For old Loyev the draft was a sickness, a mania that didn't let him rest by day or sleep at night. It cost him a fortune. How? When his son Joshua had to report to the draft board, the father first went to the provincial seat, in Chernigov, stayed a long while, and after much anguish managed to get an exemption certificate for him. This was one of several documents that exempted its possessor from military service. With such a certificate one never had to serve in the active military, only in the reserves. The cost of that piece of paper could have made a pauper wealthy. But for the sake of his son nothing was too expensive for old Loyev.

As soon as the certificate affair ended, another tumult began. The Russo-Turkish War broke out, and rumors spread that the reserves might be called up. In that case, Loyev had to get his son a white card stating that the bearer was unfit for military service. This meant that the candidate had to undergo a physical examination to determine if he was fit for duty. And, as might be expected, the examination revealed that Joshua was not suitable, and he was given the white card. In other words, disqualified, thank God.

Not only was he not qualified for military service, but the physicians also suggested that he be sent to a warm climate, to Menton and Nice, for a cure, because he had a serious heart ailment. Indeed, within several years (as we will see a bit later), Joshua died from this illness. In the meantime, however, all hell had broken loose in the house. Father and son traveled to Kaniev and became acquainted with the district police chief, with other local officials, and with doctors. The officials and the draft board doctors kept taking loans from Loyev. Friendly Jews and advice givers had also latched on to the gravy train. Everyone under the sun was pumping money into his pockets from Loyev's. In short, the only word you heard in the house was draft, draft, draft.

When Sholom had to report to the draft board, old man Loyev became nervous. He made every effort to transfer quickly the teacher's residence from Pereyaslav to Kaniev, and to register him with the Kaniev draft board, where Loyev had great influence. One's own father couldn't have been more solicitous to his son than old Loyev was to Sholom. But curiously, Sholom himself feared the draft less than the Loyevs. For him, traveling to Kaniev and reporting to the board was actually a festive occasion. He ordered a new pair of high boots and a soldier's hood; indeed, he was quite prepared to be drafted. He was certain he would excel in the army, would please the officers, and would soon become a noncommissioned officer or a sergeant-major. No Jew could attain any higher rank. But at the last minute, when Sholom had to leave, all his courage suddenly melted. He felt embarrassed and ashamed. Yet he must admit that when he had to bid farewell to the family, perhaps forever, a strange longing pressed his heart and he shut himself in his room, buried his head in his pillow, and wept bitter tears . . .

But he wasn't the only one in that house to cry bitterly. In her room, his pupil wept even more. Her eyes were swollen from crying and she couldn't even appear at the table. On the pretext of a bad headache, she remained in her room all day long and refused to see anyone.

Saying good-bye was a very sad ordeal. A Tisha B'Av mood encompassed the house. Sholom's heart was dark and desolate. In the carriage, as Andrei was about to whip the horses, our young hero looked up to the window for the last time and saw a pair of bleary eyes that silently said to him: "Go in good health, my darling, but come back quickly because I can't live without you!"

Sholom heard these words with all his senses and his eyes replied: "Be well, my beloved. I'm coming back to you because I can't live without you!" And only now did he realize how attached he had become to this house. No force in the world but death could tear him away from here.

He sank into a reverie; his heated imagination took wing, and he began to dream. When he returned he would reveal himself first to her and then to her parents. He imagined turning to old Loyev and saying: "I love her. I love your daughter. Do what you want with me!" Then the old man would embrace him and say: "It's good you told me. I've been expecting it for a long time." And then began the wedding preparations. Tailors were brought from Bohuslav and Tarashtche to sew garments for the bride and groom. They baked honey cakes and prepared fruit preserves. A huge carriage normally kept in the barn and used only for special occasions was sent for members of the groom's family. His father, Uncle Pinny and other relatives came. Though no one knew how he got there, Shmulik too appeared at the wedding. Shmulik, the rabbi's son. Shmulik the Orphan who had so many wonderful stories to tell. "Well, Sholom," he said as he kissed the groom, "didn't I tell you that the treasure was yours?"

Sweet childish dreams and golden fantasies of this kind fused in Sholom's mind until he came to Kaniev. There he stayed with a hunchbacked relative of old Loyev, a rich wine merchant who sold wines to the surrounding nobility. His name was Berach Bertchik. Sholom at once attended to his draft board affairs and presented his letter of recommendation to the local police chief. In this letter old Loyev stated: "I'm sending our tutor to the draft board with the hope that I'll have him back within a week, freed of all obligations."

The chief read the letter and gave a one-word reply: "Fine!" And that sufficed to calm Sholom. He went to the board and drew a number, which happened to be 285. True, this number was not a very high one, but the examination list at the draft board closed at 284. Sholom was free. Because of him, several other Jewish lads with higher numbers were also freed. That year there was great joy in Kaniev.

For this celebration, Sholom's father traveled to Kaniev from Pereyaslav. If I remember correctly, Uncle Pinny came too—he had an in-law in Kaniev—and the festivities grew tenfold. Berach Bertchik fetched some wine from his cellar, and the celebrant sent a telegram to Sofievke through the Baranyepolye station:

"Mazel tov. They didn't get to me. I'm free. Coming home tomorrow morning."

However, more than one day passed before our hero could leave Kaniev. For was it possible that a Jewish celebration not be marred? A certain man appeared whose name was Vishinsky or Vishnefsky. A Jew, a shouter, a loudmouth. He had a crippled son who he was sure would be disqualified. But it turned out he was declared fit for military duty. This vexed the father, and he began to raise a fuss:

"What? My crippled son will go and serve instead of those privileged snobs who bought their freedom?"

When people asked him not to yell, he shouted, "What? Am I yelling? Seems to me I'm talking rather softly."

He began to shout even louder. "I know why the chief took only cripples into the army." And he secretly told everyone the reason— but so loudly that the entire town knew it down to the last detail. Even the exact language of Loyev's letter to the chief. (There are no secrets where Jews are concerned.)

This Vishinsky or Vishnefsky proclaimed that he would not remain silent. "I'm going to bring everyone to court," he said, "the chief, the doctors, the entire draft board!"

People then called this Vishinsky aside and told him that a collection would be made and that his crippled son would be freed from military duty. But he didn't want to hear promises.

"In the Yom Kippur service, Jews bow down seven times between the words 'thus he said' and 'thus he counted.' I don't want promises. I want to see cash on hand." He then repeated these demands in Russian. Nothing helped. Then some good folk intervened. They called one meeting, another meeting, and two more meetings, and all the exempt candidates contributed. One gave fifty rubles, another a hundred, and they gathered up a sufficient sum, which would be divided among the drafted Jewish men. The largest share was taken, of course, by the shouting Jew. He argued that he deserved more than anyone else because his son was more of a cripple. Logic of course would have dictated otherwise: on the contrary, *because* he was a cripple, it would be easier to exempt him. But what could you do with such a loudmouth, shouting at the top of his lungs?

Seeing that everyone gave in to his whims, like a spoiled brat Vishinsky continually increased his demands. He began to bargain like a fishwife. Luckily, the above-mentioned relative, Berach Bertchik, had carte blanche from old Loyev to give the prospective draftee as much money as he needed. Who thought of money at such a time? Freedom was the only thing that mattered; freedom was the only blazing star. Sholom felt free only when he sat in the carriage that had been sent to the railroad station in Mironovke. Andrei the coachman brought him regards from home: everyone was well, thank God, and everything was in order.

"Giddyap," said Andrei and began a conversation with the horses in their language. The horses understood him and the carriage almost flew through the air. It was a warm, mild autumn day. The sun was hot but did not burn. It patted and caressed. Sholom's eyes closed. The web of dreams began again. Silken dreams. Castles in the air, golden castles. Soon he would be home. As soon as he arrived, he would reveal his cards to old Loyev: "I'd like to inform you that I love your daughter and your daughter loves me." Soon. Within half an hour. Fifteen minutes. Here was the familiar Baranyepolye, the forest, the pastureland, the cemetery, the windmills that looked like giants from afar, waving their hands and calling, "Come here, come here!"

A few minutes more and he saw the courtyard. The great white mansion with its two porches. There could be no greater joy than when a child comes home to his parents freed from the draft. Sholom had many, many stories to tell about the miracles and wonders of the draft—a virtual Exodus from Egypt! But he did not tell the most important matter, the one he had rehearsed. He did *not* reveal his cards before old Loyev. He postponed this for the next day, for later . . .

Meanwhile, one day passed and then another, one week and then another. Then an unexpected catastrophe struck, brought on by an outsider who opened up the old man's eyes to the ongoing romance. This person happened to be a wise, far-seeing woman, a relative of old Loyev from Berditchev named Toive. We call her "Auntie Toive from Berditchev." When you get to know her, you'll see how appropriate her name is. To her we'll devote a separate chapter.

73. Auntie Toive from Berditchev

Auntie Toive Watches the Youngsters—The Catastrophe—Out into the World—Intercepted Letter—Wandering in the Night

Actually, Toive wasn't an aunt to anyone. She was no more than a cousin to old Loyev. But, as I mentioned, the name Auntie suited her. She was a rather homely woman with a pockmarked face and a long nose. Her clever-eyed glance, however, seemed to penetrate you. People said that she wore the pants in the family. She managed the business affairs and was quite wealthy. Now, after an absence of many years, Auntie Toive came to visit the Loyevs.

Naturally, for an aunt from Berditchev the aristocratic life in the village seemed new and strange: she saw everything through her Berditchev eyes and marveled at everything. She talked familiarly to old Loyev and told him explicitly what she thought, what pleased her, and what did not.

For example, she liked the life in the village, the air, the cows, the horses, the fresh milk that smelled of the pasture, and the bread made of homegrown wheat. Everything smelled of the earth, of one's own labor. Everything was good, top-notch. She even liked Dodi, a man of nature. But she disagreed with her cousin's discipline; it smacked too much of a nobleman's antics. The way she saw it, being a Jew and a lessee of land was a contradiction. On the other hand, she liked the fact that Loyev was a good farmer and loved the earth. Why not? As long as God helps, one can make money and become a rich man. Why not? Perhaps she too wouldn't have refused this opportunity. But she didn't understand why one had to live so far from Jews. Why didn't Loyev go to Bohuslav when a Jewish holiday came? And she reproached him for his mocking a beggar with a green scarf who had wandered into the area, the sort that claimed to be a grandson of a noted Jewish scholar, when he asked for a donation. Sure, Loyev had given one, and with a generous hand too. But still, he had poked fun at the man. "Rather don't give and don't mock," Auntie Toive from Berditchev contended.

And another thing. Auntie Toive liked the teacher. Sholom was a fine lad—she had nothing against him, and he knew his stuff too. And what's more, he came from a good family—that made it even better. But where was it written that a tutor had to be so close to his pupil? In her opinion, this teacher was too chummy with his charge. How did she know this? Auntie Toive had an all-seeing eye. Auntie Toive appointed herself to watch the young couple's every step. In fact, with her own eyes she had witnessed them eating from one plate. Auntie Toive from Berditchev noticed from the very first day that the girl was dying for the lad and that he was head over heels in love with the girl.

"It's plain as day to anyone," she declared, "except for someone who's either blind in both eyes, or simply doesn't want to see what's happening under his nose. All I had to do," Auntie Toive continued, "was take one look at the two of them sitting at the table, exchanging glances, talking with their eyes. From that moment on," said she, "I didn't stop watching them for a second." Indeed, Auntie Toive zealously watched when they sat and studied, when they went for walks, or when they went riding in the carriage.

Once—so Auntie Toive told the old man—she noticed them walking into Dodi the Steward's house. That she didn't like from the start. "What business do children like that have in his poor house?" But lazy she was not, Auntie Toive from Berditchev, and she peeked in through Dodi's window and saw the young couple eating from one plate. What they ate, she didn't know. But she did see them— may she see good things the rest of her life!—eating and talking and laughing . . .

"So it's either one thing or the other. If it's a match—why well and good, but the mother and father have to know. And if it's a love affair? A romance? Then the parents should *certainly* know—for it's much healthier and better and nicer to give your daughter to a poor teacher who has no more than a couple of shirts to his name than to wait until this selfsame teacher runs off with the daughter on some dark night to set up a quick wedding canopy in Bohuslav, Tarashtche or Korsun."

These were Auntie Toive's complaints, as they later became known.

She revealed them to her cousin in absolute secrecy half an hour before her departure. Her words reverberated in old Loyev's heart, for when he left to escort his cousin, he was furious and didn't say a word to anyone for the rest of the day. He secluded himself in his room and didn't show his face.

That night, his son Joshua arrived in Sofievke and spent the night there. Something was going on. Something was brewing. They locked themselves into the old man's room, discussing something in whispers. They were evidently holding a family council. The pupil, ready to go for a walk with her tutor, was stopped at the last minute. The family didn't come to eat all at once, as usual; they came separately, at various times. Each one finished eating, rose, and went on his way. Something extraordinary was happening in the house. A strange silence that precedes a storm . . .

Who would have thought that a couple of ambiguous words from Auntie Toive from Berditchev would cook up such a storm and prompt such a revolution in the house? Had Auntie Toive known sooner what repercussion her words would cause, perhaps she wouldn't have butted in where she wasn't needed. Much later they learned that Auntie Toive from Berditchev immediately regretted the whole thing and wanted to take back what she had said, but by then it was too late. She made an about-face and began to argue with the old man that it really wasn't such a great misfortune, and that there was really nothing to get upset about. Was it the boy's fault that he was poor? "Being poor is no shame" and "Happiness is in the hands of God" were among the proverbs she fed him.

Words, however, no longer availed. The old man maintained that actually he had nothing against Sholom. But how dare they conduct a romance in his house without his knowledge? His daughter's possible engagement to a poor lad didn't bother him. Then what did? It was he, her father, who was supposed to introduce such a young man to her. And she must not choose him herself, without having consulted her father! This is what vexed him more than anything else.

The young couple became aware of all these complaints and remarks only much later. But at this time, like a pair of innocent lambs, they did not know who had betrayed them. They only felt that something was brewing. What could come of it—they would see tomorrow. The next day would tell.

The next morning when our hero awoke, he found no one at

home. Not the old man or his wife, not the son or the daughter. Where were they all? They had gone. He didn't know where and none of the people in the courtyard would say. On the table he saw a package prepared for him. He opened it, hoping for a letter, an explanation. But he found no message. Not a word. The only thing the packet contained was money—wages that had accumulated throughout his entire stay. Nothing more. In the courtyard, the sleigh stood waiting (this incident happened during the winter) with a warm sheepskin blanket to cover his legs. Sholom couldn't get a word out of the household retainers.

Even Dodi the Steward, who would have willingly chopped off his hands for Sholom and his pupil, answered all questions with only a shrug and a deep sigh. His fear of the old man overrode everything else. This made the humiliated teacher even angrier. He felt lost and didn't know where to turn. He made several attempts at writing a letter, first to old Loyev, then to his son Joshua, and then to his pupil. But the words didn't come. It was a great catastrophe. He had never expected such a slap in the face. He felt disgraced for himself and embarrassed before the others. But he didn't hesitate too long. He sat in the sleigh and let himself be brought to the station in order to leave—but where to? He himself still didn't know. Wherever his legs would take him. In the meantime, before he arrived at the railway station, he asked the coachman to stop in Baranyepolye—the post station from which Sofievke got all its mail. In Baranyepolye Sholom had a friend. You know him—the manager of the station, Postmaster Malinofsky.

By nature, Malinofsky loved to have his palm greased. And as we already know he also loved to drink. He frequently got presents from old Loyev's lands: a bag of wheat, a wagonload of straw and, in honor of the holiday, a coin or two. Malinofsky made common cause with the teacher and his pupil and, generally speaking, was a good goy.

Sholom stopped by for a short visit and unburdened his heart. Sholom wanted Malinofsky to be a smuggler of contraband—he'd send a letter to Loyev's daughter and have her reply, if there was one, forwarded to him. After hearing Sholom's request, Postmaster Malinofsky stretched out a hand and swore to God. And in case Sholom didn't believe him, he crossed himself too. He would do his absolute best. And since a business deal was being concluded between good friends, said agreement had to be wetted down with a bit of whiskey and a piece of herring. Nothing else would do. Both sat down and did not rise again until the bottle was empty and Malinofsky was full, at which he began to embrace and kiss the teacher. Once again he swore and crossed himself, and said that Sholom's letters would be given over to Loyev's daughter—rest assured. For when Malinofsky gives his word, it's his sacred oath . . .

And so it was: The first few flaming and impassioned love letters that Sholom sent him, one after another, Postmaster Malinofsky (as Sholom later learned) placed squarely in the hands of old Loyev. Hence it is easy to understand why no reply was ever received to these flaming and impassioned letters. And it is also easy to understand why he continued writing these letters—until he stopped writing.

. . . .
. . . .

What do these dots mean? They stand for a long, dark night. Everything was wrapped in a thick mist. The lonely wanderer was groping for his way. He kept stumbling over stones or falling into a pit. He fell, scrambled up, continued on his path, tripped over another stone and fell into another pit, taking no notice of the bright world around him. He did foolish things, made mistakes, one greater than the other. A blindfolded man cannot possibly find the right road. A blindfolded man must go astray—and Sholom went astray. He strayed for a long, long time. Until he found the right road. Until he found himself.

74. *The First Trip*

Arriving in Kiev—Drawn to Stars of the Haskala—The Search—
Looking for Yehalel—The Reception

Where does a homeless young man who wants to accomplish something in life go? To the big city. The big city is the center for everyone who seeks work, a calling, a profession, or a job. Where does a young man go who lost his dowry, was tired of his wife, fought with in-laws or parents, or broke up with his partners? To the big city. What does a provincial do who hears that in the stock market people turn snow into farmer cheese and gather up bags full of money? He heads for the big city to seek his fortune. The metropolitan center has a magnetic force that attracts you and does not let you go. It sucks you in like a swamp. There you hope to find what you seek.

In Sholom's region, the metropolis was the famous holy city of Kiev. That's what he set his sights on and that's where he arrived. Actually, what did he set his sights on and what was he looking for? He couldn't rightly say, because he himself didn't precisely know what his soul was yearning for. He was drawn to the big city, like a child attracted to the light of the moon. For a great town contained great people—the bright stars that shone down on us here on earth with the clear light of vast and endless skies. I refer to the great writers and divinely graced poets of the Haskala whose names made such a great impression upon—what shall I call them?—well, the young maskilim, the naive, innocent youth.

This was our hero's first entry into the big, wide world and his first trip to the metropolis. He stayed at a Jewish inn called Reb Alter Kaniever's Inn. It was in the lower part of the city, the Padol district, where Jews were permitted to reside. I said "where Jews were permitted to reside," but I must retract that lest it give the impression, God forbid, that all Jews were permitted to stay there. Oh, no! Only those Jews who had official residence permits were allowed to live there—for example, artisans, agents for businessmen of the first merchants' guild, ex-soldiers of Czar Nicholas I who had served their mandatory twenty-five years, and Jews who had children studying in the gymnasium. All the other Jews sneaked into the area for a short time, living in great fear and remaining by the good graces of the janitor, the local police chief, or the district chief. And all this was only temporary, until an inspection, when police and gendarmes would conduct a raid in the middle of the night in all the Jewish inns. This they called a spot check. And if they found contraband—meaning Jews without residence permits—they rounded them up to the police station. Then with great fanfare they escorted them on foot, along with thieves and other state prisoners, until they reached their hometowns.

But this didn't prevent anyone from going to Kiev. The Russian proverb says: "If you're afraid of the wolf, don't set foot in the forest." But despite everyone's fears of the midnight inspections, they traveled to Kiev anyway. The innkeeper saw to it that the inspections proceeded smoothly and that, God forbid, no unkosher merchandise was discovered. How? Simple. The innkeeper greased those palms that had to be greased. He got advance word of a raid and knew what to do. The forbidden goods were hidden, one in an attic, another in a cellar, someone else in a clothes closet, a fourth in a chest and a fifth in a place where no one ever dreamed that a living human being could be hidden. Best of all, when they crawled back into God's world from their hiding places, everyone laughed at the whole thing, like children at hide-and-seek. If worse came to worst, they consoled themselves with a sigh: "So what! We've lived through worse times and bigger Hamans!"

One dark wintry night, during his first trip to the great and holy city of Kiev, the author of this autobiography had the honor and pleasure of lying hidden with a few other Jews in the attic of Reb Alter Kaniever's Inn, shivering with fright. Since the raid was totally unexpected, the men didn't have a chance to grab, if you'll excuse the expression, their long underwear, and the women their undergarments. Luckily the raid ended quickly, otherwise they would have expired from cold in the attic. But on the other hand, imagine the great joy when the innkeeper, Reb Alter Kaniever, a handsome white-bearded man, called them down from the attic in an odd, rhyming, singsong fashion:

"Jews, don't fear! Come down here! The demons disappear. Inspection's done. Come, let's have fun."

And so this scare ended with a great celebration. The samovar was put up and everyone drank tea, nibbled on dried bagels and spoke of miracles and wonders—the Exodus from Egypt! But this joy was soon dashed when the innkeeper taxed each guest a ruble and a half to cover the expenses of the raid. No protests from the wives helped. Poor souls, they contended that they shouldn't have to pay a thing because they came just for pleasure and not to do business and earn money. They had come only to see the local doctor, the professor, to cure their ailments.

Then they began a saga about doctors and professors. Each woman described her sickness and which professor she had come to consult. It turned out that they all had come to see one professor, and all had one and the same illness. For whatever ailed one, all the others claimed they had too. Most astounding was the fact that all the women in the room spoke at one and the same time. Nevertheless, everyone heard everyone else. Several impressions from that night were utilized later by Sholom in one of his early works, entitled "The

First Trip" (a story about two young birds flying out into God's world for the first time).

This is how our hero spent the first night in the great and holy city of Kiev. The next morning, he set out to meet the great stars who shone down from their celestial heights: our great maskilim and poets in Kiev, among whom he knew only one thus far. That was the famous Hebrew poet, known by the acronym Yehalel, which stood for *Yehuda Leib Levin*. Sholom set out to find him, and was successful. But it wasn't as easy as you think. When he asked where to find the poet, Sholom learned that in Kiev there was a millionaire named Brodsky. This Brodsky had a mill in Padol. That mill had an office. In that office various people were employed. Among them a cashier named Yehuda Leib Levin. And this Yehuda Leib Levin was the famous poet Yehalel. And that's where the story begins.

Brodsky's mill wasn't open to everyone. Only people in the wheat or flour business were permitted to enter.

"Who would you like to see?"

"The famous poet Yehalel!"

"We don't have anyone by that name!"

One Jew, a wheat merchant, even found an opportunity to crack a nasty joke. "Oh, so you have to recite the Hallel? What's up? Celebrating a new month today?

But God performed a miracle—a tall, thin man with a long nose, wrinkled face and several yellow stumps in his mouth for teeth appeared. With his torn coat, frayed hat and big gray sailcloth umbrella he looked like Don Quixote.

It turned out this tall man, this Don Quixote, was a bookkeeper and worked alongside Yehalel. When he learned who the youth sought, the tall man took Sholom's hand and without a word led him into a building. Here Don Quixote set down his big umbrella, cast off his coat, and remained in a short jacket with frayed elbows. If not for his bowlegs the tall bookkeeper would have been even taller. But after the polite exchange that strangers use to get acquainted, the lanky bookkeeper seemed to grow even taller in Sholom's estimation.

Why? It turned out that this very Don Quixote personally knew the man whom Sholom at the time considered one of God's angels. None other than Bogrov, the author of *Memoirs of a Jew*. This tall bookkeeper knew Bogrov personally; he had worked with him in a bank in Simporopol.

"Really? Really? You mean to say you knew the great Bogrov personally?" Sholom asked ecstatically, full of curiosity.

"Young man! I'm telling you we both worked together in a bank in Simporopol and you're asking me a question like that!"

"And you actually talked to him?"

"Like I'm talking to you now. Not only did I talk to him, I played cards with him, preference in fact. He liked cards, did Grigory Isakovitch—boy, did he like, he *loved* to play cards! I wouldn't say he was actually a cardplayer, but just for the fun of it he liked a game of cards, a game of preference—why not? Oh, for a game of preference, ay, ay, ay,!"

The man raised his dry, bony hand and his frayed elbows, wrinkled his creased face even more, made a kind of semicircle in the air with the tip of his nose, and displayed the yellow stumps of what once were teeth. That was his way of smiling. But he soon became serious again. He looked out into the distance through his sparkling glasses, scratched under his collar, and spoke respectfully of Bogrov:

"Grigory Isakovitch is a great man! Nothing to sneeze at—Grigory Isakovitch! Indeed, a great man, far greater than your famous poet Yehalel, who is small, insignificant and infinitely tiny!" He brought his hand down to the ground to show how minuscule was Yehalel.

As these words were uttered, the door opened and a small man entered. He was cross-eyed, short but solidly built and with a nice-sized paunch. At first glance, compared to the long and desiccated Don Quixote, the newcomer looked like Sancho Panza, Don Quixote's sidekick. Without saying good morning, this Sancho Panza rushed through and disappeared into another cubicle on the other side of the latticework partition.

"That's him! That's your poet, Yehalel. You can go into his office, if you like. He's no big shot."

From these words, and from his earlier comparison of the great Bogrov to Yehalel, it was obvious that the bookkeeper and the cashier got along like cat and mouse. Nevertheless, this had no effect upon Sholom's veneration of his hero. With beating heart and quaking soul, he stepped across the threshold, and with the utmost deference entered the little room.

The famous writer stood in a poetic pose, hands crossed over his heart like Alexander Pushkin, or at the very least like Micah Joseph Lebensohn. Yehalel was apparently in a very rarefied poetic mood, for he paced back and forth in his cubicle, hands folded, and didn't even look at his young admirer. In fact, he responded to his "Good morning" with scarcely more than an angry glance of his crossed eyes. It goes without saying that he didn't tell him to sit, or ask who he was and where he came from. His naive admirer was confident that all poets were like this, that Alexander Pushkin also never responded to a greeting.

Sholom didn't feel too comfortable standing at the door like a fool. But there was nothing to be done. And taking offense was out of the question—after all, Yehalel was a poet! But several years later the situation changed, when the naive admirer had become not only a writer but editor of a yearbook, *The Jewish Folk Library*. When the poet Yehalel brought him a sketch, and the former admirer and present editor, Sholom Aleichem, reminded him of their first meeting and described the above-mentioned scene, the poet shook with laughter.

But then young Sholom did not laugh. One can only imagine how depressed he felt when he left the famous poet. But his first trip did not end with that. The real bundle of woes he was destined to suffer in his first great venture was just beginning.

75. *Letters of Recommendation*

The Innkeeper Speaks of Letters of Recommendation—A Visit to the Kiev Rabbiner—At the Governor General's Office—An Absent-Minded Soul—A Letter to Kupernik

Being a stranger in a large city is like being in a forest. Nowhere does a person feel more lonely. Sholom never felt as lonely as he did then in Kiev. The people in that big, beautiful city seemed to have conspired to show the young visitor no signs of hospitality or warmth. All faces were grim. All doors were closed to him. If only all the people who swam before his eyes hadn't been wrapped in furs like magnates, or ridden in magnificent sleighs harnessed to fiery steeds! And if only houses didn't radiate such wealth and luster. If only all the lackeys and servants that stood at the gates hadn't given him such snooty looks and laughed in his face! He would have overlooked everything, if only they hadn't laughed in his face.

As if in spite, it seemed that everyone made fun of him. Everyone, even the innkeeper, Reb Alter Kaniever. Because his guests didn't have official residence permits and weren't allowed in the holy city of Kiev, he had developed good connections with the police. The innkeeper never looked you in the eye when he spoke, but gazed out into the distance while a casual little smile played under his gray mustache. Speaking to young Sholom, he used neither the polite nor the intimate form of address, but, like an acrobat, cleverly wriggled around and made do without either form. Here's a conversation between the old gray-haired innkeeper and his young guest. Reb Alter smiled, looked down as he rolled a cigarette and spoke in a sugar-sweet, squeaky voice:

Innkeeper: "What's new?"

Guest: "What should be new?"

Innkeeper: "What's doing?"

Guest: "What should be doing?"

Innkeeper: "What I mean is, what's doing in Kiev?"

Guest: "What should be doing in Kiev?"

Innkeeper: "Probably looking for something in Kiev?"

Guest: "What should one look for in Kiev?"

Innkeeper: "Some kind of work or job?"

Guest: "What kind of a job?"

Innkeeper: "A job gotten through a letter of recommendation or some kind of pull, how should I know?"

Guest: "A letter of recommendation to whom?"

Innkeeper: "How should I know to whom? To the rabbi!"

Guest: "Why all of a sudden to the rabbi?"

Innkeeper: "Then let it be the rebbitsin!"

Here for the first time the innkeeper raised his eyes, looked at his young guest, and fell silent. But his young guest didn't let him go.

Guest: "Wait a minute. How come you mentioned the rabbi?"

Innkeeper: "I don't know. A modern young man coming to Kiev nowadays probably has a letter to the rabbi, I mean to the rabbiner, the crown rabbi, through whom he might be able to get a letter of recommendation. That's the way of the world. But perhaps I'm mistaken! So I didn't hit the mark!"

And then the innkeeper added in Russian: "So I didn't dance with the bear!"

Sholom liked this translation of the Yiddish proverb into Russian. But the innkeeper's last words about a letter to the rabbiner put, as they say, a bug in his ear, and he decided it might not be such a bad idea. Whether he got the letter or not, it couldn't hurt to drop in on the crown rabbi. It might even prove useful. After all, a crown rabbi was no small fry!

The more Sholom's fantasy flew, the more appealing became the plan to seek the crown rabbi's help. Clearly it was destined that a happy, brilliant idea be born of Reb Alter's mocking attitude or just plain babbling. Ideas were like that. A trifle or a coincidence brought about some of the greatest events in the world. Look at the histories of the most useful discoveries—it's a well-known fact.

After making preparations during the next few days and learning where the crown rabbi lived, one cold morning Sholom rang one of two adjoining doorbells (the right one). A door opened and a hand pointed to the left bell, which was for the office. So he rang the left bell for the office. The door opened and he entered. A few Jews, mostly poor, downtrodden, tattered artisans, sat in the room, along with a couple of disheveled, sad-looking women and a boy with a swollen face. His toes stuck out of his big, torn boots and his neck was wrapped with two scarves lest he catch cold, God forbid.

The wall was decorated with torn maps of the Land of Israel and a bad portrait of the Czar. The office, the tattered Jews, the disheveled women, the half-barefoot, swollen-faced youngster, the torn maps of the Land of Israel, the poor portrait of the Czar—all cast a melancholy pall over our hero. And if that weren't enough, behind an old, battered and stained desk sat an old man with a pale, corpselike face. If not for the pen in the old man's hand, which he occasionally dipped into the ink, one surely would have thought a corpse was sitting there, dead thirty years at least, but well preserved because he'd been marinated. The pale corpse concluded his business with all the men and women, one by one, rather quickly. It took perhaps one and a half hours until he came to the swollen-faced boy with the two scarves, who took up a half hour of his time. The boy cried. The marinated corpse shouted, and got rid of him too. Then the corpse bade the hero of this autobiography approach. He did. The corpse's voice was scarcely audible:

"What would you like?"

"I have to speak to the rabbiner."

The corpse consulted the appointment book. His voice sounded otherworldly.

"Birth certificate?"

"No."

"A wedding?"

"No!"

"Registering a baby boy? Baby girl?"

"No."

"Did somebody die?"

"No."

"Contribution?"

"No."

"Then what would you like?"

"Nothing. I'd like to see the crown rabbi."

"Well, why didn't you say so?"

The marinated man rose, tottered slowly from the desk, and disappeared into a side room. Fifteen or twenty minutes later he came back with a neutral look on his face and sad news.

"The crown rabbi is not at home. Please be good enough to come another time."

Sholom attempted to see the Kiev rabbiner several times. Finally, he found him at home. He received a very warm welcome, although perhaps at first it wasn't that friendly. The crown rabbi seemed to be frightened. It took some doing until he learned what his young visitor wanted. Sholom, however, felt that the Kiev crown rabbi should have known at once what he wanted and what he needed. But the upshot was that the rabbiner looked him straight in the eye, innocent as a babe, and Sholom had to chew each word for him and spoon-feed him. And after all the long-winded explanations, it turned out he could do nothing anyway. Absolutely nothing. The only thing he could do—was to write him a letter of recommendation.

"A letter of recommendation? That's fine! That's good enough for me. What more do I need? I need nothing more than a letter of recommendation."

The visitor looked at the Kiev crown rabbi and compared him to the crown rabbis of the smaller towns he had known. A whole gallery of crown rabbis appeared before him, ugly do-nothings, one of whom was absolutely bald. Compared to them, the Kiev crown rabbi was a magnate. Compared to him, they were monkeys, midgets. He was a giant. A good-looking man. His one flaw was he had a sallow complexion and was phlegmatic. He spoke slowly, moved slowly, thought slowly. A man without fire. People like him live to be a hundred. They're in no rush to die—they have plenty of time.

"So you'd like to have a letter of recommendation? To whom?"

"To whom? Why don't you decide?"

Well and good. He'd think about it. And then the crown rabbi asked again who his visitor was, where he came from, and what he would like. Then, a long silence. He pressed a button and the old, pale, well-marinated corpse shuffled in from the office. The crown rabbi told him to write a letter to a friend of his—Sholom didn't hear the man's name—perhaps he could do something for this young man. Then the rabbiner told Sholom that the letter was to Herman Markovitch Baratz, one of the lawyers in town, a Jewish intellectual who advised the governor-general.

Done with this laborious task, the rabbiner heaved a sigh of relief. One could see that a stone had fallen from his chest. Indeed, it was a bit of hard work. But he had done a very useful thing—drafting a letter of recommendation for the young man, and what a letter it was—to the Jewish adviser at the governor-general's office. Sholom's overwrought fantasy had never imagined this! The letter of recommendation in his chest pocket warmed his body and made him walk on air. He went straight to Baratz at the governor-general's office. Things would surely work out there. He imagined that this Jewish adviser would be like a professor, bemedaled like a general.

A rill of shivers ran down his spine as he rang the doorbell and was admitted into a room lined with sacred texts and secular books. His teeth chattered. A few minutes later, a man with sparse side-whiskers dashed into the room. He was extremely myopic and seemed to be in a dither. Could this be the Jewish adviser to the governor-general? If not for the bare chin, Sholom would have sworn that he was a Hebrew teacher or a Talmud instructor. This Jewish adviser spit when he spoke and seemed to be quite scatterbrained. Sholom later discovered that all kinds of stories and anecdotes circulated about him in Kiev. For example, he was never able to find his own house until he saw his nameplate: HERMAN MARKOVITCH BARATZ. One day, Baratz stared at his name and saw a sign beneath it that said: RECEPTION 3–5 P.M. He looked at his watch and saw it was only two. Baratz is probably out, he thought. And since Baratz wasn't home, what should Baratz do? So Baratz took himself for a walk in the park.

In a word, it was said of Baratz in Kiev that Baratz sought Baratz and couldn't find him. This morning Baratz happened to be in quite a daze and ill-tempered too. He was in a hurry to get somewhere: he gesticulated and spit and sprayed as he spoke. After reading the crown rabbi's letter recommending the young man to him, the Jewish adviser clapped his hands to his head and began to pace back and forth in the room. He muttered and spit and pleaded for mercy. "Leave me alone. I don't know anything and I'm not going to do anything."

It was pitiful looking at this Jewish adviser. Sholom began to justify himself. "I meant no harm . . . All I wanted was . . . well . . . if possible . . . a letter of recommendation."

"I know exactly what you want," Baratz cut him short. "But I'm angry at the crown rabbi. Day after day he keeps sending me young men. What can I do for them? What do I know? Who am I? What am I? I'm not Brodsky!"

Brokenhearted and dispirited, Sholom slipped out of the Jewish adviser's office. As he reached the last step he heard someone calling him back. The very same Baratz. He had come to the conclusion that, although he himself couldn't do anything for Sholom, he could give him a letter of recommendation to a friend and colleague named Kupernik.

"I want you to know that Kupernik can do quite a bit for you. A lot, in fact! Kupernik is nothing to sneeze at! With a letter of recommendation from him you can break through brick walls, move the greatest people!"

And without further hesitation, Baratz sat down and wrote a card to his best friend and colleague, the noted lawyer Lev Abramovitch Kupernik.

76. *Kupernik*

Sholom Looks for the Famous Attorney—One of Kiev's Noted Streets—Kupernik's Office—In the Regional Courthouse—The Effect of the Letter—A Little Mistake

 The name Kupernik or, as the Jews called him, Kopernikov, was almost as well known as Alexander von Humboldt in Europe or Columbus in America. The famous blood-libel case in the town of Kutais, whose Jews Kupernik successfully defended, made him as famous as Oscar Grusenberg when he took on the Mendel Beilis case several years later. And as with Grusenberg, so in Kupernik's time they told wonders about him and wrapped his deeds in legends.

With a letter of recommendation to a man like Kupernik one could indulge in flights of fantasy and the sweetest dreams. There was also no reason to hurry. Especially since he didn't know Kupernik's address. So Sholom slowly climbed up the steep Kreschatik Street, Kiev's most beautiful boulevard, where our hero had no difficulty finding Kupernik's office. Entering the courtyard opposite the Hotel Europa, he saw a Russian sign: KUPERNIK'S EXCHANGE OFFICE. Puzzled, he wondered why the attorney Kupernik ran a money-changing business. But the mystery was soon resolved.

In Kupernik's office he saw a young man with blue glasses and a Lithuanian Jewish woman in a white wig.

"Who would you like to see?"

"Kupernik."

"Who sent you?"

"The Jewish adviser. I have a card from Herman Markovitch Baratz."

"You have a card from Baratz? Let's see it."

The young man with the blue glasses took the card and gave it to the woman in the white wig. She took the card, put on her glasses, read it, and threw it away.

"It's not to me, it's to my son."

"Where is he?"

"Who?"

"Your son."

"Where's my son? What do you mean where? Go to the regional courthouse—that's where you'll find him."

Looking for a lawyer in the regional courthouse was like looking for a needle in a haystack. The regional courthouse was a massive old building with iron steps and so many rooms, halls and cubicles that a stranger could get lost there and not find his way out.

For the first time in his life our hero saw a throng of people in black frock coats carrying large briefcases. All were lawyers who had taken the oath. Go guess which one was Kupernik. Stopping one to ask was impossible. All of them were so busy. They all bustled around with briefcases, this one here, that one there, like madmen. But

Sholom dared to stop one man with a very sympathetic face. He wasn't in a black frock coat but carried a huge yellow briefcase.

"Where can I find Kupernik?" Sholom asked.

"Why do you need Kupernik?" replied the man.

"I have a card for him from the Jewish adviser, Herman Markovitch Baratz."

"Ah! From Baratz? Why don't you sit down? I'll be back in a minute."

The man pointed to a long, polished bench, turned and slipped away. Sholom sat down on the long, polished bench and waited half an hour, an hour, one and a half hours. But no one came. Not Kupernik, not anyone else. He rose from the polished bench, about to leave. The crowd had thinned out. Here and there a solitary black frock coat was seen. Then he spotted the man with the yellow briefcase.

"Ah, you still here? Actually, why do you want Kupernik?"

So Sholom told him once more:

"I have a card from Herman Markovitch Baratz."

"And where's the card?"

Sholom showed him the card. The man read it.

"What is it you want from Kupernik?"

"I don't know myself . . . Perhaps he'll give me a job."

"What can you do?"

"I know how to write Yiddish and Russian."

"Russian too? Follow me."

Should he doubt any longer that this was Kupernik? As they left the regional courthouse, the man hailed one of the rubber-wheeled carriages and said: "To the Hotel Russia." With the speed of an arrow, the vehicle brought them to the hotel. They entered a room thick with smoke. Kupernik sat his guest down at a table, lit a cigarette, handed Sholom a sheet of paper, a pen and ink, and suggested that he write a couple of lines.

Sholom dipped the pen into the ink, but before he began to write, asked Kupernik:

"In what language do you want me to write, Yiddish or Russian?"

"Russian, of course."

As Sholom set to work, the merit of his teacher, Reb Monish of the golden hand, stood him in good stead. He had hardly finished the first line when Kupernik stopped him.

"I'm satisfied with your handwriting. Have a cigarette."

Sholom declined the cigarette. "I hope you'll forgive me, Mr. Kupernik, but I don't smoke."

"I hope you'll forgive me, my dear young man, but I'm not Kupernik. My name is Appelbaum."

"Appelbaum?"

"Yes, yes, Appelbaum. Moshe Appelbaum from Byelotserkov, attorney-at-law, member of the bar."

It was fated. Who could have known that a Kupernik from Kiev would turn out to be a Moshe Appelbaum from Byelotserkov! But this Moshe Appelbaum from Byelotserkov showed himself to be a true gentleman. He didn't bargain over wages. He agreed to everything. He even promised the young man that he would train him to be an attorney and then would write letters of recommendation not only to Kupernik but to many others greater than Kupernik. For he knew the most notable men in Kiev, in Moscow and in Petersburg, and had connections with all the cabinet ministers.

"If you like, we can even leave for Byelotserkov today. I just have to drop in for a short while to the governor-general. And since I'm seeing the governor-general, I'll also have to drop in to see the regional governor. These dogs are terribly jealous of each other. Actually, I should also drop in to see the police chief of Kiev, but I wouldn't mind if the police chief came to see me. There's nothing wrong with his legs."

Attorney-at-Law Appelbaum rushed out of the room and left Sholom on his own. The entire adventure pleased the young traveler. He was enchanted by Appelbaum's personality. Sholom hardly had time to consider thoroughly his situation, when Appelbaum returned in a carriage full of packages stuffed with all kinds of goodies: herring, sturgeon, caviar, fruits and cigarettes.

"Do you think I bought these? They're all gifts. Presents from the governor-general's wife, from the regional governor's wife and from the police chief's wife."

"Then you dropped in to see the police chief too? But you told me that—"

"God forbid! Not from his wife but his mistress. I'm her lawyer. I'm handling a suit of hers for half a million rubles. She's a multimillionaire, but terribly stingy. She'd sooner hang herself than spend a kopeck. But when it concerns me, nothing's too expensive. They'll all do anything for me! . . . So then, off to Byelotserkov?"

"Off to Byelotserkov!"

77. A Job as Secretary

*Sholom Travels with His New Patron to Byelotserkov—A Warm
Reception—Family Idyll—Reb Levi—The Boss Teaches His Secretary
Law—A Surprise—A Letter to His Father*

On his way to Kiev from Byelotserkov, Attorney-at-Law
Appelbaum played the role of the grandee. He acted like a
rich landowner, spared no expense, and bought first-class
seats. At the station in Pastov he squandered money at the snack
bar. He tipped the waiter at the buffet generously. He introduced
our young hero to his friends as his secretary. And what he told his
family at home about the secretary only God in heaven knows.

One can only assume that the lawyer praised his secretary to the
sky to members of his household. Only a long-awaited guest, or a
rich kinsman from America, or a relative whose inheritance everybody has his eyes on, could hope for such a warm, magnificent
reception. Moshe Appelbaum's wife, a saintly woman and an excellent housekeeper, put on her Sabbath best and scrubbed the children.
For supper she prepared a meal fit for the Czar. Appelbaum's elder
son, Levi, a snippety youngster who was called Reb Levi at home,
couldn't restrain his enthusiasm. As he rose from the table he patted
his stomach and remarked:

"Too bad we don't have such guests every day and have such
wonderful meals."

At which Moshe Appelbaum graced him with a slap in the face.

"Too bad you're not a bit smarter, Reb Levi, and too bad you
have such a long tongue."

Then, addressing his secretary, he added:

"Well, what do you think of my son and heir, Reb Levi? Some
gem! May no evil eye befall him, he's accomplished in everything!
Grass will be growing over me when he finally learns the Kaddish . . ."

Everyone laughed at this joke, including Rev Levi. Nevertheless,
the mother found it necessary to defend her son. After all, she was
a mother! But her intervention almost precipitated a conflict.

"I'm quite sure," Madame Appelbaum said openly, "that when
Levi is as old as his father is now, he's going to be just as smart as
his father."

"And maybe even smarter than Father!" Reb Levi himself added.

His father flew into a rage. Luckily, Reb Levi beat a quick retreat, otherwise a nasty situation would have developed.

"Although I'm against corporal punishment," Moshe Appelbaum admitted, "and although it's my view that beating is a barbaric custom inconsistent with the principles of civilization, nevertheless I find it necessary that a profligate and impertinent son like Reb Levi get the taste of the whip at least once a week. I consider this an inviolable rule."

Reb Levi was evidently well acquainted with this rule, for he himself had his own rule: just as the father was about to mete out his sentence, he upped and disappeared—go and find him! Reb Levi's disappearance did nothing to quiet the storm. The battleground moved, literally speaking, to another area. A minute ago, it was between father and son. Now, instead, war broke out between husband and wife. Moshe Appelbaum threw the entire blame upon his wife.

"You're the one who's totally to blame, my dear, devoted wife, may you live and be well. You're to blame because you're standing up for your lovely sonny boy."

But his wife, Madame Appelbaum, didn't let herself be spit in the face.

"I'd like to remind you, my dear, devoted husband, may you live a long life, that when you were your son's age, you were a bigger boor than Levi is now. And if you, my dear, devoted Moshe Appelbaum, have any memory whatsoever, you'll recall that when you were young, they didn't call you Moshe Appelbaum, but Moshe Bagel . . ."

It was rather unpleasant for a guest to be an unwilling witness to such a family scene and watch the dear, devoted couple wash their dirty linen in public. However, Sholom was surprised that neither of the battling sides, not husband, not wife, seemed to be upset; in fact, they were quite calm. They looked as if they had just returned from their honeymoon and, not having anything better to do, began exchanging sweet compliments. There are all kinds of people in God's world, and all kinds of idylls!

After the magnificent supper, Attorney-at-Law Appelbaum sat his guest and secretary down at a desk and handed him a sheet of paper to copy, while he himself lay down for a snooze. After his nap, he smoked a cigarette and began a conversation with his young secretary. I swear it was so interesting, it would be a sin before God to omit it. After so many years, it will be hard to reconstruct the conversation word for word, but in essence it went something like this:

"Now listen here, young man, here's the story. You're a youngster, I see you're no dummy, and your penmanship is superb. You're no slouch in Russian either. All this shows that your goal can be achieved. What I mean is, you're a born lawyer. Only one thing is needed—willpower! If you really want to be a lawyer, you'll succeed. Knowledge is secondary. Above all, don't lose your self-confidence if somebody knows more than you. You must smash the other guy's case with your tongue. You're not supposed to let on for a minute, not even a second, that you're in awe of someone greater than you. Because you are the greatest. You just have to keep talking.

"Your tongue has to work harder than your head. You have to inundate the other guy with so much blather that he becomes confused, loses his train of thought, and no longer understands a thing. Then you pelt him with thousands of bombshells from the law books and from rules of procedure, none of which ever existed. What I've just said is directed at the judges. Now as regards your client—clients are sheep that let themselves be fleeced. Cows that let themselves be milked. Horses that love to be ridden. With them you surely don't have to stand on ceremony. They don't go for namby-pambies who preach morality. They have more respect and deference for a fresh lout than for a learned professor who, like a bag filled with chaff, is stuffed with the fine points of law.

"Don't dare show your face outside without carrying a huge briefcase—even if you only keep old newspapers or dirty collars in it. In the privacy of your home you can play with the cat all day long. But as soon as the doorbell rings, you must grab the thickest book you can find, immerse yourself in it, and rub your forehead. Don't dare let a client slip out of your hands until you've squeezed him dry. And remember, there is nothing under the sun to which you'll admit 'I don't know'—because you know everything!"

After such a fine lecture, Sholom should have realized what sort of creature was this Attorney-at-Law Moshe Appelbaum. But Appelbaum had such a clever, sympathetic face that he enchanted you with his eyes, seduced you with his talk, until, unwillingly, you were captivated heart and soul. That very evening, after he had taken his nap, Appelbaum took his walking stick and briefcase, ready to go out. Here another conflict broke out between the dear, devoted husband and wife.

"Where are you going?" asked the wife.

"I'm going to the club for half an hour," replied the husband. "I have to see someone there."

"I know your half an hours," the wife said. "I hope you'll show up for lunch tomorrow. And I know this person you're supposed to see quite well too. It's no person," she said, "but little peoplekins, all of whom are kings and queens and jacks . . ."

"Seems you've forgotten to include the aces, my dear, the aces! What kind of a game is it without aces?"

The wife did not respond to this. But she gave him such an icy look that another man would have preferred sinking into the earth alive. But Moshe Appelbaum pretended not to notice. He approached his young secretary, bent down to him as he was writing, and softly asked him:

"How much money do you have with you?"

The secretary patted his pockets and showed Appelbaum how much money he had. Appelbaum thought for a while, then stretched his hand out to his secretary.

"Could you perhaps lend it to me for a few minutes? I'll return it when I come back from the club."

"Oh! With pleasure!" Sholom replied and gave him all his cash.

After Appelbaum left, Madame Appelbaum began questioning Sholom:

"How did you get to become my husband's secretary, and what's your connection to Brodsky?"

"With which Brodsky?"

"With the Kiev millionaire Brodsky!"

"What has Brodsky got to do with this?" Sholom asked.

"Isn't Brodsky your uncle?" she asked.

"What made you think that Brodsky is supposed to be my uncle?"

"Then how is he connected with you?"

"Who?"

"Brodsky!"

"Who said he's connected to me?"

A short pause. Appelbaum's wife and Sholom exchanged astonished glances. Each thought his own thoughts. A minute later, Madame Appelbaum asked the secretary once more:

"Really? Didn't you also work for Brodsky?"

"Where did you get the idea that I worked for Brodsky?"

"And don't you even know him?"

"Who?"

"Blast it! We talk and talk and we can't get to the point! Tell me at least who you are and how you got here."

The next day a new surprise awaited our naive hero. His patron, Moshe Appelbaum, still had not returned from the club. Reb Levi had a mission—to go to the club and call his father home for supper. But Reb Levi had no strong desire to be on the receiving end of undeserved slaps, especially on an empty stomach. So his mother had to give him a slap-fee as an advance payment. Reb Levi soon returned with the news that his father had gone straight from the club that morning to the railway station and had left for Kiev.

This struck our hero like a thunderbolt out of the blue. It was a double blow: his stomach hurt and his face flamed with humiliation. Only then did he begin to inquire about his patron. He learned that Appelbaum had never become a full-fledged member of the bar. He was only a paralegal adviser, the sort that were called street-corner lawyers. When the name Appelbaum was mentioned in Byelotserkov, it always elicited a little smile.

Meanwhile, our hero's situation started to deteriorate. He was at the point of feeling hunger once again. With an embittered heart, he sat down and wrote a long letter in florid Hebrew to his father in Pereyaslav. One might say that this fancy Hebrew saved him. With hyperbole one can write much and say little.

Only at the end of the letter did he briefly mention that he would return home if only he had enough change for travel expenses. His father responded without delay and enclosed a few rubles. In his letter he ordered Sholom to come home as soon as possible, for there was an opening for a crown rabbi in a town near Pereyaslav and his chances for getting the post were good. His father also concluded the letter in florid Hebrew:

"Make haste! Speedily on thy way! Fly like an arrow, on the wings of eagles! Quickly, look not behind thee! Come, and may all thy efforts be crowned with success!"

78. The Elections

How a Crown Rabbi Is Chosen—The Previous Rabbiner in Luben—An Old Acquaintance—Reb Nachman Kahana and His Young Protégé— Reactions to the Sermon—The Vote—To Pereyaslav—A Promise

 The town that sought a new crown rabbi was Luben. The word "sought" is just a fanciful exaggeration. A town seeks a rabbiner with the same enthusiasm as one seeks a grave-digger. The whole institution of crown rabbi is actually a superfluous one, imposed by the Czar's regime upon Russian Jewry, who hold on to it as if it were something good and proper. The nicest thing is that a crown rabbi is not sent directly by the government to rule over the Jews; the Jews themselves have to elect him. But the elections are mandated from above. The authorities send a letter to the Jews stating that on such and such a date the Jews are to assemble in such and such a place and choose a rabbiner.

Candidates sprout up from all over. Every candidate has his party and all the parties have their arsenals and their strategies to win public favor. One has a fine letter of recommendation. Another has money to spend. A third offers liquor. No one sleeps. The town is in a tumult and everyone is in a dither. People get excited! There is a feeling of exultation on the Jewish streets. Joy and celebration— they're choosing a rabbiner! They vote, they cast their ballots. A merry to-do! A hullabaloo! Sometimes this takes weeks. Occasionally, months.

To guarantee that the elections are run fairly, the authorities send an official to make sure there is no fraud, God forbid, in the counting of the ballots. But the real fun begins after the elections. Since the governor has to certify and approve the election results, the losers then run to the governor's office with denouncements and character assassinations. If they succeed in invalidating the elections, the entire tumult starts again from scratch. New candidates, new parties, new elections, new denunciations and new invalidations.

Among those who announced their candidacy for the rabbinic post in Luben was the former rabbiner, Shimon Ruderman, who was the son of the teacher Moshe David Ruderman. If you recall, he had almost converted to Christianity in Pereyaslav, and Jews saved him and sent him to the rabbinical seminary in Zhitomir. Apparently he wasn't a very popular rabbiner in Luben. Its citizens looked forward to new elections as to the Messiah.

But the Jews of Luben weren't too well versed in politics or tact. If they liked someone, they told him: "We like you." And if they didn't, they said, "Good-bye, we don't like you." They had long ago informed Crown Rabbi Ruderman, and none too subtly either, that he could start looking for another position. And if perchance he thought they were joking, they rented his seat in the synagogue to one of the local householders. When the rabbiner came to pray on Sabbath, he had no place to sit and had to stand on his feet for the entire service. That's why he brought the police on the following Sabbath, and by force retrieved his seat in the front of the synagogue along the eastern wall. One can imagine how enchanted everyone was by this. The whole world knew of the incident.

In addition to an article about the affair in the Hebrew newspaper *Ha-Melitz,* the editor, Zederbaum, added his own editorial, which was three times as long as the news report itself. He laced into both the crown rabbi and the congregation, and sermonized about the desecration caused by letting the police into a holy place. Jews ought not behave this way, he concluded, citing several midrashim and quoting a line from the Book of Esther: "And there will be endless wrath and humiliation." Zederbaum, may he rest in peace, was a master at that kind of writing!

Nonetheless, Ruderman did not withdraw his candidacy for the rabbiner's post in Luben. The other candidates worked with their parties, each of which had its own weapons. The battle began. Then, almost at the very last moment, a couple of days before the elections, the hero of this autobiography appeared in town like a bolt out of the blue. He brought a letter from his Uncle Pinny, whose in-law Nachman Kahana was one of the most respected citizens in Luben. He was an old, wealthy man from a distinguished family, the kind who sits at the very front of the synagogue. The cantor dared not repeat the Silent Devotion until Reb Nachman had finished saying it first—even though he stretched it out forever. If it happened that Reb Nachman would come late to shul (an almost weekly Sabbath occurrence), he sent a messenger saying: "Don't wait for me." But the polite congregation knew that he probably *wanted* them to wait before beginning the service. In a word, he was an ornament to the community, the sort the Talmud describes as "learned and prominent."

The young candidate met Kahana poring over some passages in the Mishna. After reading Uncle Pinny's letter, the distinguished old man fixed his spectacles and began inspecting the young man head to toe. It seemed that the youngster, clad in a modern short jacket, didn't meet with his approval. Nevertheless, Sholom's connection with Uncle Pinny stood him in good stead and Reb Nachman asked Sholom to be seated. He engaged him in conversation and soon discovered that his visitor was no ignoramus in the fine points of Jewish learning. He knew a chapter of the Mishna and occasionally injected a Hebrew word into the conversation. This delighted the old man. He smiled and gave an order: "Please bring something to eat." A servant brought in a tray with a little dish. In this dish, all alone, like a little orphan, lay a tiny piece of sugar cake. And in the middle of this tiny piece of sugar cake was a little raisin.

"Say the blessing and eat!" old Kahana said and asked the young candidate about his hometown of Pereyaslav. "When I was there about sixty years ago it was a Jewish town. How is the Yiddishkeit there today?"

"In good shape," the guest replied and declined the little piece of cake, not because of the blessing but because later he probably would have been ordered to say the special grace for snacks, a prayer he had never learned by heart. Before Sholom left, old Kahana wished him success.

"And, God willing, you no doubt will succeed, because when I give a blessing," old man Kahana assured him, "it comes true. You see, I'm a kohen."

That same day the news spread in town that another candidate had been added to the list. Despite his youth, he was a bright chap with all the right attributes. First of all, he came from a good family. One of Reb Nachman Kahana's own. Moreover, he knew the Bible, was an excellent calligrapher, and knew the Talmud with all its commentaries. And since people's imaginations had already become overheated, others added that Sholom was an ordained rabbi, that he was authorized to answer rabbinic questions, and that he could put the local rabbi and three others like him in his back pocket. In short, he was a golden peacock from golden peacock land! When Sholom appeared on the street and walked past the shops, people pointed at him.

"Is that him?" he heard them say behind his back.

"Who?"

"The new rabbiner."

"Such a young tyke?"

"His mother's milk isn't dry on his lips yet."

"And what long hair he has!"

"Long on hair, short on brains!"

Nevertheless, Sholom had enough brains to make half a dozen visits to the leading citizens of town, to the very crème de la crème, to the families Bachmutsky, Kanievsky, Rogachefsky and all the other representatives of the Luben bourgeoisie. And if that wasn't enough, he also went to the synagogue on the Sabbath prior to election day. He was seated up front and was inspected from all sides. A couple of hundred people shook hands and greeted him, and he was honored with the Maftir of the weekly Torah portion.

This was a kind of examination. And the young fellow gave them a Haftora the like of which they had never heard before! But this was nothing compared to what happened at the elections. Here's the story:

The hall of the town council was full of Jews. Just before the voting began, the youngest candidate stepped forth and delivered a speech, in Russian no less, in which he quoted Biblical verses, parables, and selections from the Midrash which were as much to the point as a square bagel. But this sermon proved to be so popular that the young candidate was chosen to be crown rabbi without resorting to a vote.

Immediately thereafter, Sholom sent a telegram: "Mazel tov, I was unanimously chosen." Then the chosen young rabbiner went to old Reb Nachman Kahana to express his gratitude. The old man was truly touched that his recommendation was so efficacious.

"I'd very much like to hear the sermon you delivered to the audience."

"I'd be glad to repeat it for you," Sholom said, "but there's really nothing to hear."

"Then how come everyone says that the crowd was licking its fingers?"

"With your permission, I'd like to tell you a story."

"Why, go right ahead! As long as it's relevant to the matter." Old Kahana put on his glasses and settled back to listen. The young crown rabbi began:

"The story I'm about to tell you concerns a priest. A young priest, fresh from the seminary, came to the bishop for his blessing and for advice as to what kind of sermon to preach at Eastertime in church. The bishop blessed him and told him to tell his congregation about miracles that saints had experienced. 'For example, the miracle of the forty saints who were lost in the forest three days and three nights and almost died from hunger. God performed a miracle and they found bread. So all forty saints sat down to eat the bread. They ate and ate, and ate and ate, and still there was enough left for the morrow.' When Easter came, the young priest told the assembled gentiles in church about this miracle, but with some slight changes. He said that one saint got lost in the woods for three days and three nights and almost died of hunger, whereupon God performed a miracle and he found forty loaves of bread. He sat down to eat, and he ate and ate, and ate and ate, and still there was enough left for the morrow. Later the bishop scolded the young priest:

" 'How can a priest make such a terrible mistake?'

"To which the young priest responded: 'For the goyim in my town my version is also a miracle.' "

Old Kahana shook with laughter. He enjoyed talking to the rabiner and had a wonderful time, as though Sholom were a member of the family. But this mood did not last too long. The feeling of joy was quickly marred, as we shall soon see. In the meantime we shall follow our young crown rabbi to his hometown of Pereyaslav.

Sholom imagined that Pereyaslav would be beside itself with joy at his election. Such a success at so young an age was no trifle. But the upshot was—nothing. Only the family celebrated. And not fully either. The joy would come only when the governor certified the elections. Meanwhile, it was still up in the air. Sholom would have to go to the government offices in Poltava, to run around and grease palms. This alone sufficed to cool the uplifted spirits. And if that was not enough, our hero had to bump into Chaite Ruderman, the Luben crown rabbi's younger brother. Chaite walked around looking chipper, hands behind his back, his yellow jacket draped across his shoulders, and his sleeves rolled up. Not feeling in any way guilty, Sholom stretched out his hand in greeting. The other fellow didn't reciprocate, but stepped to the side and continued walking as if Sholom were a stranger. One brother stands up for another, the aggrieved party thought, trying to justify Chaite's behavior; then he fled to pour out his heart to another friend, Avreml Zolotushkin.

It turned out that Zolotushkin, though he was at daggers drawn with Chaite Ruderman, maintained that Chaite was right and told his friend straight to his face: "Anyone in his right mind wouldn't offer his hand for two reasons: First, because you're a crown rabbi, and a rabbiner is a hypocrite, a two-faced bootlicker of the rich and a lackey of the government. Second, a decent man doesn't take away another person's livelihood, doesn't go tearing the bones out of another person's mouth like a dog . . ."

Short, sharp words. Our hero felt there was some merit to those remarks. He remembered a scene that had taken place the day of the elections when he met the ex–crown rabbi of Luben, Shimon Ruderman. The latter paled, a frightened look in his eyes, as though to ask: "What have you got against me?" The tragic look on his face was like that of a tattered and bitten dog who is driven to the winds by other dogs. Sholom felt his heart in a vise; he was deeply affected by this meeting. There was a moment when he was ready to cast his arms about the unfortunate Shimon Ruderman's neck, beg his pardon, and relinquish to him the town of Luben with its fine upstanding citizens and his candidacy for the crown rabbi's position. That would have been the proper—perhaps too proper—thing to do. But this feeling lasted all of a minute. Soon the egoistical "I" surfaced—and the "I" had the upper hand . . .

One can imagine how Sholom felt when he left his friend Zolotushkin. What could be worse than knowing that his friend was right and he was wrong? Chekhov described this feeling well: "He felt like someone who had eaten soap." But there was one thing that Sholom could not understand: Why should a crown rabbi be a hypocrite and a bootlicker of the rich and a lackey of the government? Sholom promised that he would *not* be like that! He would not be a crown rabbi like all the others. What he wanted to be was a mentch!

GLOSSARY

Prepared with the assistance of Shulamit Leviant

Afarsemon. A sweet-smelling balsam mentioned in the Talmud.

Afternoon Service. One of the three daily services. The other two are the Morning Service and the Evening Service.

Ato Horeyso. Prayer recited on Simchas Torah, prior to the Hakofes.

Bar Mitzva. Ceremony at the age of thirteen, when a Jewish boy is called to the Torah for the first time and assumes adult responsibility for his conduct.

Bes Medresh. A house of study; also used as a place for prayer.

Bris. The circumcision ceremony of a baby boy on the eighth day after his birth.

Challa. The braided bread made of white flour and eggs, used for Sabbath and holidays.

Cheder. Hebrew school. In European villages, usually a room in a teacher's house, where children are taught Hebrew, prayers and the Pentateuch.

Code of Law (Shulkhan Arukh). Compiled by Joseph Caro and published in 1565, it contains all the laws observed by Orthodox Jews.

Crown Rabbi. A government official, not necessarily an ordained rabbi, who served in Russia, mainly to record births, deaths, marriages, etc.

Days of Awe. The ten-day period of High Holy Days from Rosh Hashana through Yom Kippur.

Days of Repentance. The ten-day period beginning with Rosh Hashana and ending with Yom Kippur; a time when the Jew is supposed to examine his moral and religious state of being and change his ways.

Elul. The last month of the Jewish year (August–September); the month preceding the season of High Holy Days, Rosh Hashana and Yom Kippur.

Feast of Leviathan. The legendary banquet in the World to Come, where the righteous will eat the Leviathan, the Wild Ox, and drink the Preserved Wine.

Gabbai. A trustee in a synagogue.

Ganev. Thief.

Goy. Gentile; or a nonobservant Jew.

Gut Shabbes. Good Sabbath.

Gut Yontev. Good, or happy, holiday.

Gymnasium. A European high school.

Haftora. A chapter from the Prophets, chanted on Sabbaths and holidays.

Hakofes (sing. Hakofeh). The Torah circuits on Simchas Torah.

Hanuka. Feast of Lights (November or December) celebrating the rededication of the Temple by the Maccabees in 165 B.C.E.

Hanuka gelt. The money children are given during Hanuka.

Hasid. A follower of a Hasidic rebbe. The Hasidim were known for their accent on joy, dancing and singing in their worship of God, rather than on religious study.

Haskala. The Enlightenment, which sought to bring to the Jews secular learning and knowledge of languages.

Havdala. Prayer said at the end of the Sabbath.

Holy Ark. The ark where the Torah is kept in the synagogue.

Hoshana Rabba: The seventh day of Sukkos. Tradition has it that on this day God's judgment of man, sealed on Yom Kippur, receives final confirmation.

Intermediary Days. The half-holiday days between the first two and last two festival days of Passover and Sukkos.

Kabbala. A body of mystical lore and scriptural interpretation developed by the Kabbalists, who through study and meditative speculation sought communion with God.

Kabbalist. One who studies Kabbala.

Kaddish. A prayer that marks the conclusion of a unit in the service; it is also recited as a prayer for the dead.

Kadkod. Hyacinth or ruby. First mentioned as a precious stone in Isaiah 54:12.

Kapores. Expiatory ritual on the eve of Yom Kippur.

Kiddush. Blessing recited over wine at the beginning of the Sabbath or holiday evening meal.

Klezmer. Musician.

Kohen (pl. Kohanim). A descendant of the Levites; a member of the priestly class. Blesses the congregation and is called first to the Torah.

Kvass. A frothy sour brew made from fermenting rye flour or rye bread, malt and sugar. As typically Russian as vodka or borscht.

L'Chayim. Toast: "To life!"

Levites. Descendants of the tribe of Levi; assisted kohanim at Temple services.

Litvak. Jew who comes from Lithuania. Litvaks are traditionally thought of as being more reserved and scholarly than Jews from other regions.

Machzor. A festival or High Holiday prayer book.

Maftir. The concluding section of the Torah portion read on Sabbaths and holidays. It is a distinct honor to be called up to the Torah for Maftir.

Maskil (pl. Maskilim). A follower of the Haskala, the Jewish Enlightenment movement.

Megilla. A scroll; usually the scroll of the Book of Esther.

Mentch. A decent human being.

Mezuza. A rolled piece of parchment containing Torah verses and inserted in a wooden or metal case; affixed on the doorpost of Jewish homes and synagogues.

Midrash (pl. Midrashim). Rabbinic commentary and explanatory notes, homilies, and stories on scriptural passages.

Minyan. The quorum of ten adult males needed for synagogue services.

Mishna. The body of oral law redacted c. 200 C.E. by Rabbi Judah.

Mitzva. A Torah precept or commandment; a good deed.

Mizrach Decoration. A folk-art wall decoration placed on the eastern wall of a house to indicate where a man should face when praying.

Mohel. The man who performs circumcisions.

Nudnik. Pest.

Prayer of Deliverance. Recited when a person has safely crossed an ocean or escaped a peril.

Preserved Wine. See Feast of Leviathan.

Rabbiner. See Crown Rabbi.

Reb. Mister.

Rebbitsin. Wife of a rabbi.

Ritual Fringes. A four-cornered, poncholike garment put on over the head and worn underneath the shirt by male Jews who observe the Biblical commandment to wear a garment with fringes (Numbers 15:37–41).

Rosh Hashana (lit., Head of the Year). The Jewish New Year, celebrated the first and second days of Tishrei (September). Next to Yom Kippur, these are the most solemn days of the year.

Seder. The festive home ritual of the first and second nights of Passover, at which the Hagada is recited.

Shamesh. Beadle of a synagogue.

Shema, Shema Yisroel. The "Hear O Israel" prayer; the Jew's affirmation of faith in one God.

Shemini Atzeres. A festival that comes at the end of Sukkos, on the day before Simchas Torah.

Shiva. The seven-day period of mourning for a close relative.

Shofar. Ram's horn, blown on Rosh Hashana.

Sholom Aleichem (lit., Peace to you). Used as a greeting in Yiddish; also a Friday hymn sung at home when the men return from the synagogue.

Shul. Synagogue.

Siddur. Prayer book.

Silent Devotion. One of the central prayers in the Jewish service, recited while standing.

Simchas Torah. The festival immediately following Sukkos on which the reading of the Torah is completed and begun anew. This joyous holiday is traditionally celebrated with singing and dancing.

Sukka. The booth with the thatched roof used during Sukkos.

Sukkos. The Feast of Booths, celebrated for seven days (nine, including Shemini Atzeres and Simchas Torah), starting the fifteenth of Tishrei. Sukkos commemorates the Jews' living in booths (sukkos) during their wandering in the desert and is, in addition, the fall harvest festival.

Tallis. Prayer shawl.

Talmud. The body of written Jewish law, comprising the Mishna (in Hebrew) and the Gemara (mostly in Aramaic) and compiled c. 500 C.E.

Talmud Torah. The school in which children are taught Hebrew, the prayers and the Pentateuch.

Tefillin. Phylacteries used in morning prayers. These are square boxes, containing scriptural passages, with leather thongs worn on the arm and head during morning prayer daily, except Sabbath and holidays, by male Jews over thirteen.

Tisha B'Av. The ninth day of the month of Av (July–August), marking the destruction in 586 B.C.E. and 70 C.E. of both Temples in Jerusalem.

Torah. Not only the Five Books of Moses—and, by extension, the entire Bible—but the entire complex of Jewish learning, comprising the Talmud, the Commentaries, rabbinic writings, etc.

Tsimmes. Vegetables simmered in honey or sugar; usually carrots or potatoes and prunes.

Wild Ox. See Feast of Leviathan.

Woman of Valor. The verses from the last chapter of the Biblical Book of Proverbs, chanted by the man of the house in honor of his wife on Friday evening before Kiddush.

Yarmulke. Skullcap.

Yiddishkeit. The entire complex of Judaism.

Yom Kippur. The Day of Atonement, the holiest day in the Jewish year.

Yorzeit. The anniversary of a loved one's death.

Yoshfe. First mentioned in Exodus 28:20 as one of the twelve precious stones in the breastplate of the High Priest, it is the gem representing the tribe of Benjamin.

Zemiros. The table hymns chanted during the three Sabbath meals.

PERSONALITIES AND JOURNALS

Auerbach, Berthold (1812–82). German Jewish novelist and a leader of Jewish emancipation.

Beilis, Mendel (1874–1934). Victim of famous blood-libel charge in Russia, 1911.

Bogrov, Grigory (1825–85). Assimilated Russian Jewish author. Wrote *Memoirs of a Jew.*

Chernyshevsky, Nikolai (1828–89). Russian socialist reformer and writer.

Chmielnicki, Bogdan (1595–1657). Ukrainian Cossack leader, responsible for massacres of Polish Jewry in 1648–49. Sholom Aleichem's hometown, Pereyaslav, was among the cities where Jews were brutally massacred in the Ukrainian slaughters of 1648.

Dubzevitch, A. D. (1844–99). Hebrew writer.

Erter, Isaac (1792–1851). Polish-born Hebrew writer and maskil.

Gottlober, Abraham Baer (1810–99). Hebrew poet.

Grusenberg, Oscar (1866–1940). Russian lawyer who achieved his greatest renown in his world-famous defense of Mendel Beilis at his blood-libel trial.

Guenzburg, Mordecai Aaron (1795–1846). Influential Hebrew writer and leader of Vilna Haskala.

Ha-Cohen, Adam (1799–1879). Pen name of A. D. Lebensohn, poet and dramatist.

Ha-Maggid. Earliest of the nineteenth-century Hebrew periodicals; founded in 1856.

Ha-Melitz. Hebrew periodical founded by A. Zederbaum in 1860.

Judah Halevi (1085–1142). Hebrew poet; author of *The Kuzari.*

Kaminer, Isaac (1834–1901). Hebrew writer and physician, active in Haskala movement.

Kupernik, Lev (1845–1905). Prominent Russian lawyer. Though a convert (in order to marry a Christian woman), defended Jews in the village of Kutais accused of a blood libel.

Kutais. *See* Kupernik, Lev.

Lebensohn. *See* Ha-Cohen, Adam.

Lebensohn, Micah Joseph (1828–52). One of the noted Hebrew poets of the Haskala, he was the son of Adam Ha-Cohen.

Levin, Yehuda Leib (1845–1925). Hebrew poet, known as Yehalel.

Levinsohn, Isaac Ber (1788–1860). The father of Russian Haskala.

Maimonides, Moses (1135–1204). Major Jewish philosopher and codifier of laws.

Mandelkern, Solomon (1846–1902). Russian-born poet and translator; best known for his Hebrew concordance to the Bible.

Mapu, Abraham (1808–68). First to introduce novel into modern Hebrew literature.

Mazepa, Ivan (1640–1709). Cossack leader in the Ukraine.

Mendelssohn, Moses (1729–86). German Jewish thinker, writer and founder of the German branch of the Jewish Enlightenment.

Montefiore, Moses (1784–1885). English philanthropist, patron of Jewish scholarship, helper of oppressed Jews all over the world.

Mysteries of Paris, The. See Sue, Eugène.

Rashi (1040–1105). Greatest medieval commentator on the Bible and Talmud.

Schulman, Kalman (1821–99). Hebrew novelist.

Shatzkes, Moshe Aaron (1825–99). Yiddish writer.

Slonimsky, Chaim Zelig (1810–1904). Hebrew writer; popularizer of science.

Smolenskin, Peretz (1842–85). Hebrew novelist, critic, editor.

Spielhagen, Friedrich (1828–1911). German novelist who wrote on political and social themes.

Spinoza, Baruch (1632–77). Dutch Jewish philosopher.

Sue, Eugène (1804–57). French author of popular tales of the Parisian underworld, including *The Mysteries of Paris* (1842–43). He also wrote the famous novel *The Wandering Jew.*

Weissberg, Isaac Jacob (1840–1904). Hebrew writer.

Yehalel. *See* Levin, Yehuda Leib.

Zederbaum, Alexander (1816–93). Hebrew journalist and editor.

CHRONOLOGY

1859 Sholom Aleichem born on March 3 in Pereyaslav, in the province of Poltava in the Ukraine.

1872 Bar Mitzva. Death of Sholom's mother.

1873–76 Educated in the Pereyaslav Russian school.

1876 Tutor in Pereyaslav and Rzhishtchev.

1877–79 Tutor in home of wealthy farmer, Elimelech Loyev, where he meets Loyev's daughter, Olga, whom he later marries. First publications in Hebrew, in 1879.

1880–83 Crown rabbi in Luben.

1883 Marriage to Olga Loyev. First Yiddish short story and first use of pen name Sholom Aleichem.

1885 On death of father-in-law, Loyev, inherits vast sum of money.

1884–90 Articles, stories and novels in Yiddish, Hebrew and Russian.

1888 Founds a Yiddish literary annual, *Di Yiddishe Folksbibliotek* (The Jewish Folk Library), to which many noted writers contribute. Published in 1889.

1890s Involved in unsuccessful business ventures and stock speculation, which cause financial hardship.

1892 First story in *Menachem Mendl* series.

1894 First of the *Tevye* stories.

1899 Becomes steady contributor to various Yiddish weeklies and dailies in Warsaw and St. Petersburg.

1900–5 Prodigious output. At height of his fame. However, he still lives in poor financial circumstances.

1906 Begins to give readings of his work. Trip to the United States.

1907 Returns to Europe, disappointed by stay in New York and by failure of his two plays on the Yiddish stage. Continues to draw large crowds for his readings. Diagnosed as having tuberculosis. First of the *Mottel the Cantor's Son* stories.

1909 Fiftieth birthday, marked by worldwide celebrations. Translation of his works into Russian and Hebrew.

1910–14   Health improves. Summers in Switzerland or on the Italian Riviera. Prolific literary activity.

1914   Returns to New York. Financial straits. Health declines. Continues to write *Mottel the Cantor's Son* and his autobiography.

1915   Serialization of the autobiography in a New York Yiddish daily.

1916   Death in New York, on May 13. Funeral attended by more than 150,000 people.